WRITING FOR MULTIMEDIA AND THE WEB

Second Edition

WRITING FOR MULTIMEDIA AND THE WEB

Second Edition

Timothy Garrand

Focal Press
Boston Oxford Auckland Johannesburg Melbourne New Delhi

Focal Press is an imprint of Butterworth–Heinemann.

Copyright © 2001 by Butterworth–Heinemann

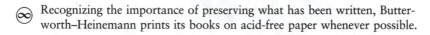 A member of the Reed Elsevier group

 Butterworth–Heinemann supports the efforts of American Forests and the Global ReLeaf program in its campaign for the betterment of trees, forests, and our environment.

Library of Congress Cataloging-in-Publication Data
Garrand, Timothy Paul.
  Writing for multimedia and the Web / Timothy Garrand.—2nd ed.
    p.   cm.
  Rev. ed. of: Writing for the Web. c1997.
  Includes bibliographical references and index.
  ISBN 0-240-80381-7 (pbk. : alk. paper)
  1. Interactive multimedia—Authorship.   2. World Wide Web.   I. Garrand,
Timothy Paul. Writing for the Web.   II. Title.
  QA76.76.I59 G37 2000
  808′.0660067—dc21

                                                                00-056180

British Library Cataloguing-in-Publication Data
A catalogue record for this book is available from the British Library.

The publisher offers special discounts on bulk orders of this book.
For information, please contact:
Manager of Special Sales
Butterworth–Heinemann
225 Wildwood Avenue
Woburn, MA 01801-2041
Tel: 781-904-2500
Fax: 781-904-2620

For information on all Focal Press publications available, contact our World
Wide Web home page at: http://www.focalpress.com

10 9 8 7 6 5 4 3 2 1

Printed in the United States of America

I dedicate this book to my mother, Virginia Garrand, who encouraged me to reach for my dreams.

Sometimes I've reached those dreams, and sometimes I've come up a bit short. Win or lose, I can always count on her love and support.

Writing for Multimedia & the Web
The Book at a Glance

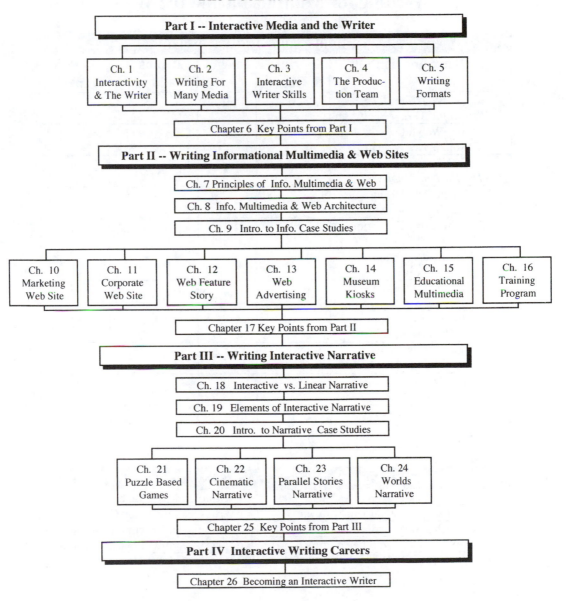

Part I -- Interactive Media and the Writer

Ch. 1 Interactivity & The Writer	Ch. 2 Writing For Many Media	Ch. 3 Interactive Writer Skills	Ch. 4 The Production Team	Ch. 5 Writing Formats

Chapter 6 Key Points from Part I

Part II -- Writing Informational Multimedia & Web Sites

Ch. 7 Principles of Info. Multimedia & Web

Ch. 8 Info. Multimedia & Web Architecture

Ch. 9 Intro. to Info. Case Studies

Ch. 10 Marketing Web Site	Ch. 11 Corporate Web Site	Ch. 12 Web Feature Story	Ch. 13 Web Advertising	Ch. 14 Museum Kiosks	Ch. 15 Educational Multimedia	Ch. 16 Training Program

Chapter 17 Key Points from Part II

Part III -- Writing Interactive Narrative

Ch. 18 Interactive vs. Linear Narrative

Ch. 19 Elements of Interactive Narrative

Ch. 20 Intro. to Narrative Case Studies

Ch. 21 Puzzle Based Games	Ch. 22 Cinematic Narrative	Ch. 23 Parallel Stories Narrative	Ch. 24 Worlds Narrative

Chapter 25 Key Points from Part III

Part IV Interactive Writing Careers

Chapter 26 Becoming an Interactive Writer

Writing for Multimedia and the Web

The CD-ROM at a Glance

Additional Case Study Material

Genre and Title	Scripts & Charts	Images	Demos & Videos	WWW Links *
Web Site *Prudential Verani Realty*	√	√		√
Web Site *T. Rowe Price Web Site*		√		√
Web Feature Story *The Harlem Renaissance*	√	√		√
Online Advertising *ZDU Campaign*		√	√	√
Museum Kiosk Simulation *The Nauticus Shipbuilding Co.*		√		√
Multimedia Training *Vital Signs*	√	√		√
Multiplayer Narrative *Boy Scout Patrol Theater*	√	√		√
Puzzle-Based Game *The 11th Hour*	√	√	√	√
Cinematic Narrative *Voyeur*	√	√		√
Parallel Stories Narrative *The Pandora Directive*	√	√		√
Worlds Narrative *Dust*	√	√	√	√
Worlds Narrative *Titanic: Adventure Out of Time*		√		√

Background	Reference
Playback/Delivery Systems	Glossaries of Media Terms
Production Systems and Software	Writers & Production Companies
Accessible Multimedia & Web Pages	Info. for the Teacher & Student
Multimedia & Web Legal Primer	Links To Writing Related Software

* Links to sites on the World Wide Web can be accessed if the reader has an Internet connection.

BOOK CONTENTS

CD-ROM CONTENTS

PART V   SOFTWARE

Links to software useful to the interactive writer including
software for scriptwriting, flowcharting, and WYSIWYG Web
editors

N.B. All sections of the CD-ROM will include links to pertinent sites on the World
Wide Web that can be accessed if the reader has an Internet connection.

ACKNOWLEDGMENTS

I'd first like to thank the editors and staff at Focal Press for their help and support writing and producing this book and CD-ROM, especially my editor Terri Jadick and publisher Marie Lee, who initiated the first edition of this book.

I also want to thank the readers of the first draft: Annette Barbier and Glorianna Davenport.

This book could not have been written without the generous donation of script samples and images by the copyright holders. Many thanks to CyberFlix Inc., Trilobyte Inc., Chedd-Angier Production Company, T. Rowe Price Associates, Access Software Inc., National Scouting Museum of the Boy Scouts of America, Ziff-Davis, Houghton Mifflin Company, Harvard Pilgrim Health Care, Encyclopaedia Britannica, Philips Media, and Prudential Verani Realty.

Equally crucial was the time generously donated by the many writers and designers interviewed for this project. In the informational programs they include Andrew Nelson, Kevin Oakes, Deborah Astudillo, Steve Barney, John Cosner, Fred Bauer, Matt Lindley, John Hargrave, Peter Meyerhoff, Tom Michael, Emmett Higdon, and Peter Adams. The storytellers are Madeleine Butler, Jane Jensen, Shannon Gilligan, Tony Sherman, Matt Costello, Dave Riordan, Lena Marie Pousette, Aaron Conners, and Andrew Nelson. A full list of all who contributed may be found at the back of the book.

I owe a special debt to writer Maria O'Meara, who contributed interviews and material for case studies and critiqued the first edition manuscript.

Of course, none of this would have been possible without the patience and support of my wife, Anne Fenn, and my daughter, Danielle. I owe them my deepest gratitude.

INTRODUCTION

This is a book on writing for multimedia and the Web . . . and much more.

To be effective, an interactive writer has to be more than just a great wordsmith. The interactive writer must also understand the architecture, tools, and capabilities of interactive multimedia. This book addresses this need by providing a detailed explanation of the process of conceptualizing multimedia and Web sites that both the newcomer and media industry professional will find valuable. A wide variety of Web sites and multimedia programs are discussed including: marketing, portals, reference, features, education, training, games, and online advertising.

Part I, "Interactive Media and the Writer," examines the particular demands that multimedia and the Web make on the writer, including interactivity, writing for many media, organizational tools, and script formatting.

Part II, "Writing Informational Multimedia and Web Sites," and Part III, "Writing Interactive Narrative," are devoted to in-depth case studies of a wide variety of projects, ranging from Web sites, to training, to games. Some of the top writers and designers for multimedia and the Web reveal their secrets for creating powerful programs. Their ideas are documented with extensive script samples, flowcharts, and other writing material.

Part IV, "Interactive Writing Careers," outlines the challenges the interactive writer faces and provides tips for developing an interactive writing career.

The attached CD-ROM includes script samples, screen shots, program demos, multimedia production information, links to scriptwriting software, a video on the creation of a multimedia program, and more.

Read this book and CD-ROM interactively; choose what is valuable to you.

If you are a *NEWCOMER,* start at the beginning of the book and browse through the background material on the CD-ROM.

If you are an experienced *INTERACTIVE MEDIA PROFESSIONAL,* focus on the later chapters and the case studies to see how some of the top multimedia and Web professionals work their magic.

If you are or want to become a *WEB WRITER or DESIGNER,* you will benefit from the chapters about Web sites and from the other multimedia case studies as well, because many of the techniques used in disc-based programs can now be applied to Web-based multimedia.

If you are a *GAMER,* read the last part of the book to learn how some of the classic games were created.

If you are a *MEDIA SCHOLAR*, study the entire book for a solid grounding in the principles and practices of interactive media.

If you are a *JOB SEEKER*, check out Part IV, "Interactive Writing Careers," for suggestions on how to develop an interactive media writing career.

So turn the page or pop in the *Writing for Multimedia and the Web* CD-ROM, browse the contents, and choose the material that suits your needs.

Tim Garrand
tpg@interwrite.com

PART I

INTERACTIVE MEDIA AND THE WRITER

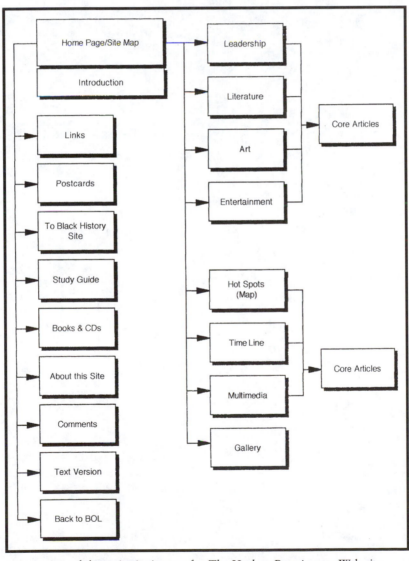

A portion of the writer's sitemap for *The Harlem Renaissance* Web site.
© 1999 by Encyclopaedia Britannica, Inc.

C H A P T E R   1

INTERACTIVITY AND THE WRITER

CHAPTER OVERVIEW

This chapter defines important terms and explains the key concepts relating to interactivity including:

- Interactivity versus control
- Thinking interactively
- Linking
- High-level design
- Interactive devices

DEFINING INTERACTIVE MULTIMEDIA AND THE INTERACTIVE WRITER

The first edition of this book was called *Writing for Multimedia*. At that time, Web sites were primarily text with a few pictures, and CD-ROMs had "true multimedia," with text, images, video, sound, animation, and sophisticated interactivity. Because of this, the word "multimedia" made many users think of CD-ROMs and later DVDs, not Web sites. But now true multimedia has come to the Web with the increased online use of the rich media and interactivity once reserved for CDs. For this reason I have greatly expanded the coverage of the Web in this edition. To make this clear I changed the book's title to *Writing for Multimedia and the Web*. Strictly speaking, this doesn't make much sense because the Web is just one way to present multimedia along with CDs, DVDs, and other platforms, but I included "the Web" in the title for the many readers who still think of multimedia as programs on CD and the World Wide Web as something completely different.

Maybe by the time the next edition is published the language will have caught up with usage, and I can simply title the book Writing for Multimedia and everyone will know that it includes all ways of presenting multimedia.

It is that broad meaning of the words "multimedia" and "interactive multimedia" that I would like to use in this book.

- "Multimedia" and "interactive multimedia" encompass all computer delivered media that use some combination of text, images, video, sound, animation, and sophisticated interactivity. This includes all the disc based (CD, DVD, etc.) programs and most of the Web sites in this book. It would also include many major sites on the Web today.

- "Interactive Media" has traditionally been a much broader term than multimedia, describing all media with interactivity. Most of the time this term is used to refer to computer delivered interactive media, such as multimedia programs and non-multimedia Web sites (limited interactivity and no animations, video, or sound). Interactive media can, however, refer to all types of interactive media, such as "choose your own adventure" books that allow readers to pick from multiple endings. (For more on other types of interactive media, see the Introduction to Multimedia article in the "Background" section of this book's attached CD-ROM.)

Based on the above definitions, I will generally use the terms "multimedia" or "interactive multimedia" in this book to indicate my major focus is on CD-ROMs, Web sites, and other projects that use some combination of rich media and complex interactivity. I will also discuss some traditional, pictures-and-text, non-multimedia Web sites because they still comprise a large percentage of sites on the World Wide Web.

TYPES OF INTERACTIVE MULTIMEDIA

Web sites are a growing platform for multimedia. Material is presented on sites through multiple media, including pictures, text, and sometimes video, audio, or animation. The site interacts with the user by allowing the user to control what material will be presented and in what order. The user controls the flow of information or performs tasks usually through clicking with a mouse on the computer screen.

In addition to the World Wide Web, multimedia is presented on online services, such as America Online; local networks, such as corporate intranets; computer hard drives, such as museum kiosks; interactive television, such as Web TV; dedicated gaming systems, such as Nintendo; and discs, such as CD-ROMs and DVDs. Interactive multimedia has dozens of uses, with the most common being marketing, sales, product information, entertainment, education, training, and reference material.

THE ROLE OF THE INTERACTIVE WRITER

The interactive writer may create proposals, outlines, sitemaps, treatments, walkthroughs, design documents, scripts, and all the other written material that describes a multimedia or Web site project. This can include developing the information architecture, on-screen text, overall story structure, dialogue, characters, narration, interface, and more. The key difference between writing for linear media, such as television and movies, and writing for interactive media is interactivity, which allows the user of the program to have control over the flow of the information or story material.

INTERACTIVITY VERSUS CONTROL

POTENTIAL INTERACTIVITY

Interactivity means that the user can control the presentation of information or story material on the computer. The potential interactivity of multimedia is awesome. It is possible to interact not merely by screen or page, but by controlling the presentation of individual objects within a screen, such as a single character's actions in a scene, the color of a part of an image, or the presentation of a line of text.

LIMITS TO INTERACTIVITY

There are practical limits to the potential of a particular user's interactivity. The viewer's equipment has to be powerful enough to support the level of interactivity. And even if the viewer has the best system in the world, if the source material is a CD-ROM, a DVD, or some other closed system, the player is working with a finite number of options. He or she can access only what the makers place on the disc. This limitation disappears when multimedia is delivered online, through the World Wide Web or an online service, which allow users to link instantly to thousands or perhaps millions of other sources throughout the world. However, for Web surfers who still use a modem, the slow download speed can make the online multimedia experience sometimes frustrating. (See the "Playback/Delivery Systems" article in the Background Section of the *Writing for Multimedia and the Web* CD-ROM for a detailed discussion of this issue.)

Is unlimited interactivity the most effective way to communicate with multimedia, if technically possible for the user? It depends to a great degree on what your goals are. If, for example, you are trying to tell a story, such as the interactive narrative *Voyeur* (profiled in Chapter 22), the degree of interactivity you can allow and still create believable characters, intriguing plot, and suspense will be far less than if you are simply creating a world for viewers to inhabit, such as *SimCity 3000*. Similarly, a Web site with the focused goal of getting you to buy a car will have far less interactive options than an online encyclopedia that wants you to explore its information. *Voyeur* designer David Riordan echoes the feeling of many multimedia developers when he says, "Infinite choice equals a database. Just because you can make a choice doesn't mean it's an interesting one" (Riordan). He says that the creators of multimedia must maintain some control for the experience to be effective.

THINKING INTERACTIVELY

THINKING OF ALL THE POSSIBILITIES

The stumbling block for most new interactive writers is not limiting interactivity and maintaining control over the multimedia experience. Most new writers have the opposite problem of overly restricting interactivity and failing to give users adequate control over the flow of information or story material. This is because limiting options is what most linear writers have been trained to do. In a linear video, film, or book, it is essential to find just the right shot, scene, or sentence to express your meaning.

In writing for interactive media, "the hardest challenge for the writer is the interactivity—having a feel for all the options in a scene or story," says Jane Jensen, writer-designer of the Gabriel Knight series (Jensen). Tony Sherman, writer-designer of *Dracula Unleashed* and *Club Dead* agrees. Unlike a linear piece in which it is crucial to pare away nonessentials, in interactive media, the writer must "think of all the possibilities" (Sherman).

VIEWER INPUT

It is difficult to predict how the viewer will interact with all the possibilities in a piece. Jane Jensen warns that this can sometimes make multimedia "a frustrating and difficult medium. . . . You have this great scene, but you have to write five times that much around it . . . to provide options. When your focus is on telling the story, that can feel like busy work and a waste of time" (Jensen).

For example, you have a telephone in one scene that your player must dial to call his or her uncle and find out who the murderer is. This is near the end of the game and getting the telephone number itself has been one of the game's goals. The writer needs to anticipate all the things players might try to do with that telephone. What if players get the telephone number from having played the game earlier, and they then jump ahead to the telephone scene? What should happen when they dial? Should they get a busy signal? What if they dial the number after they have gotten it legally in the game, but they don't have all the information they need, such as knowing that the one who answers is their uncle? Should the writer give them different information in the message? What if they dial the operator? What if they try dialing random numbers?

This can be equally complex in an informational multimedia piece where you must anticipate the related information that the viewers will want to access and all the different ways they may want to relate to the key information. *Compton's Interactive Encyclopedia*, for example, allows users to explore a particular piece of information through text, pictures, audio, videos, maps, definitions, a time line, and a topic tree. The design of the program allows all of these different approaches to be linked together if the viewer desires. This means that students studying Richard Nixon can mouse-click their way from an article about Nixon, to his picture, to an audio of his "I am not a crook" speech, to a video about Watergate and Nixon's resignation, and finally to a time line showing other events happening during his presidency.

KNOWING THE USER

A key way to anticipate users' input is to know as much about them as possible. This is also important in linear media, but it is even more crucial in interactive multimedia because the interactive relationship is more intimate than the more passive linear one. Knowing the audience is absolutely essential. Knowing what the user considers appealing will affect every element of a production, from types of links to interactive design.

LINKING

Links are the connections from one section of an interactive media program to another section of the same program or, if online, to a totally different program. When the information for a program or site is stored in a database, then the linked material can be even smaller or more granular. It is possible to link users' actions to single program elements, sentences, or even words. The simplest link is a text menu choice that the user clicks to bring up new information. When writers develop links, they must make a number of decisions:

- What information, program elements, pages, chapters, or scenes will connect with other sections of the program?

- How many choices will the user have?
- Which choices will be presented first?
- What will be the result of those choices?
- Will the links be direct, indirect, or delayed?

IMMEDIATE OR DIRECT LINKS: AN ACTION

In an immediate or direct link, the viewer makes a choice, and that choice produces a direct and immediate response that the viewer expects. For example, in the detail in Figure 1–1 from the T. Rowe Price investment company's Web site, when the user clicks on the "Mutual Funds" link near the top of the left menu, they expect to and will get a page of information about mutual funds.

INDIRECT LINKS: A REACTION

Indirect links, also called "if-then" links, are more complex. Users do not directly choose an item, as in the example above. Instead, they take a certain action that elicits a reaction they did not specifically select. The following example is taken from the walkthrough for the interactive movie *The Pandora Directive*. The walkthrough describes the program's story and the main interactive options for the user. At this point in the story, you, the user, are trying to escape with the woman Regan, but you have been cornered by the villains Fitzpatrick and Cross.

EXCERPT FROM THE PANDORA DIRECTIVE WALKTHROUGH

```
You get the choice of shooting Fitzpatrick, shooting
Cross, or dropping the gun. If you try to shoot
Fitzpatrick, you get trapped alongside Regan and Cross;
then everybody dies, safely away from Earth. If you try
to shoot Cross, he kills you before you ever get into
the ship. If you drop the gun, you get to the
spaceship.
```

An example of an indirect link in an informational piece is a student who fails a test in a certain subject area and is automatically routed to easier review material, instead of being advanced to the next level. The student did not make this direct choice. It is a consequence of his or her actions. Figure 1–2 shows how a student who could not answer an arithmetic question in a math tutorial might be sent back to an arithmetic review module as opposed to being advanced to the more difficult algebra material.

Indirect links can also cause multiple things to happen when the user clicks one choice. This is most common in a program or Web site where the information is dynamic because it is stored in a database. What this means is that the information is not static in large sections, like the pages and chapters of this book or a traditional HTML Web page. If this book was a database-generated Web site, every paragraph or sentence in it would be a separate piece of information. Depending on what actions the user took on the Web site, these separate pieces of information could be sorted, organized, and displayed in the order requested by the user. For example, on the *T. Rowe Price* Web site, users can fill out a form and establish the list of mutual funds

T. Rowe Price

MARKET UPDATE	10/19/1999	11:09am ET
DJIA	10327.77	+211.49 ▲
Nasdaq	2727.31	+38.16 ▲
S&P 500 Index	1278.51	+24.38 ▲
Russell 2000	414.32	+5.42 ▲

Access My Account

Daily Prices

FIND OUT ABOUT
Mutual Funds
Asset Manager Account
Brokerage Services
Retirement / IRAs
College Funding
Tax Info / Strategies
Service Area / Forms
Tools & Insights
Site Help
Contact Us

SPECIALIZED SECTIONS
Retirement Plans @ Work
Small Business

WHAT'S NEWS   October 19, 1999

▶ Retired? Almost there? See how Retirement Income Manager^{SM}, a new advisory service from T. Rowe Price, can help with your toughest retirement decision.

▶ The fall editions of the T. Rowe Price Report newsletter and our quarterly Performance Update are now available for download.

▶ Need help building the right portfolio for you? Visit our Investment Strategy Planner.

FIGURE 1–1

Detail from the *T. Rowe Price* Web site home page. © 1999 T. Rowe Price Associates, Inc.

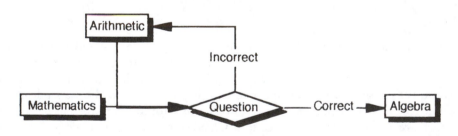

FIGURE 1–2

Indirect links: A reaction to user input.

and stocks that they are most interested in. After they have done this once, when they log on to the site in the future, they are activating a program that searches out the most current data on their topics in the database, organizes this data, and presents it to them. Chapter 11, "Corporate Web Site Case Study: *T. Rowe Price* Web Site," profiles this site and describes dynamic information flow and customization in more detail.

In the T. Rowe Price example, the multiple actions (sorting, organizing, etc.) are finally displayed in one location, but a single indirect link can also create multiple actions throughout a site or program. For example, on a well-designed Web site for an auto dealer, when a salesperson sells a car and enters the final sales form into the system, the car is automatically removed from the display on the public Web site and from the dealer's inventory list. The site might also automatically generate an E-mail message to the customers thanking them for their business.

INTELLIGENT LINKS OR DELAYED LINKS: A DELAYED REACTION

Intelligent links remember what choices the user made earlier in the program or on previous plays of the program and alter future responses accordingly. These links can be considered delayed "if-then" links. In a story, intelligent links create a realistic response to the character's action; in a training piece, they provide the most effective presentation of the material based on a student's earlier performance.

In *The Pandora Directive*, for example, you as the player are a detective who is trying to get in touch with Emily, a nightclub singer. You meet Emily's boss, Leach, well before you meet her. If you are rude to him, he mistrusts you. Later in the script when you try to rescue Emily, he will block your entrance to her room, and she will be strangled. If, however, you are nice when you first meet him, he lets you in, and you save her.

Certain Web sites record every click you make and gradually define your preferences. This allows the sites to personalize their presentation to you so that they only show you information and products of interest to you. One example is Amazon.com recommending new book titles to repeat users based on past purchases. The most sophisticated sites might also personalize the way the information is presented. For example, a user who always jumps right to the online videos would be presented with pages containing more multimedia. Customization and personalization will be discussed in more detail later in this book in Chapter 7, "Principles of Informational Multimedia and Web Sites."

HIGH-LEVEL DESIGN

The complexity that interactivity and linking add to a multimedia project demands strong high-level design for the program to be coherent and effective. High-level design determines the broad conceptual approach to the project, including the structure, interface, map, organizing metaphors, and even input devices.

STRUCTURE AS AN INTERACTIVE DEVICE

The overall structure of a piece is one of the main ways interaction can be motivated in a narrative. In *Voyeur*, the player is a voyeur in an apartment building across from a mansion. The character's only reason for existing is to peer into the mansion's windows. In the narrative informational piece *A la rencontre de Philippe*, the player is motivated to learn about Paris through the role of helping Parisian friends find an apartment.

The overall structure and navigation of an informational multimedia piece is called the information or interactive architecture. This is a large topic that will be dealt with in more detail in Chapter 2, "Writing for Many Media," and in the case studies, but it is worth mentioning here. Poorly structured information will cause the user either to fail to interact with the program at all, or to get confused and give up part way through. For example, good information architects knows what information to put on the top level of the interactive program, such as a Web site's home page, to hook the user. After hooking the user, this top-level information has to lead the user logically to the information that the user wants.

INTERFACE DESIGN

Another way to help users find their way through the complex structure of an interactive media production is through good interface design. The interface is simply the "face" or basic on-screen visualization of the information or story material in a program. The interface governs how we will interact with multimedia. An interface can be as simple as a list of words in a clickable menu that organizes the information into content categories, such as the T. Rowe Price menu in Figure 1–1. The interface can also be more graphical, such as the time clock and icons from *The Harlem Renaissance* site in Figure 1–3.

The interface can also be much more complex, such as the interface for the interactive narrative *Voyeur*, which allows the user to interact with the story material in a variety of ways using items in the voyeur's apartment (Figure 1–4). The camera can be used to spy on the mansion across the street; the TV can be watched for back ground information; the FedEx envelope can be clicked on to mail evidence; and the telephone can receive calls.

The amount of input the writer is allowed to give regarding the interface design depends on the designer and the project, but the writer must consider interface design

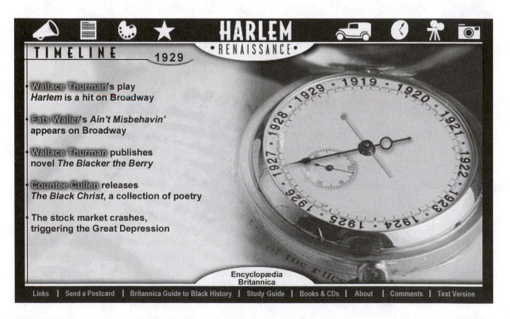

FIGURE 1–3

Timeline and icons from Web site *The Harlem Renaissanse*. © 1999 by Encyclopaedia Britannica, Inc.

FIGURE 1-4

Interface for *Voyeur*. Courtesy of Philips Media. © 1993 Philips Interactive Media.

when writing. Interface design is crucial in deciding how multimedia content will be organized. It affects the structure of the script for the writer and dictates how the viewer will interact with that content.

The interface also affects the navigation of the piece—how the viewer can travel through the information or story and the order in which the information will be presented. The navigation is often demonstrated through flowcharts and diagrams. (See flowchart that introduces Part I.) The CD-ROM *Clinton: Portrait of Victory* uses a simple hierarchical menu for navigation in which users can first choose one of the following: "The Assignment," "The Candidate," or "The Campaign." "The Campaign" choice yields further options: "The Primaries," "The Convention," "On the Road," "The Debates," and "A Bold Finale."

MAP OR SITEMAP

An element of good interactive design is a sitemap or map that represents the overall structure of a piece in a concrete manner. A sitemap illustrates how the player should interact with the interface and navigate through the program. It can be as simple as a text menu that lists all the key pages of a Web site broken down by categories. This type of sitemap is used on the *Prudential Verani* Web site profiled in Chapter 10, "Writing a Marketing Web Site from Proposal to Meta Tags: *Prudential Verani Realty*." Sometimes the map is a flowchart of the entire production, as in the Oakes Interactive training piece for Fidelity Investments retirement counselors. In this program, a student can bring up the flowchart of the whole program and access any area of it by clicking on one of the labeled boxes. (The "Book at a Glance" at the beginning of this book uses a flowchart to provide an overview of book contents.) The sitemap can even be a literal map, as in *Dust: A Tale of the Wired West*, in which the player can consult a map of Diamondback, New Mexico, to get oriented and decide where to go next. (The actual interface of the game is a 3-D animation of the town's buildings and citizens, with whom the viewer can interact.)

METAPHORS

The maps of Diamondback, the voyeur's telephone and TV, and the training program flowchart are types of metaphors that help the audience understand the organization of an interactive piece. For software developers, the metaphor is a concrete image or other element that represents an abstract concept, making it clear and comfortable to the user. Perhaps one of the best-known software metaphors is the desktop. Windows PCs and Macs present the abstract concepts of computer files, directories, and software as file folders and documents that users can arrange and work with on the desktop.

Metaphors are also used to design individual screens and navigational aids. According to designer Aaron Marcus, "Consistency and clarity are two of the most important concerns in developing metaphors" (Marcus 98) Familiarity to the viewer is a third item that could be added. Consistency means that users should not have to use buttons as the main navigational tool on one screen and then suddenly have to switch to a different approach, such as clicking on pictures, in the next screen. Both of these are valid metaphors for linked information, but they are confusing when mixed. Consistent placement of the same types of information in the same place on the screen is also important.

Creating familiar metaphors ties into knowing your audience. A valid metaphor for the structure of an elementary school education CD-ROM or Web site might be a street in a town. This is something students are familiar with. It makes sense for them to click on a library to get information or a movie theater to see a film. On a micro level, a common metaphor is a book that opens. Click a dog ear to turn a page. Click the table of contents to go to a chapter. Sometimes a metaphor can add to the mood of a piece. *The Harlem Renaissance* Web site profiled in Chapter 12, "Research Portal Web Site and the Online Feature Story: Britannica.com and *The Harlem Renaissance*," uses a tourist metaphor to help make the user feel that they are visitors to another era. The metaphor is strengthened with items such as street maps, E-mail postcards, and evocative full-page visuals.

Familiar metaphors help orient viewers, but this certainly doesn't mean that metaphors have to be cliched or boring. Certainly a designer who can push the envelope without losing the audience should by all means go for it. There is lots of room to be creative. It is important to make even the minor elements of a production work well. For example, one of the frustrating things in multimedia is the "wait-state" image. Many programs are content to give the standard clock or hour glass, but there is no rule that the wait-state image cannot be fun. *A.D.A.M. The Inside Story*, an anatomy program, shows a skeleton with a cup of coffee. Some children's programs have scurrying animals.

INPUT DEVICES

Writers might also consider how the users will input their responses to the program. Standard choices include the keyboard, mouse, and touchscreen, but sometimes the input device can be integrated into the material. Instead of a mouse, *Welcome to West*

Feedback, a music game, uses a toy guitar plugged into the computer as the input. *Redbeard's Pirate Quest* uses a model pirate ship loaded with electromagnetic sensors. Speech recognition is also finally coming of age. This could have a major impact on interactive narratives. Even more exciting are the potential applications for multimodal interaction. "Multimodal systems process combined natural input modes—such as speech, pen, touch, hand gestures, eye gaze, and head and body movements—in a coordinated manner with multimedia output" (Oviatt 74). For interacting with complex multimedia programs such as virtual worlds populated with intelligent animated characters, a multimodal system will be far superior to the conventional Windows-Icons-Menus-Pointer (WIMP) interface.

INTERACTIVE DEVICES

In addition to the high-level design elements, the designer and writer must develop specific interactive devices that will make users aware of the interactive possibilities they have created. These devices include on-screen menus, help screens, icons, props, other characters, and cues imbedded in the story or information.

ICONS

Various types of icons are used for interactive devices. In *Voyeur* they are used to inspire viewers to look into the rooms of the mansion that are visible from the voyeur's apartment. If the voyeur moves the camera over a room in which there is action to view, an eye icon appears. If there's something to hear, an ear appears. If there is evidence to examine, such as a letter, a magnifying glass appears. Clicking on the icons causes the material to be presented.

In Britannica.com's Web site *The Harlem Renaissance*, icons are used to efficiently indicate the main sections of the site in the Web site's navigation bar (see Figure 1–3). The megaphone is for leadership, the page is for literature, the palette is for art, and so on. The meaning of the icons is clarified through the use of rollovers that show text labels when the mouse passes over one of the icons.

MENUS AND OTHER TEXT

The text menu and the navigation bar are traditional and still effective ways to access material in informational multimedia. Figure 1–1 shows the main menu from the *T. Rowe Price* Web site home page. Clicking on one of these menu items leads to other pages that also have menus. In addition to static text, menus can also be presented as popup or drop-down menus that take less screen space (Figure 1–5). They only appear when the user clicks on them. Text links can also be highlighted directly on a page as in Figure 1–3 on page 10 where the names of important figures of the era are links to additional information.

Although text menus can work well in an informational piece, they can disrupt the flow of a narrative. However, some designers are willing to accept that disruption to achieve a high degree of interactivity. In *Under a Killing Moon*, written by Aaron Conners, menus allow the player a wide variety of action options, including *look, get, move, open*, and *talk*. The player can even choose the tone of the lead character's dialogue by picking menu choices such as "Rugged Banter," "Indignant," and

FIGURE 1–5

Drop-down menu from the *T. Rowe Price* Web site home page. © 1998, 1999 T. Rowe Price Associates, Inc.

"Reeking of Confidence." (See Chapter 23, "Parallel Stories Narrative Case Study: *The Pandora Directive*," for a more detailed discussion of response attitudes.)

Sometimes words on the screen are optional. In *Under a Killing Moon*, players can pull down an optional hints window. This helps orient them in the game and tells them their interactive options. Sometimes written material is integrated into the story itself. Shannon Gilligan's *Who Killed Sam Rupert?* includes an investigator's notebook that keeps track of what the detective-player has done so far in the game.

PROPS

Props are a popular interactive device. In *Under a Killing Moon*, the character can click on objects in the room to get information. Depending on the object, a player might hear a voice-over wisecrack about a painting, or even see a full-motion video flashback that shows the detective's relationship with the object. In the educational CD-ROM *Sky High*, users can click on various props in a scene, such as toy helicopters and birds, to bring up additional information related to that aspect of flight.

Props that a character can actually use as they might be used in real life are particularly effective. The player in *Voyeur* has a camera with a zoom lens to use for exploring and recording evidence of the crime. Telephones are also used to give clues in this game and others. *Sky High* has a camera that students can use to take shots of the information on the screen.

CHARACTERS

Characters are another way to guide interactions. Sometimes this is the primary function of the character. The investigators in *Who Killed Sam Rupert* and *Gabriel Knight* both have assistants who remind them of appointments, give them telephone messages, or suggest people to talk to. Other characters, who are not primarily information givers, might say things that suggest a location to visit or a person to interview. This technique is frequently used in *Dracula Unleashed*.

A character can also be used as a guide to lead the viewer through the material. This can be successful in both narrative and nonnarrative pieces. For example, children's educational programs frequently have a character that suggest what actions to take and what information to explore. More subtle guides are used on the health information Web site drkoop.com. Most sections of this site are hosted by different experts who help lead the user to the information they need on the site. In the narrative video game *Astronomica*, the daughter of the doctor who disappeared approaches you, the user, directly by banging on your bedroom window and asking you to help find her father. She leads you to her father's lab, where she works on the main computer, and sends you into the exploratorium to solve the problems there. She also appears now and again on a small communications monitor in the exploratorium to give you tips and encouragement.

CHALLENGE OF THE INTERACTIVE DEVICE

The challenge of the interactive device is to design something that will motivate interaction without radically disrupting the flow of information or story material. A well-designed interactive device will not pull us out of the dream state of storytelling or disrupt our train of thought as we pursue information. In short, interactive devices must be well integrated into the material.

CONCLUSION

This chapter has provided a broad overview of some of the key interactive issues the writer must consider when developing a multimedia informational or narrative program. Although the elements discussed above, such as interface design, are not always under the control of the writer, the writer must understand these concepts if he or she is to write effectively for interactive media. This chapter has discussed the "interactive" component of interactive multimedia. The next chapter will address the "multimedia" aspect of interactive multimedia. Writing for multimedia or many media is another key challenge for the writer.

REFERENCES

Davenport, Glorianna. "Bridging Across Content and Tools." *Computer Graphics* 28 (February 1994): 31–32.

Drkoop.com Web site. http://www.drkoop.com, 1999.

Halliday, Mark. "Digital Cinema: An Environment for Multi-threaded Stories." Master's thesis, Massachusetts Institute of Technology, 1993.

The Harlem Renaissance Web site. http://www.britannica.com/harlem, 1999.

Jensen, Jane. Telephone interview with the author, July 1994.

Marcus, Aaron. "Making Multimedia Usable: User Interface Design." *New Media* 5 (February 1995): 98–100.

Oviatt, Sharon. "Ten Myths of Multimodal Interaction." *Communications of the ACM* 42 (November 1999): 74–81.

Prudential Verani Web site. http://www.pruverani.com, 1999.

Riordan, David. Telephone interview with the author, June 1994.

Sherman, Tony. Telephone interview with the author, July 1994.

T. Rowe Price Web site. http://www.troweprice.com, 1999.

C H A P T E R 2

WRITING FOR MANY MEDIA

CHAPTER OVERVIEW

The multimedia writer must be able to write effectively for a variety of media. This chapter outlines some of the basic principles for writing:

- Text
- Audio
- Video

THE SKILLS OF THE INTERACTIVE WRITER

The necessity of writing for many media in the same production is as demanding on the multimedia writer as is dealing with interactivity. Unlike a print writer who can focus on honing communication skills with the written word, or the screenwriter who can specialize in communicating with images, the writer of interactive multimedia must be expert in a variety of techniques: writing to be read (journalism, poetry, copywriting); writing to be heard (radio, narration); writing to be seen (presentations, film, video); plus writing for the special demands of the computer screen. This is because multimedia can easily incorporate many types of media in a single production or even a single screen, and multimedia can manipulate these media in ways not previously possible.

Depending on the project, a multimedia writer may write on-screen text, audio narration, video action and dialogue, and other material. Often writers also write ancillary material, such as hints files and help screens. There are basic style differences in each of these types of writing. Following are a few guidelines, but if there is an area where you feel you are particularly weak, consult some of the references listed in the "References" section of the CD-ROM.

TEXT

The World Wide Web has brought a major resurgence in the writing and reading of text in multimedia programs. Even with the increased use of Web video, audio, and animation, on-screen text still plays a major role on most Web sites. Text is also used in disc-based multimedia, such as CD-ROMs and DVDs, where it is most common in informational, educational, and training pieces.

A multimedia writer writing blocks of text in an informational program or Web site can take a few tips from print journalists:

- Be accurate, check your facts, and be sure you understand what you are writing.
- Keep sentences short and use simple sentence construction.
- Use the lead or first sentences to tell simply and clearly what the following text is about.
- Use the active voice (for example, "The dog bit the man," not, "The man was bitten by the dog").
- Use descriptive nouns and verbs; avoid adjectives and adverbs.
- Choose each word carefully, and avoid jargon or technical terms unless you are writing for a specialized audience.

There are also a number of text-writing techniques that are unique to writing for the computer screen. The main reason for using many of these techniques is that most people cannot read as quickly and as comfortably on a computer screen as they can from the printed page. Adding to the problem of writing for computer screens is that many readers use multimedia and the Web for quick information. They do not want to sit down and read a six-page essay. They want to get the information they want quickly and then go about their business.

Some intriguing Web site usability studies by Dr. Jakob Nielsen, usability engineer and information architect, discovered that many users don't read Web sites, rather they scan them for the information they need. To write effectively for these scanners, Nielsen suggests in *The Alertbox: How Users Read on the Web* that Web writers use:

- highlighted **keywords** (hypertext links serve as one form of highlighting; typeface variations and color are others)
- meaningful **subheadings** (not "clever" ones)
- bulleted **lists**
- **one idea** per paragraph (users will skip over any additional ideas if they are not caught by the first few words in the paragraph)
- the **inverted pyramid style**, starting with the conclusion
- **half the word count** (or less) than in conventional writing

These concepts are particularly true on the first couple of levels of a Web site or multimedia program where users are trying to find the information they want. Once they have located their information deeper in the site, users may be content to read longer text material.

Andrew Nelson, the writer of *The Harlem Renaissance* site profiled in Chapter 12, "Research Portal Web Site and the Online Feature Story: Britannica.com and *The Harlem Renaissance*," suggests that when writing for the Web you should remember that most people view the Web as one person sitting in front of a computer. To connect to your site users, it is important to "write as if you are talking to an individual, not a collective group of anonymous Web surfers (Nelson, E-mail).

The following excerpt from the *T. Rowe Price* Web site illustrates many of the elements of good text writing for the computer screen described above, including the inverted pyramid, concrete statements, simple sentence construction, reduced amount of text, highlighted text, different fonts, bulleted lists, one idea per paragraph, and conversational style. Note that the underlined text in the sample below are blue hyperlinks on the actual Web site.

ONLINE COLLEGE PLANNER

This on-line College Planner can help you learn about meeting the costs of college. Our five-step *College Planning Calculator* calculates how much money you'll need to save, and suggests ways to invest your savings. Meanwhile, our *College Planning Library* gives you more information on other helpful resources, including:

- Tax Issues
- Education IRAs
- State Tuition Assistance Programs
- Sources of Financial Aid
- Ways that Grandparents Can Help

A wealth of additional college planning information is available on-line. See our *Additional Sources of Information*.

Courtesy of T. Rowe Price Associates. © 1999 T. Rowe Price Associates, Inc.

AUDIO

Writing in which the audio carries the bulk of the meaning, as it does in radio, occurs fairly often in multimedia for two practical reasons: (1) Audio is much cheaper to produce than video; and (2) Audio files are much smaller in size than video files. Because of this, it is much easier to include substantial audio material on a disc or to transmit audio files on Web sites than it is to use video. Writing such as this, where audio carries the primary meaning, demands the skills of the radio writer, or the ability to write to be heard as opposed to being read. In addition to the print writer's skills of being accurate, simple, and clear, the radio writer must:

- Write conversationally, the way people talk. Radio is the most intimate medium. When most radio announcers talk through the mike to thousands of people, they imagine they are talking to just one person, because that is how most people experience radio: one person and a radio. This is the same intimate way most multimedia is experienced: one person and a computer.

- Write material to be understood on the first play. Unless an instant replay is designed into the program, audio is more difficult to replay than text is to reread.

- Keep it simple. Be aware that the writing will be heard and not read. Avoid abbreviations, lots of numbers, unfamiliar names, and anything else that cannot be easily understood just by hearing it.

- Read all your work out loud when you are rewriting, or better yet, have someone read it out loud to you. You'll be amazed at how much of your perfectly acceptable written prose is unspeakable as dialogue or incomprehensible as narration.

- Write visually. A well-written audio-only piece can stimulate vivid images in the audience's minds. A famous radio ad once convincingly portrayed a ten-story-high hot fudge sundae being created in the middle of Lake Michigan. Create such pictures in the audience's mind by using:
  - Concrete visual words
  - Metaphors and other comparisons to images the viewer already knows
  - Sound effects
  - Different qualities of voices (sexy, accents, etc.)
  - Music
  - Words and phrases that appeal to other senses, such as touch, smell, and taste

EXAMPLES OF AUDIO-ONLY SCENES

Examples of audio-only or audio-dominant multimedia include Web audio interviews and seminars; audio and image scenes in which narration carries the bulk of the meaning; and even streaming Web video, which can easily degenerate to a series of still pictures with audio voice-over if the user has a slow connection or if the network is congested.

Narrative scenes sometimes emphasize audio to save space or for dramatic effect, such as the following example from the interactive narrative *Voyeur*. In this scene the player is looking at closed window blinds and listening in. Notice the use of visual writing, sound effects, and different voices to create images in the audience's mind. (These items are in boldface type.)

```
CHLOE'S ROOM, LARA AND CHLOE. SLIGHT KNOCK ON DOOR.

                         LARA
                   (knock on door)
         Chloe?


                         CHLOE
         Yeah. Come on in Lara ...


                         LARA
                   (embarrassed)
         Oh, I'm sorry I didn't know you weren't dressed
         ...
```

CHLOE

No, no, no don't worry about it, man, don't worry
about it.

LARA
(nervous **laughter**)
Maybe if I had a **tattoo** there, Zack would take a
closer look ...

CHLOE

Yeah? You like that? I'm not sure what hurt more,
the tattoo or the hangover ...

LARA

What am I doing wrong with him?

CHLOE

Oh, Lara would you stop it right now! Don't buy
into Zack's bullshit. You're a babe. You're
gorgeous. You've got a **terrific body**. You just don't
know how to package it. . . . I have got the most
terrific outfit for you. It's going to look killer
on you. I swear to God.

RIIING! She's interrupted by phone call.

CHLOE

Look, . . . Hold on a minute.
(into phone)
Yeah? . . . Oh, hi. . . . Well, not exactly . . . Hey man
I'm working on it. . . . will you give me a fucking
break . . . Hold a sec.
(to Lara)
Lara, could you . . . come back here tonight ...

LARA

I don't want to be a pest ...

CHLOE

Oh, come on, come on, it'll be fun . . . please, come
on, come by around eight.

LARA

OK. . . . see you then . . . **(door closes)**

CHLOE
(back to phone)
Like I told you, give me a couple a more days . . .
I'll get you the damn money. Fine.

Courtesy of Philips Media. © 1993 Philips Interactive Media.

VIDEO

Writing for video is an important skill for the multimedia writer because DVDs can accommodate considerable full-motion video and animation. Likewise on the Web, breakthroughs in compression, streaming tools, and faster user connections have made Web video a reality.

In a video, the viewer is **seeing** the results of the writing, not just reading or hearing them as in print and radio. Writing for video is a complex subject, about which many books have been written. Further complicating this topic are the very different demands on the scriptwriter of writing documentaries and fiction. It is difficult to reduce the specifics of scriptwriting to a few rules, but some of the scriptwriter's concerns include:

- Show, don't tell. Discover action to present the information. Don't have long-winded interviews about poverty in the ghetto; show scenes of poverty in the ghetto. Don't have your character tell us about how sad they are; have them do something that shows this.

- Structure. Have a clear grasp of how to structure a video. Academy Award-winning screenwriter Sheridan Gibney once said that scriptwriting has more in common with architecture than with writing. He said that screenplays are built, not written. Shots build scenes, scenes develop sequences, and sequences create plots and subplots (Gibney). Much of film and TV follows established structures that writers should be familiar with. (These structures are discussed in Part III, "Writing Interactive Narrative.")

- Setup. Exposition is one of the hardest elements to portray in video, and without proper exposition, characters are shallow, themes are undefined, and the setting is unclear. Exposition includes background information on the characters, setting, and the back story (events in the story that happened before the beginning of the current narrative). An example of important back story occurs in the classic film *Casablanca*. This film begins in Casablanca, a port city in Morocco, but essential back story includes the lead characters' romance that occurred in Paris a year earlier. Setup is equally important in an informational video, where we need to understand the context of the material that is being presented. Unlike print, where it is fairly easy to "tell" the reader about background information, in video this material needs to be shown. In multimedia, novice video writers often either have the characters talking incessantly about things that happened years ago, or they dump the entire back story into a separate background file and assume everyone has read it. Such a background file might be accessible from a program's help or hints menu.

- Characterization. There are a limited number of original stories but an unlimited number of unique characters. Finding and developing unique characters is essential in most fiction films and many documentaries.

- Conflict. Conflicts must be clearly defined. Most video focuses on conflict, whether it is a fictional battle between humans and aliens or a *60 Minutes* documentary on the concerned citizens of India versus their nuclear power industry.

- Cost. Unlike radio and print writing, video production is costly, and scriptwriters must be aware of this. Even though digital video cameras and desktop video-editing software have brought costs down, a writer with a limited multimedia budget probably will have to either forget about blowing up that rocket ship, do it as an animation, or use stock footage.

VIDEO EXAMPLE

The following video script example is by writer Matthew Costello from the opening of the video game *The 11th Hour*. Note how the characters, setting, background story, and key conflicts are set up quickly and visually.

```
INTRO-1 INT / DENNING'S COUNTRY HOME—AFTERNOON*

CARL DENNING is watching television. His handsome face
is grim and determined, bathed in the flickering light
of the TV's images. On the TV screen, an anchorwoman
is reading the evening news.

                    ANCHOR
   State Police have called off the intense search for
   producer Robin Morales of television's CASE
   UNSOLVED.

She continues to speak in voice-over as the screen is
filled with an image of an intelligent-looking woman
with compelling beauty. The words "ROBIN MORALES—CASE
UNSOLVED PRODUCER" are superimposed across the bottom
of the screen.

                    ANCHOR (V/O)
   Morales was researching a story about the famed
   haunted house in the small town of Harley on
   Hudson—the abandoned mansion of Henry Stauf.

The anchorperson continues to talk over images of old
newspaper stories from the 1920s and mysterious photos
of HENRY STAUF and his ill-fated guests. The screen
switches to current images of the main street of Harley
on Hudson.

                    ANCHOR (V/O)
   Police have expressed concern that Morales'
   disappearance may be connected to a series of
   killings that have plagued the Hudson Valley this
   year.

Another IMAGE, a BODY, lying in the grass. Signs of
violence, blood, the skin discolored, leaves and twigs
stuck to the body.

                    ANCHOR (V/O)
   So far, four women and three men have been victims
   fitting a pattern of homicide, and several others
   are missing.
```

Another image of Robin comes onto the screen.

                    ANCHOR(V/O cont'd)
  Robin Morales has been missing for more than three
  weeks and seems to have vanished without a trace.

The anchorwoman again appears on the screen.

                    ANCHOR
  She is the producer for the very popular and
  flamboyant CASE UNSOLVED reporter Carl Denning.

An image of Denning fills the screen, smiling, confident.

                    ANCHOR (V/O)
  Denning is said to have been in seclusion in his
  country home in Connecticut since Morales'
  disappearance. It's rumored that the two were
  romantically involved before ...

Denning clicks off the TV with a remote switch. He
slumps back in his chair and massages his temples. He
looks up at the sound of a doorbell ringing, gets out
of his chair and crosses the room and opens the door.
A UPS truck is pulling away and a package is on the
doorstep.
  Denning crouches down and picks it up and goes back
inside. He returns to his chair and opens the package,
revealing a small, portable computer of some kind. He
switches it on, and a game flickers to life on the
machine . . . "Funhouse From Hell"—Cartoony images of
mayhem, monsters . . . Slowly, the computer game changes
to an image of Robin looking frightened in the basement
of an old house. She speaks to him from the small
screen.

                    ROBIN
  Carl . . . help me . . . please! . . . I can't get out . . .
  I . . .

The image of Robin fades away and the video screen
goes blank as if the game has shut itself off. Denning
shakes the box and clicks it on and off but it seems
to have died.

                    DENNING
  What is this! . . . ?

He sets the game computer on the arm of the chair,
gets to his feet and begins to pace. The game starts
beeping. He grabs it and switches it on. An image of
the Stauf mansion appears briefly and fades away and the
game shuts down again.

```
                         DENNING
     Damn!


     Then the screen comes alive for another brief moment:
     An image of Robin appears. She mouths the word "Help"
     but there is no sound and the picture quickly fades.
     Denning pulls on a leather windbreaker and stuffs the
     game in his pocket as he crosses the room and leaves
     in a rush.
```

Script courtesy Trilobyte Inc. © 1994 Trilobyte Inc.

CONCLUSION

A writer who is a master of all the types of writing described above will be an asset on a multimedia production team, but additional skills will make you truly invaluable. These are outlined in the next chapter.

REFERENCES

Gibney, Sheridan. Lecture. University of Southern California, Los Angeles.

Nelson, Andrew. E-mail to the author, October 1999.

Nielsen, Jakob. *The Alertbox: How Users Read on the Web.*
    http://www.useit.com/alertbox/9710a.html.

O'Meara, Maria. Notes to the author, February 1996.

T. Rowe Price Web site. http://www.troweprice.com, 1999.

CHAPTER 3

HIGH-LEVEL DESIGN, MANAGEMENT, AND TECHNICAL SKILLS USEFUL TO THE INTERACTIVE WRITER

CHAPTER OVERVIEW

Understanding interactivity and the ability to write well for many media are essential for the interactive writer, but writers who want to get more control over their material and expand their career options should consider developing additional skills. The skills this chapter discusses include:

- Information and Interactive Architecture
- High-Level Narrative Design
- Project Management
- Content Expertise
- Writing to the Search Engines
- Flowcharting and Other Techniques for Organizing Content
- Creating Web Pages

HIGH-LEVEL DESIGN, CONTENT, AND PROJECT MANAGEMENT

INFORMATION AND INTERACTIVE ARCHITECTURE

Information architecture is the overall structure and navigation of an informational multimedia piece. Structuring multimedia is far more challenging than structuring a linear piece, such as a book or a video, because multimedia is made up of many discreet units of information that can be connected in a myriad of ways, as was discussed in the last two chapters. Key issues for the information architect are:

- clearly identifying the project's communication goals
- understanding the key needs of the targeted user, including what specific tasks they need to accomplish
- organizing the information into categories and subcategories
- deciding how the different categories and pieces of information will be linked so that the user can easily navigate among them and interact with them
- establishing the types of interaction and functionality that will be allowed and what technology (databases, simulations, etc.) will facilitate the needed interactions

An information architect has to not only have a librarian's eye for organizing information, but the architect also needs a broad understanding of current technologies available for interactive multimedia. For example, the information architect should clearly understand how databases work and how dynamically driven database information can be presented on a Web site or multimedia program. This topic will be discussed in the case studies in Chapters 11 and 15. Some types of programs require information architects who specialize, such as instructional designers who focus on training and education programs.

A well-designed information architecture not only helps users find the information they want, but it is also one of the most effective ways to initiate interaction with a program. For example, good information architects know how to hook the user by placing the most appropriate content on the top level of the interactive program, such as a Web site's home page where most users first arrive. After hooking the user, this top level information has to lead the user logically to the information that the user wants or that the designers want them to see, such as the purchasing section of the site. Structuring your site so that there are several ways to access information is also important.

An interactive architect performs most of the same duties as an information architect, but he or she is also expected to contribute to the overall user experience on the project. This includes making suggestions about the interface, design, usability, and online applications. These activities are usually the primary responsibility of other team members, but it is one of the duties of the interactive architect to make sure all these elements work together effectively with the information architecture. In actual practice, the titles "interactive architect" and "information architect" may not be as clearly defined as I have suggested above. Sometimes an information architect's role will closely resemble what I have described above for the interactive architect.

Just as film writers become directors to gain more control of their work, interactive writers should consider moving up to the information or interactive architect role. This book has considerable discussion of the information architecture or structure of multimedia to give writers some insight into this practice.

HIGH-LEVEL NARRATIVE DESIGN

Similar to the information architecture in an informational program, the high level-design of an interactive narrative defines the major elements and organization of the project, including:

- the story structure
- the characters
- the role of the player in the narrative and what they will be able to do
- the granularity of the interactions. For example, will the player be able to choose scenes, shots, or the dialogue of the characters.

The writer's participation in the high-level design process of a narrative varies considerably from project to project. Sometimes the designer develops the story idea and the basic structure of the piece before the writer comes on the project. It is the designer who determines what the player will be able to do and how the interactions will work. Sometimes the writer's role is even more restricted; the designer may do much of the writing and bring in a writer to handle just a few scenes. But even in this diminished role, the writers need to be aware of how the scenes they are writing relate to the overall piece. Other designers bring the writers in early and encourage their contribution to the overall design. Many writers feel this is the best way to go, particularly when dealing with stories.

As writers gain experience in multimedia, many learn high-level story design and take more control of their material. This is actually a growing trend with the all-powerful designer disappearing on many projects and being replaced by a designer-writer. This was the case for the interactive narratives that are profiled in Chapters 23 and 24.

PROJECT MANAGEMENT

Once a writer becomes responsible for the high-level story design or information architecture, he or she has an overall grasp of the project that is equal to or surpasses any other member of the team. Considering this, it is not a big leap from information architecture or high-level design to project manager, if the writer has organizational and people management skills. The project manager manages the budget, the personnel on the project, the client, and the coordination of all the elements.

CONTENT EXPERTISE

In informational multimedia, writers are more valuable if they have familiarity with certain types of content. It certainly doesn't hurt for a writer to have a specialty or several specialties, such as finance, medicine, or science. But all writers should be careful to maintain enough flexibility so that they don't get pegged into just one type of work.

WEB SITE MARKETING: WRITING TO THE SEARCH ENGINES

If you write the most amazing Web site and no one can find it, then you have failed. Most users find information on the Web through major search engines, portals, and directories. A Web site writer needs to be able to write a site in such a way that when users search for the Web site's topic, the search engine presents the Web site near the top of the search results list. This requires clever writing of site titles, site text, and meta tags. Meta tags are text on a Web page that is hidden from the user but that has a major impact on search engine placement. To the writer, the two most important meta tags are the description and key words tags. The description tag briefly describes the site's content; the key words tag list words that users might use when they search for the site. For a detailed discussion of writing for search engines see "Search Engines and Key Words" in Chapter 10, "Writing a Marketing Web Site from Proposal to Meta Tags: *Prudential Verani Realty.*"

TECHNICAL SKILLS

If the writer wants to expand his or her role beyond writer into information architect, project manager, and the other duties described above, learning a few technical tools can be quite helpful.

FLOWCHARTING

One of the handiest tools for visualizing and organizing the branching structures of most multimedia programs and Web sites is the flowchart (Figure 3–1). It is also a useful device to visualize processes, such as the flowchart illustrations used throughout this book. Fortunately, the software for creating flowcharts is inexpensive and easy to learn. Numerous examples of flowcharts as preproduction documents for multimedia productions and as illustrations appear in this book.

Flowchart Functions and Variations

A flowchart can have several functions and variations for the same multimedia production:

- To design interactions. Lines with arrows drawn between the labeled boxes on a chart make it possible to understand what links with what and in what way. For example, does the link work in both directions? Is it viewer-initiated or automatic?

- To see the effects of revisions. Continuity is a monstrous issue in interactive media. In linear media, changes in one scene may affect only the scenes immediately following it, but in interactive media, changes in one screen will affect all of the material that is linked to it. It is hard to determine these effects without a chart.

- To chart character development. Some writers create separate charts to track character development, particularly in parallel branching structures where the writers must be sure that the character change is properly set up and consistent in each plot line.

- To present material to clients. A complex interactive script can be inscrutable to a client, particularly one who has no interactive background. A one-page flowchart overview can do wonders to explain a project.

- To communicate with the production team. A production team chart is far more complicated than a client chart, especially a chart for the programmers, in which boxes are labeled with complicated programming code.

- To track large productions. Flowcharts combined with project management software can help chart the progress of a large production, keeping track of what has been accomplished and who is responsible for what lies ahead.

- To form the basis for the user's sitemap. Sometimes the chart itself is the user map, as in Fidelity Investments' retirement counselors' training program, where

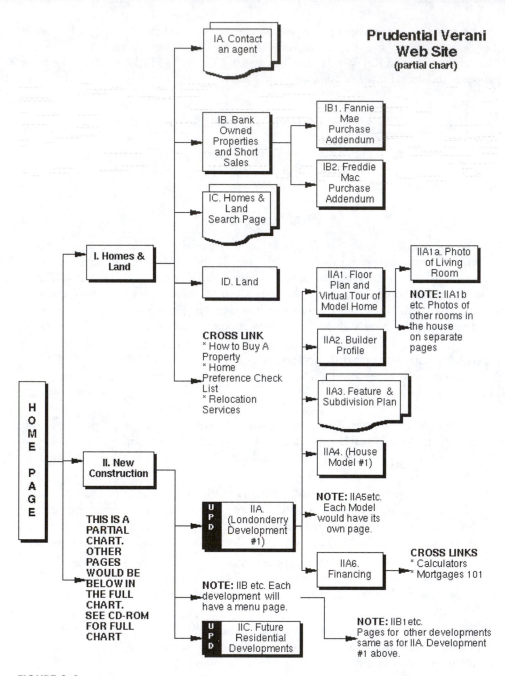

FIGURE 3-1

Partial Flowchart/Sitemap for the *Prudential Verani* Web Site. Flowchart courtesy of Prudential Verani Realty. © 1999 Prudential Verani Realty.

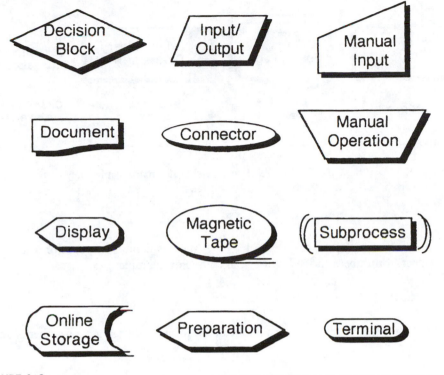

FIGURE 3–2

Flowcharting symbols. Symbols courtesy of Inspiration Software. © 1999 Inspiration Software, Inc.

students can bring up the flowchart at any point and click on a labeled flowchart box to go to that section of the course.

Flowchart Symbols

A number of developers have suggested flowchart symbols to help make charts more useful. The medium being charted is usually distinguished by the shape of the boxes. The type of interaction is usually indicated by the types of lines and arrows. The symbols shown in Figure 3–2 are part of the list from Inspiration flowcharting software (see References at end of chapter).

Text Labels: Gannt Charts

Instructional designer Rodger Gantt suggests labeling each box in a flow chart with a text label. These charts are often called Gantt charts. Some examples of Gantt code are:

INTRO = Introduction

DEMO = Demonstration

REV = Review

KEY

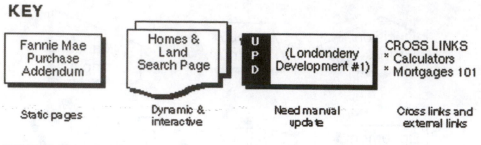

FIGURE 3-3 ————————————————————————————————

Symbol Key for *Prudential Verani* Web Site Flowchart/Sitemap. Symbol key courtesy of Prudential Verani Realty. © 1999 Prudential Verani Realty.

If there is more than one item of a type, such as demonstrations for a lesson or a product, a number is added before the code. For example,

> 1DEMO = Product 1, Demonstration

In this example, if there is more than one demo for a product, then a number is added after the code:

> 1DEMO2 = Product 1, Demonstration 2 (Iuppa, 34)

Writers don't usually go to this level of detail in their flowcharts, but if some variation of the Gantt code helps you clearly see the structure of your project, by all means use it.

Custom Symbols and Labels for a Project

The goal of using flowchart symbols or text labels is to increase clarity, but if there are too many complex symbols, they may add confusion. In my experience, a universal set of symbols has not been accepted. Instead, writers and developers seem to adopt symbols and labels that work well for them on a particular project. For example, Aaron Conners of Access Software uses shaded boxes to distinguish characters in his interactive dialogue. (See *The Pandora Directive* flowchart, Figure 23–2. For the *Prudential Verani* Web site, the symbols illustrated in Figure 3–3 were used.)

Flowchart Design Tips

The goal is for the flowchart to be a clear visualization of the project structure. There are a number of techniques that help make it a more useful tool. The following points are illustrated in the Prudential Verani flowchart in Figure 3–1.

1. Give every page of the site a unique number and name. This makes communication with clients and production staff much clearer. Give pages in a specific section of the site the same first number with different second letters. In the flowchart

example in Figure 3–3, standard outline conventions were used with numbers and different case letters. For example, the menu page for the Homes and Land section is roman numeral I. The Contact an Agent Page, which is linked to that page, is page IA, and so on.

2. For ease of printing and presentation to a client or on a review Web site, run the chart vertically, as in the sample in Figure 3–1, instead of horizontally. If this becomes a problem because your site is more than five levels deep, you may want to reexamine your information architecture and divide your material into more main categories. If a site has too many levels, it can cause navigation problems.

3. Simplify where you can. If there will be multiple sections that will be designed in the same way, it is OK to say that in a note. No need to draw out all the boxes for repetitive pages. There are several examples of this on the chart in the New Construction section where each housing development will be presented on the site the same way.

4. Make it easier to see the main sections by writing those pages in bold text with drop shadows on the symbols.

5. Indicate cross-links (links to pages within the site that are already on the chart) and external links (links to other Web sites) as text only. This helps make the chart more readable and makes it clearer how many pages have to be produced for this project. If there are multiple cross-links or external links from the same page, use asterisks or bullets to separate them.

6. Visually indicate the pages that will have special functions, for example, pages that will have interactive elements or that will be generated dynamically from a database. Do not, however, make your chart confusing with two many different types of symbols. Three or four symbols with a simple key at the top is adequate. See the key sample in Figure 3–3.

Flowcharting Software
The key characteristics of a good writer's flowcharting program are that it can:

- Easily and quickly create and edit flowcharts.
- Export the chart in a standard image format, such as JPEG or GIF, and the outline as HTML for Web publication. On almost every project that I have worked on, the client expects you to post work on a Web site for review. A flowchart program that will automatically convert the charts and outline for Web publishing is essential.
- Be used cross-platform. There should be both Windows and Mac versions of the software. The files should also be cross-platform because your client or other members of your team may need to work with the outlines and flowcharts, and they may be on different platforms than you are.
- Convert the chart into an outline and vice versa. This conversion is useful because:
  - some clients prefer outlines
  - a chart can be converted into an outline, and then that outline can be used as the basis of a script for a program
  - an outline can be imported from another program and then converted to a flowchart.

Software Recommendation   There are lots of tools that you can use to create flow-charts including word processors, draw programs, authoring programs, and presentation software, but like any dedicated task you are going to be much better off getting software designed specifically for flowcharting. There are many good flow-charting programs on the market. My favorite flowcharting software is Inspiration, but if you are already skilled with another one, by all means use it. Major flow-charting software includes: SmartDraw, Visio, FlowCharter, MacFlow/WinFlow, and Inspiration.

The most advanced (and most expensive) flowcharters are more than specialized drawing programs, they are environments for creating applications, but the writer does not generally need this kind of power. Inspiration is a good choice for the writer because it has all the characteristics described above and is not expensive. All the charts in this book were drawn with Inspiration.

I also use Inspiration in my work as a Web interactive architect.

OTHER ORGANIZATIONAL TOOLS

Outlines

Some writers prefer to start their project with a simple hierarchical outline, as in a linear piece. I find that an outline combined with a flowchart is a useful way to describe the content in a Web site (see Chapter 10). Some story writers find outlines one of the easiest ways to keep the story line and character development clear. Aaron Conners, whose interactive movies *Under a Killing Moon*, *The Pandora Directive*, and *The Black Pearl* are among the most complex being written, uses an outline in the early stages of writing.

Storyboards

Storyboards are an excellent organizing tool. A storyboard contains images of the main screens of a program or Web site combined with text explanations of the elements and how they will work together. The storyboard is also a useful way to present a program to a client. Storyboards can be very elaborate for complex programs, but often the client just needs a rough visualization of the proposed screens. There are dedicated storyboard programs, such as Boardmaster, but other multi-use programs will work equally as well for the writer. A WYSIWYG (What You See Is What You Get) HTML editor, such as Microsoft's FrontPage and Macromedia's Dreamweaver, can create quick Web pages that function like storyboards and even link the pages to give a simulation of the planned interactivity. Sometimes just a rough sketch done in your word processor's draw program is adequate, such as the screen in Figure 3–4, which was done in Microsoft Word for a CD-ROM on careers. Some designers call simple storyboards, like this, wire frames.

Database

Although the word "database" might strike fear in the hearts of many nontechnical writers, database programs have become much easier to use. They can be a useful tool when writing, organizing, and managing large, complex projects. For example, my former company InterWrite developed a geology Web site and CD-ROM for the textbook company Houghton Mifflin. The project was large, had numerous assets (video, graphics, audio, animations), several content experts, and a number of editors. Developing a coherent script that would clearly describe and organize all these ele-

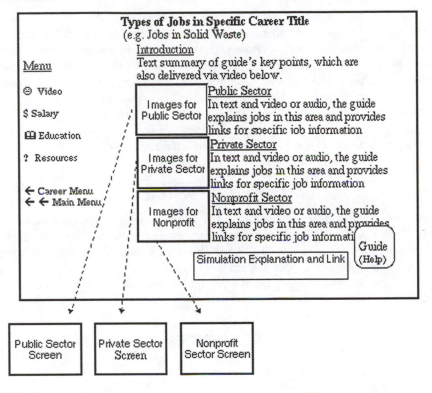

FIGURE 3–4

Rough storyboard or wire frame for a CD-ROM done in Word. Storyboard courtesy of the Environmental Careers Organization. © 1996 The Environmental Careers Organization.

ments, plus allow all the content people and editors to add their comments to the script, was a challenge. The solution was to develop the script as a FileMaker Pro database that allowed us to have one master script as well as to sort and export various special versions of the script for different team members. See the end of Chapter 5 for a description of this solution and a sample page from the script.

WYSIWYG HTML EDITORS

A WYSIWYG HTML editor is a software program that allows the user to create Web pages without knowing HTML, the markup language or programming code that is the basis of most Web sites. A WYSIWYG HTML editor's features include text formatting, image layout, linking, and much more. These editors are as easy to use as word processing software.

There are a couple of reasons why a writer should be able to create Web pages. On almost every project that I work on, one of the first things that the client wants done is the creation of a review Web site or extranet. This is a Web site where I post scripts, flowcharts, images, and other production documents for the client to comment on. Sometimes it is also useful to rough out a complex section of a project in HTML to help the client visualize it.

Basic WYSIWYG HTML editors are inexpensive and adequate for most of a writer's tasks. Microsoft is probably the best inexpensive editor. Windows even includes a limited version of FrontPage with their operating system. If you are already skilled with a major word processor, such as Word or WordPerfect, then you may not have to spend any money at all. Most major word processors have converters that will convert your text into HTML. In most cases, however, these are not as versatile as a dedicated HTML editor. If you think you will get seriously involved in creating Web pages, you might want to buy a more expensive and more powerful HTML editor, such as Adobe GoLive or Macromedia's Dreamweaver.

CONCLUSION

A multimedia writer does not have to learn all the skills described above to be successful. Many writers in large organizations are happy just writing content, but to increase your chances of success and your ability to handle any writing or organizational challenge, the more tools in your arsenal the better. On the other hand, don't forget to maintain your primary focus—presenting compelling information and exciting stories.

REFERENCES

Inspiration Software. http://www.inspiration.com.
Iuppa, Nicholas V. *Interactive Video Design.* Boston, MA: Focal Press, 1982.
O'Meara, Maria. Notes to the author, February 1996.
Prudential Verani Realty Site. http://www.pruverani.com, 1999.

C H A P T E R   4

THE MULTIMEDIA AND WEB SITE PRODUCTION TEAM

CHAPTER OVERVIEW

No matter how multiskilled the writer is, he or she will usually work as part of a production team. Understanding who these team members are and how to interact with them can add to the writer's success and ultimately that of the project. This chapter discusses the following members of the multimedia and Web site production team:

- The Designer
- The Art Director or Creative Director
- The Project Manager
- The Information Architect or Interactive Architect
- The Programmer
- The Video Director
- The Photographer/Videographer
- The Content Expert
- The Product Manager

THE DESIGNER

On a large project, there may be several types of designers, for example, instructional designers, graphic designers, and interface designers. These categories are sometimes lumped into one title: creative designer or just designer. Because of overlapping duties, these titles frequently become meaningless. In most cases, a designer's responsibilities include the visual look of the project and sometimes also the interface design. The designer's relationship with the writer is different from production to production.

THE ART DIRECTOR OR CREATIVE DIRECTOR

The art director, sometimes also called the creative director, oversees and sometimes creates visuals: backgrounds, interface screens, graphics, and animations. Individual designers are supervised by the art director. The writer should work closely with the art director/creative director, especially if considering more complex visuals, such as animations. He or she can make the writer aware of the communication potential of the graphic tools being used on the project.

THE PROJECT MANAGER

On large projects, this is a separate position, but sometimes is combined with other positions, as described in Chapter 3, "High-Level Design, Management, and Technical Skills Useful to the Interactive Writer." The project manager (PM) manages the budget, the client, the personnel on the project, and the overall assembly of the elements.

THE INFORMATION ARCHITECT OR
INTERACTIVE ARCHITECT

As described in the Chapter 3, the information architect is the person responsible for the overall structure and navigation of an informational multimedia piece.

THE PROGRAMMER

The programmer is the computer expert. He or she writes the code or uses the authoring program to make the dreams of the writer, designer, and other production members become reality on the computer screen. Establishing good rapport with the programmer is essential for the writer to understand what type of information or story element manipulations are possible with the tools available for this program. For example, the programmer can help the user better understand the potential of dynamic information flow through the use of databases and other tools. (Dynamic information flow is discussed in detail in Chapter 11.) If a programmer's skills are limited to HTML and Java Script for Web sites, the team member is sometimes called a site developer. Site developers often also have graphic skills.

THE VIDEO DIRECTOR

The video or film director is in charge of creating live-action video. The director may also be in charge of developing the original audio for stock footage. The writer's relationship to the director varies with each individual, but in many cases it is a collaboration that starts with the director's commenting on early drafts of the script, and extends into production, with the writer performing last-minute rewrites.

THE PHOTOGRAPHER/VIDEOGRAPHER

Another key person is the photographer or, if there is video, the videographer. On smaller projects, there will not be a separate video director. The writer has to be sure that the photographer or videographer can capture the images needed for the project. The writer must be able to adequately describe the project's visuals needs and to understand the capabilities of the photographer/videographer and the limitations of their equipment.

THE CONTENT EXPERT

The content expert is an important person in informational or educational multimedia because he or she can be an invaluable source of information. For example, medical pieces often have physicians as content experts. Nevertheless, content experts are not necessarily writers. Knowledge of a subject does not mean that one knows how to present it well. That is the job of the writer.

THE PRODUCT MANAGER

On large projects, the product manager works with the client and deals with marketing issues if the program is aimed at the mass market. Sometimes the roles of product manager and project manager are combined. A writer who is brought in early can test ideas with the product manager, who often knows the client's needs or the intended market best. But writers should never completely abdicate their creative vision in favor of market research. If the marketing people could always predict what would be successful, then they would all be rich.

CONCLUSION

Not all of the individuals discussed above will be on every project. Many projects will have some of these duties combined. Very large projects will have even more positions. To get a sense of the types of positions evolving in multimedia and the Web, go to the careers section on the Web site of a big production company or recruiter and review their job listings.

The core creative team for most projects includes writers, designers, and programmers. Because of the complexity of multimedia, the writers must think of themselves as part of this team and learn all they can from their team members so that they push the communication potential of multimedia and the Web to the limits needed for each project.

REFERENCE

O'Meara, Maria. Notes to the author, February 1996.

C H A P T E R 5

SCRIPT AND PROPOSAL FORMATTING

CHAPTER OVERVIEW

Multimedia and the Web's use of many media and interactivity makes script formatting difficult. Nevertheless, it is essential for writers to present their ideas effectively on paper so that clients and production team members can visualize their ideas. At this point in the industry, there is no one set format for all situations. The format chosen depends on the demands of the individual production. After discussing scriptwriting software, this chapter defines the following formats:

- Web Site Outlines
- Treatments
- Proposals and Design Documents
- Single-Column scripts
- Double-Column scripts
- Triple-Column scripts

SCRIPTING SOFTWARE

There are number of software programs dedicated to script formatting. Some of the better known ones include Final Draft, Movie Magic, and ScriptThing. Some writers swear by these programs and think that it makes the writing process much easier. My own feeling is that if you are competent with a major word processing program, such as Word or WordPerfect, you don't really need a dedicated scriptwriting program. The key is becoming skilled with tables and learning how to create macros. Macros allow you to automate certain formatting functions and make writing a script much easier. If you don't know how to use macros, go to the help section of your software, search for macros, and follow the instructions. There also are some word processor add-ons that can help with macro creation, such as Macro Concepts.

Using your current word processor will not only save you money and the time it would take to learn a new program, it will also insure compatibility. Scripts and other documents are often shared with other member of the multimedia team. If you write in a major word processor, chances are that other members of the team will be able to open your files and edit your documents. If you use a specialized script formatting software, accessibility may not be the case, unless the software can export to a standard format.

PRELIMINARY DOCUMENTS: OUTLINES, PROPOSALS, HIGH-LEVEL DESIGN DOCUMENTS

A project's script or detailed design document includes every word of text, narration, and dialogue; descriptions of all the images, video, and animation; and explanations of the linking and functional elements. Fortunately, projects almost never start with a script. Usually some sort of preliminary written document is presented to the client and other members of the production teams before the final script is written. This is useful for clients who may have difficulty understanding an interactive script. It also insures that the basic goals of the project are being achieved before the fine details are worked out in the script. Sometimes the preliminary form itself, such as a Web site outline, is adequate to get the production green-lighted with the client.

WEB SITE OUTLINES

For many of my Web sites, I have found that a complete script of the site is not needed. Usually a flowchart and a detailed outline of the content is sufficient to explain the site to the client. With a large Web site, many clients may not even want to read a full script in the planning stage.

Flowcharts were discussed in detail under "Flowcharting" in Chapter 3, "High-Level Design, Management, and Technical Skills Useful to the Interactive Writer." The flowchart illustrates the overall navigation, structure, and size of the site; the outline provides more details about the actual content and functionality of the individual pages. The outline sample that follows is most effectively used with an accompanying flowchart. The client consults the chart for overall structure, then reads the outline for the details. The structure of each page on the outline below is fairly simple. The outline should be adjusted to match the specific project. The elements include:

- Title: The page title, which should be the same as what is on the flowchart
- Image: Describes possible images for the page, including animations or video
- Text: Describes on-screen text
- Links: Includes all the links on this page from text within the page and from the navigation bar or menu
- Navigation: The specific buttons that will have to be created for the navigation bar or menu
- Functionality: This describes what the user can do on this page besides click and read. For example, if it is a real estate site, as in the example below, can they search for properties or calculate their mortgage?

A useful feature of Inspiration software, which I use to create my outlines, is that it will convert the outline to HTML for publishing to a client's review site on the Web. Part of this conversion is to create a clickable menu at the top of the outline for every page in the site, so the client can quickly jump to the page they want. See the Chapter 10 section on the *Writing for Multimedia and the Web* CD-ROM for a working example of this menu.

Partial Outline of the *Prudential Verani* Web Site

HOME PAGE

TITLE: PRUDENTIAL VERANI REALTY: The Real Estate and Relocation Resource for Southern NH

IMAGE: Images that demonstrate that Verani is a professional, friendly place. Possible images: Prudential logo, friendly Verani staff, Verani office, people enjoying a beautiful home. Might have other images on page to lead user to some of our key features, such as a calculator image for the tools and an E-mail icon for our custom E-mail notification service. Images will be small or designed in such a way that the page will load quickly.

TEXT: Explain that we are part of Prudential, one of the largest corporations in the world, but also a family-owned company with strong roots in Southern New Hampshire. We have the resources to sell your property effectively and/or make your home search efficient and successful. Also should introduce some of the key features of the site, such as our searches, custom E-mail notification tools, extensive information resources, and so on. Near the bottom of the page should be a short disclaimer stating that we have made every effort to make the information on this site accurate but are not liable for any errors or omissions; please see our Terms of Use Policy.

LINKS: Homes & Land, New Construction, Commercial & Industrial, Relocation Services, Verani Mortgage and Title, Real Estate Information & Resources, News & Special Events, Search/Site Map, About Us/Contact.
   Might also have a link from a calculator image to the tools and calculator section.
   In text on the bottom of the page and on every page will be links to Terms of Use, Privacy Statements, and a WebMaster E-mail link.

NAVIGATION BAR: Homes & Land, New Construction, Commercial & Industrial, Relocation Services, Verani Mortgage and Title, Real Estate Information & Resources, News & Special Events, Search/Site Map, About Us/Contact.

The text sample courtesy of Prudential Verani Realty. © 1999 Prudential Verani Realty.

I. HOMES & LAND

TITLE: Homes & Land

IMAGE: Small image of attractive house. This could be the same picture all the time or a regularly changing featured house.

TEXT: Briefly explain the range of properties we offer and the area we cover. Direct the user to the search page and other services that will help them in their moving and home buying, such as Relocation Services, the How to Buy a Property Section, Home Preference Check List/Questionnaire, & New Construction.

LINKS: Home, Search, Contact, Relocation Services, the How to Buy a Property Section, Home Preference Check List/Questionnaire, & New Construction.

NAVIGATION BAR: Home, Search, Contact

IA. CONTACT AN AGENT

TITLE: Contact Us

IMAGE: Photo of friendly agent.

TEXT: Phone numbers, addresses, and E-mails for all offices. Plus a form that user can fill out and submit so that we can contact them.

LINKS: Home Page, Search, Contact, Homes & Land.

NAVIGATION BAR: Home Page, Search, Contact, Homes & Land.

FUNCTIONALITY: Users can fill out form with their address and E-mail, click the type of information they want, write a short note and submit it to us. Message will go to different people at Prudential Verani depending on what type of information the user requests.

TREATMENTS

Although a treatment could be used for a preliminary description of a Web site, it is more commonly used for CD-ROM or DVD multimedia programs. The treatment, a form borrowed from linear film or TV writing, describes the structure and key elements of a project in a form similar to an essay or a short story. Guidelines for treatment writing include:

- Use the third person (e.g., "He shambles," not "I shamble" or "you shamble").
- Use the present tense ("he shambles," not "he shambled").
- Write visually. Be descriptive, but don't call shots.

- Capitalize:
  - Character names when they first appear.
  - Major sound effects.
  - Technical directions, such as ROLLOVER, LINK, etc. (but don't use unless necessary).
- Usually summarize on-screen text, dialogue, and narration, although a few bits of dialogue or narration are allowed if they help present the material.
- Usually double-space treatments, although sometimes they are single-spaced, with chapter or section headings in all capitals.

Multimedia Informational Treatment Sample

The following sample is from the conclusion of the treatment for *The Nauticus Shipbuilding Company*, a multimedia program about shipbuilding presented on a museum kiosk. (The entire treatment may be found under "The Proposal" in Chapter 14, "Museum Kiosk Case Study: *The Nauticus Shipbuilding Company*.")

> **Conclusion:** After the last component has been selected, a 3-D animation sequence depicts the launching of the vessel. If the design is suitable for the mission, the visitor will see a depiction of their design successfully carrying out the mission. If the design is fundamentally flawed, the vessel will be shown sinking. Some evaluation will be provided as to the ability of the visitor's design to carry out the selected mission. Finally, the visitor will be given the opportunity to print out their design and evaluation.

Narrative Treatment Sample

A narrative interactive treatment is sometimes called a walkthrough. Following is a section of the walkthrough for *The Pandora Directive*. (See "*The Pandora Directive* Narrative Walkthrough" in Chapter 23.)

> In the introductory conversation with Gordon Fitzpatrick, you learn that he is looking for a Dr. Thomas Malloy, who recently stayed at the Ritz Hotel. Fitzpatrick and Malloy used to work together (where, unspecified). Fitzpatrick then says he saw a photograph of Malloy in the Bay City Mirror and found out that the photograph had been taken at a local university (San Francisco Tech). Fitzpatrick gives Tex a copy of the photo.

PROPOSALS AND DESIGN DOCUMENTS

A treatment is usually only one component of the first detailed description of an interactive project. This preliminary description is sometimes called a high-level design document proposal, a design proposal, or just a proposal.

Format for an Informational Design Document Proposal

A design document usually includes the following elements in this order. See Chapter 14 for a complete design document.)

- Design objective. This is a short description of what the program hopes to accomplish. It is sometimes no more than a paragraph, but it is important because it is the first chance to grab the reader.
- Creative treatment. This is a detailed description of the entire program. It will run for many pages, depending on the size of the project.
- Navigation. This is a description of the interface and how the user will navigate through the program. It often includes a navigation flow chart. The navigation is also described in the treatment.
- Production and marketing. Design documents often have sections dealing with the project schedule or, if it is a mass-market piece, ideas for marketing the program to the public. Biographies of the writer, designer, and other key personnel are sometimes included here.

Format for a Narrative Proposal

A proposal for a multimedia program that includes a story would follow much of the same format as above. It may, however, call the treatment a "story summary." There may also be sections describing the characters.

SCRIPTS AND FINAL DOCUMENTS

Unlike the preliminary documents discussed above that summarize the key features of a program, the script details every element of a piece. The examples that follow are only a few of the interactive script formats in use, but they present enough options that you should be able to find something that can be adapted for your production.

Be aware that many productions don't use traditional scripts at all and instead use combinations of flowcharts, dialogue lists, walkthroughs, and other types of written material. These materials and other script samples are documented in more detail in the case studies in Part II, "Writing Nonnarrative Informational Multimedia and Web Sites," and Part III, "Writing Narrative Multimedia."

LINEAR SCREENPLAY FORMAT

Many approaches to formatting scripts for interactive multimedia use linear screenplay or teleplay format as their basis and then add variations, so it is useful to understand the specifics of the linear screenplay format.

Script format is important because the running time of a video is judged by the number of pages. One page, if it is typed in proper format, is roughly, one minute of screen time. There are variations on the example below, such as greater use of double-spacing in television writing, but the example is a standard screenplay format that can readily be adapted to different situations. Note that margins and line spacing are distorted in the example below to allow space for the directions.

DIRECTIONS
Top margin = 1″. Number pages in upper right-hand corner.
No number on page 1.

Slug lines are typed in CAPS at the beginning of each scene,
telling whether scene is INT. or EXT. (interior or exterior),
location of scene, and day or night.

Scene Description: Left margin 1.75″, right margin 1″ (7.5″
if measured from left)

Break long descriptions into several short paragraphs. The
first time a character's name appears in the scene
description, type it in CAPS.

Single-space within scene description or dialogue. Add a
blank line space between dialogue passages, scene
description paragraphs, and slug lines.

Dialogue: left margin = 3.0″, right margin = 2″ (or 6.5″ if
measured from left.)

Name of person speaking dialogue is in CAPS and centered
over the dialogue. No space between speaker's name and
dialogue.

                              THE MULTIMEDIA WRITER

FADE IN:

INT. ARNOLD'S BEDROOM DAY

The room is a wreck. The floor is
covered with papers and trash, the
bed is unmade, and cigarette butts
litter the desk and window sills.

ARNOLD throws the door open and
stumbles into the room. **CAMERA
DOLLIES BACK** with him. Arnold is in
his early twenties, thin, and
unkempt. His once handsome features
are contorted in agony. He clutches
what appears to be a multimedia
manuscript in his hand.

He stumbles to the floor and falls to
his knees, pulling the script to his
bosom. He falls back with a scream
and hits the floor in agony, dropping
the script.

The title of the manuscript is
revealed to be The Great American
Video Game.

                    ARNOLD (OS)*
                     (whispering)
          Why me?

DISSOLVE TO:

EXT. ARNOLD'S APARTMENT DAY LONG **SHOT**

The door of the apartment swings open
and Arnold stumbles out clutching his
script.

                        ARNOLD
          I keep asking myself:
          What is the secret?

The booming, powerful, authoritative
voice from the unseen NARRATOR of our
film is heard.

Dialogue direction is typed in small letters, centered under speaker, and placed in parentheses.

NARRATOR (VO)**
(booming)
Arnold never did learn the secret. He should have read Tim Garrand's Writing for Multimedia and the Web.

Camera movements, such as tilt, pan, track, dolly, and zoom typed in CAPS in the scene description.
On right side of page are placed: Fade out and Dissolve to.
On left is Fade in.

THE CAMERA QUICKLY ZOOMS IN TO Arnold. He tosses away his script in the trash and runs off.

His script sits on the top of the trash can, its pages fluttering sadly in the breeze.

Bottom margin = 1/2–1″. It depends on how dialogue breaks. Don't break dialogue over 2 pages.

FADE OUT.

*(OS) next to the speaker means off-screen. The character is part of the action, but we do not see him or her in this particular shot. A character yelling from the bathroom while the camera focuses on the bedroom is an example of an off-screen voice. Or, as in the example above, the camera could simply be focused on an object in the same room as the character, leaving the character nearby but off-screen.

**(VO) next to the speaker means voice-over. This indicates that the speaker is not a part of the film or video's action. Peter Jennings narrating a World War I documentary is an example of VO.

SINGLE-COLUMN, IF-THEN INTERACTIVE FORMAT

Use: Narrative or informational programs with limited interactivity, usually at the scene level. Because it is a single-column script, it would not be well suited to a program with extensive voice-over narration. That usually requires a multi-column script, which is explained later in this chapter under "Double-Column Format" and "Triple-Column Format."

Description: This script is similar to the linear screenplay described above, except that at various points in the script the user is given two or three choices of different scenes. This type of script can be used when the interactivity is fairly simple. The following example is part of an interactive museum piece located at the National Scouting Museum in Murray, Kentucky. In this story, the characters have to choose whether to search the school, the farm, or the neighborhood for a missing child. The situation is first outlined in a linear fashion, and then the options follow: first the school scene option, then the farm scene option. The neighborhood option is not included in this sample. The complete script is included in the "Boy Scout Patrol" area of the Chapters section of the book's CD-ROM.

BOY SCOUT PATROL THEATER

by Maria O'Meara

SCENE 2
TROOP HQ

```
2-1. WS GROUP


                        ALEX
   Okay. We all know why we're here. Bob has divided
   the map up into areas. We're going to use the
   buddy system to cover each one.


                        BOB
   Here's a map of the area we're searching.

2-2. MAP GRAPHIC


                   BOB (voice-over)
   This is where she was last seen—the school. Here's
   where she lives. Between the two is the old Wilson
   Farm.

WHICH PART DO YOU WANT TO SEARCH?
A. THE SCHOOL
B. THE FARM
C. THE GIRL'S NEIGHBORHOOD


IF A. THE SCHOOL
SCENE 2A
2A-1. CU ALEX


                        ALEX
   Chas and Don, you guys go see if she's not still
   hanging around the school.

M-1.
TRANSITION MONTAGE TO SCHOOL
1. POV HALLWAY
2. POV SCIENCE ROOM
3. POV POOL
4. POV STAIRS


SCENE 3
3-1.2 SHOT BOYS enter a classroom.
```

[Scenes have been deleted. The boys search the school and fail to find the girl. They return to scout headquarters and must choose again.]

```
WHICH PART DO YOU WANT TO SEARCH?
A. THE SCHOOL
B. THE FARM
C. THE GIRL'S NEIGHBORHOOD


[IF B. THE FARM]


2B-1. 2 SHOT ALEX AND BOB
```

```
                              ALEX
          Greg and Hal—search the farm.

          M-2.
          TRANSITION MONTAGE TO FARM AREA
          1. POV WOODS

          They happen upon their science teacher who is looking
          for mushrooms in a field. He looks very scientific, and
          has a sample bag, notebook, magnifying glass, etc. He
          is humming a little song.
```

SINGLE-COLUMN, CODED INTERACTIVE FORMAT

Use: Extensive interactivity at the scene level. This is best suited for a narrative, but it could also be used for an informational program that did not have extensive voice-over or other audio that would require a multicolumn script. In this script there are many more options available to the user at each branching program than in the previously described script.

Description: This format follows standard screenplay format pretty closely, but the big difference is that each scene starts on a new page and carries a number code at the top. This allows the program to be interactive at the scene level. Depending on what actions the user chooses, different scenes will be presented. This format is not adequate for interactivity below the scene level.

Depending on the production, the actual code on each scene has different information, such as which story path this scene belongs to, what other scenes it is linked to, and when in the program it plays. (In the example below, the "Z3" indicates that it is the third scene played simultaneously in the "Z" time zone; the 520 indicates it is Jessica's story path.) Once the scenes are coded, they are then presented in a linear fashion with a flowchart or some sort of guide to help the reader understand the possible paths of the story.

The following example is from *Voyeur*, an interactive narrative in which the player is a voyeur who lives across the street from the mansion of a corrupt politician, Hawke, who is preparing to run for the U.S. presidency. The goal of the game is for the voyeur to expose Hawke's corruption without getting anyone (including the voyeur) killed.

VOYEUR

by Lena Maria Pousette and Jay Richardson

```
Z3/115/520-Jessica exposes Reed Hawke
EXT. HAWKE MANOR/ALLEY—NIGHT—APPEARS ON
PLAYER'S TV

Graphic SPECIAL BULLETIN appears on the TV screen.
```

Handheld shaky-cam as the reporter and cameraman run to
Jessica and Masa.

                         REPORTER #1
        Excuse me, Miss Hawke, why are you leaving...

                           JESSICA
        I have material that proves that Hawke Industries,
        with my father's knowledge, was responsible for
        poisoning an entire village in Japan.

                         REPORTER #1
        Is this going to affect your father's decision to
        run for president?

                           JESSICA
        Well, I intend to present this evidence at the
        highest level in Japan, where I am sure criminal
        charges will be filed. But that's all I have to
        say.

                         REPORTER #1
        But what about the reports—

They exit.

_____

© 1993 Philips Interactive Media.

SINGLE-COLUMN, SCREEN-BASED INFORMATIONAL SCRIPT WITH ELEMENT LABELS

Use: This script is best suited to an informational program that has considerable
interactivity and a variety of media, such as narration, text, and video. Screen elements are clearly defined in the script by labels.

Description: This script was used in the training program *Vital Signs*, which teaches
medical technicians how to perform various tasks. Each script page is one screen of
material. The script page has three parts divided by horizontal lines. The top part
describes the lesson and topic. The middle part describes the actions. The bottom part
describes the feedback (reaction to the actions) and linking.

                         VITAL SIGNS

        Unit: u1
        Lesson: Blood Pressure
        Topic:
        Title:
        Screen: u1.4.13p
        Type:
        Graphic File:

(**GRAPHIC/VIDEO:** Colette looking apprehensive)

Text:

Meet Colette, age 7.

You're going to take her blood pressure. You've explained the procedure to her. What do you use next?

(CAPTIONS)

    Cuff   Ball Pump   Valve on cuff   Doll

(**AUDIO: NARRATOR VO**): Now it's your turn. Meet Colette, age 7. You're going to take her blood pressure. You've explained the procedure. What do you use next—the cuff, the ball pump, the valve on the cuff, or the doll? SELECT your choice now.

Feedback: (VO and text)

Cuff, Ball Pump, Valve = (SFX: Little Girl's Voice) (**VO audio ONLY**): No. I don't want that. It's going to hurt!

NARRATOR (VO): Apparently, Colette didn't buy your explanation. Try again.

Doll = **NARRATOR (VO):** You're good. That's right. From the look on her face, you can tell Colette didn't buy your explanation, so you demonstrate on a doll. (SELECT "GO AHEAD" to continue.)

Branching: u1.4.14p

Special Instructions:

© 1995 Harvard Pilgrim Health Plan.

SINGLE-COLUMN, SCREEN-BASED INFORMATIONAL SCRIPT WRITTEN IN A DATABASE

Use: This type of script could be used for a narrative or information piece with substantial interactivity. It would only be needed for a complex program with many team members or where the final pages were dynamically generated from script segments in a database.

Description: My company InterWrite developed a geology Web site and CD-ROM for the textbook company Houghton Mifflin. The project was quite large, had numerous assets (video, graphics, audio, animations), several content experts, and a number of editors. Developing a coherent script that would clearly describe all these elements and allow all the content people and editors to add their comments to the script was a challenge.

The solution was to develop the script as a FileMaker Pro database (see following for a sample page). Each of the elements below, such as screen text or visual layout, were separate fields or units of information in the database. This allowed us to have one master script with all the elements, but by using the databases sort and export functions, we were able to create multiple custom scripts and documents from that master script. These documents included: a list of scenes and a flowchart for the project manager; a table of assets needed for the media researcher; a script (free of internal comments) for an outside vendor; a detailed list of instructions for the animator; and so on. This database script could also be used as the basis of an asset database so that video, graphics, and other elements could be easily found for future projects.

GEOLOGY EXPLORER

Page Number. **Title Date**	VIII-2b Relative Ages
Screen Text	Now see if you can determine the year in which the car in the center was released. Write your answer in the space provided and then hit "Continue." If you have absolutely no idea, just hit "Continue."
Visual Layout	Layout 2 Text top, Graphic bottom. The graphic consists of the three cars in a row. A text input box labeled "Car Release Date" is above the 1955 Ford.
Screen Action	Input date; hit "Continue."
Feedback	
Links	Correct Answer + Continue. → VIII-2b1 Incorrect Answer + Continue. → VIII-2b2.
A: Graphic 1	D1) Model-T Ford
A: Graphic 2	D2) 1955 Ford
A: Graphic 3	D3)1999 Lexus
A: Animation	
A: Audio	
A: Video	
A: Shockwave	Three pictures are arranged in a horizontal row with a text input box above D2)1955 Ford.
Assets Notes	
Notes Internal **Notes to Author**	No need to actually register whether the student is right. We can just give the correct answer.
Notes to Vendor	

DOUBLE-COLUMN FORMAT

Use: Informational projects with substantial interactivity and voice-over narration.

Description: This format is similar to what is used for documentary video. It has two columns, with images on the left and audio and text on the right. An unusual aspect of this particular script is that it is illustrated, which works very well to present the feel of the completed project. Most double-column scripts do not include images.

This program is displayed in an interactive kiosk at the National Maritime Center in Norfolk, Virginia. This production teaches shipbuilding principles by having the player build a ship. In the following section, users can choose to get information on various hull types and then must pick one of these hulls for the ship they are building. Because there is only a small amount of material on each hull, all the choices are listed sequentially. See Chapter 14 for the full script.

THE NAUTICUS SHIPBUILDING COMPANY

IMAGES	AUDIO & TEXT
	"Press a number to learn about a hull"
	CHOICES:
	1) Air Cushion
	-Flat hull rides on cushion of air
	-Capable of high speeds
	-Needs flat water conditions
	-Flat, rectangular deck, easy to load
	2) Planing Hull
	-V-shaped hull capable of high speeds
	-Performs best in flat water conditions
	-High stress levels on hull
	3) Displacement Hull
	-Deep, rounded hull, very stable in all conditions
	-Very large cargo capacity
	-Stable platform for large propulsion systems
	-Needs very large propulsion system
	4) SWATH (Small Waterplane Area Twin Hull)
	-2 submerged hulls, very stable
	-Flat deck provides good work area
After selecting a hull to use, cut to Design Assembly	Loudspeaker VO: "Planing hull being moved into position."

```
           screen, animation of
           hull rollout.

           Cut to POV animation      Background sound of motors
           moving to propulsion      whirring and machinery
           subassembly area.         clanging. "Next,  you'll need
                                      to choose a propulsion
                                      system."
```

© 1994 Chedd-Angier Production Company.

TRIPLE-COLUMN FORMAT

Use: Informational scripts with substantial interactivity and a variety of media.

Description: Some writers like to use a triple-column format, such as the one for the educational CD-ROM *Sky High* illustrated below. This approach separates the visuals in one column, the narration and dialogue in another, and the music, sound effects, and links in the third column. This type of format helps the production people clearly isolate the different production elements.

PANEL II-MEDIEVAL AND RENAISSANCE TIMES

CLOSE-UP—KING ARTHUR'S COURT—600 A.D. Click on the castle and go inside!

VISUAL	NARR/SYNC	MUSIC/SFX
Animation [PHAZ.QT.ANM] Castle—On the wall, an ancient-looking calendar with moving phases of the moon	Narration [PHAZ.QT.NARR]	SFX [PHAZ.QT.SFX] [BK 2.2]
VISUAL	**NARR/SYNC**	**MUSIC/SFX**
Video [ECLP.QT.VID] CASTLE VIDEO-Méliès FOOTAGE, from "The Astronomer's Dream," will probably need to be speeded up a little. ARCHIVE FILMS	Narration [ECLP.QT.NARR]	Music [ECLP. QT.MUS] Music [BK 02.3]
VISUAL	**NARR/SYNC**	**MUSIC/SFX**
Animation [CATP.QT.ANM] Castle—Ye Olde Gravity Lab—enter lab and play animated game catapulting different balls. Take catapult to the moon, Mars, and Jupiter to see differences.	Narration [CATP.QT.NARR]	Music [CATP.QT.MUS]

© 1995 D.C. Heath and Company.

CONCLUSION

As you have seen in the variety of script and other document formats in this chapter, there is no one way to format for multimedia and Web documents. The primary requirement is to make sure that whatever format you choose, it is clear to your client and everyone on your production team. And as with most things, keep it as simple as you can. Your format should be self-explanatory.

CHAPTER 6

KEY POINTS FROM PART I: INTERACTIVE MEDIA AND THE WRITER

MULTIMEDIA DEFINED (CHAPTER 1)

Interactive multimedia is a computer-delivered, communication medium that uses any combination of sound, pictures, video, animation, and text to communicate to the user interactively. Multimedia is presented on the World Wide Web; online services, such as America Online; local networks, such as corporate intranets; computer hard drives, such as museum kiosks; interactive television, such as Web TV; dedicated gaming systems, such as Nintendo; and discs, such as CD-ROMs and DVDs. The interactive writer creates proposals, outlines, sitemaps, treatments, walkthroughs, design documents, scripts, and all the other written material that describes a multimedia production.

THINKING INTERACTIVELY (CHAPTER 1)

Unlike linear media in which the writer must limit options, in multimedia and the Web, the writer must have a feel for all the possible interactions in a narrative scene or for all the different ways that information can be linked together in an informational program. Complicating the interactivity is the need to anticipate user input—the different ways that users will want to take advantage of the interactive options the writer has provided.

LINKING (CHAPTER 1)

A link is the way that one element of a program is connected to another element in the same program or a completely different program. There are three basic types of links:

1. Immediate or direct links: An action.
2. Indirect links: A reaction.
3. Intelligent or delayed links: A delayed reaction.

HIGH-LEVEL DESIGN (CHAPTER 1)

The complexity that interactivity and linking add to a multimedia project demands strong high-level design for the program to be coherent and effective. High-level design determines the broad conceptual approach to the project, including the architecture, navigation, interface, map, organizing metaphors, and even input devices.

INTERACTIVE DEVICES (CHAPTER 1)

The designer and writer must develop specific interactive devices that will make users aware of the interactive possibilities they have created. These devices include on-screen menus, help screens, icons, props, other characters, and cues embedded in the story or information.

WRITING FOR MANY MEDIA (CHAPTER 2)

The interactive writer must be expert in a variety of techniques: writing to be read (journalism, copywriting); writing to be heard (radio, narration); writing to be seen (film, video); plus writing for the special demands of the computer screen. This is because multimedia can easily incorporate many types of media in a single production or even a single screen, and multimedia can manipulate these media in ways not before possible.

HIGH-LEVEL DESIGN AND MANAGEMENT SKILLS USEFUL TO THE INTERACTIVE WRITER (CHAPTER 3)

Writers who want to get more control over their material and expand their career options should consider developing additional skills, such as:

- Information Architecture
- High-Level Narrative Design
- Project Management
- Content Expert

FLOWCHARTING AND OTHER ORGANIZATIONAL TOOLS (CHAPTER 3)

To organize the complex elements of a multimedia or Web production, the writer must learn organizational tools. Flowcharting is a particularly useful way to visualize an interactive program for clients and production team members. Other organizational and visualization tools commonly used by writers are outlines, storyboards, databases, and index cards.

WRITING AS PART OF THE PRODUCTION
TEAM (CHAPTER 4)

No matter how multiskilled the writer is, he or she will usually work as part of a production team. Understanding who these team members are and how to interact with them can add to the writer's success and ultimately that of the project. The core creative team for most projects includes writers, designers, and programmers, but larger projects may have many other positions.

SCRIPT FORMATTING (CHAPTER 5)

The preliminary forms for many multimedia programs are proposals, design documents, and outlines. The elements of an informational design document include design objective, creative treatment, navigation, and production and marketing. A narrative proposal might also include a story summary and characters. There is a wide variety of script formats including single-column, double-column, and triple-column scripts.

PART II

WRITING INFORMATIONAL MULTIMEDIA AND WEB SITES

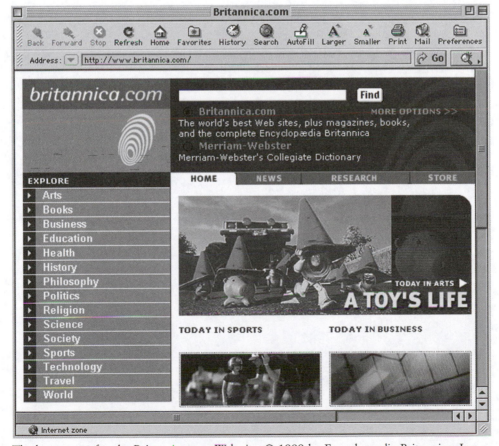

The home page for the Britannica.com Web site. © 1999 by Encyclopaedia Britannica, Inc.

C H A P T E R 7

PRINCIPLES OF INFORMATIONAL MULTIMEDIA AND WEB SITES

CHAPTER OVERVIEW

This chapter introduces multimedia and Web sites that communicate information without using fictional storytelling techniques. The aspects of informational multimedia and Web sites examined in this chapter include:

- Definitions of nonnarrative informational multimedia and Web sites
- Passive versus active information delivery: getting beyond click-and-read
- Informational multimedia and Web site communication goals
- Learning to learn: educating toolmakers

INFORMATIONAL MULTIMEDIA AND WEB SITES DEFINED

Most multimedia is designed to communicate information or to allow users to perform information-based tasks. Multimedia informational titles include many Web sites, educational and reference CDs and DVDs, corporate training programs, museum exhibits, and even online advertising.

If the information being presented is about something concrete, such as a person or a place, informational multimedia follows the documentary tradition of presenting its information through the actual locations and individuals studied. For example, *Compton's Interactive Encyclopedia* shows a video of Babe Ruth hitting a home run in Yankee Stadium, as opposed to having an actor portray Ruth in a studio. *The Harlem Renaissance* Web site (see Chapter 12) has photos and video of Harlem in the 1920s.

If the information is more abstract, such as the process of buying a home, the material can be explained through text; visualizations, such as charts; and even interactive devices, such as calculators. See the case study in Chapter 10, "Writing a Marketing Web Sit from Proposal to Meta Tags: *Prudential Verani Realty*."

There would be nothing wrong with an informational program that used an actor to play Babe Ruth, and many informational programs are created using narrative fiction. Examples include dramatic re-creations of historical events, or character-driven training programs in which an actor takes on the role of a typical employee. Narrative fiction and informational programs using narrative have special concerns of their own and will be dealt with later in Part III, "Writing Narrative Multimedia." The focus of Part II, "Writing Informational Multimedia and Web Sites," is informational multimedia programs that do not use fictional storytelling techniques.

PASSIVE VERSUS ACTIVE INFORMATION DELIVERY: GETTING BEYOND CLICK-AND-READ

PASSIVE INFORMATION DELIVERY

Too many interactive informational writers deliver their content in a way that requires no user action beyond click-and-read. A common structure is for viewers to click a series of menu items and read the linked content. This approach dominates most Web sites. It is perhaps a functional way to access information, but it keeps viewers at a distance by not making them use or think about the information. Figure 7–1, for example, shows the structure of a click-and-read approach to a project about shipbuilding. In this case, the writer simply organized the information according to categories and subcategories, so users can click an information category and view material about it. This information is presented in a clear manner, but it is not very engaging.

ACTIVE INFORMATION DELIVERY

Active or dynamic information delivery demands more of the user than simply click-and-read. A video or an animation that the user can play and replay is a small step in the right direction, but interactive media can do much more. For example, the same shipbuilding program charted in Figure 7–1 could easily be developed as a program that involves the user interactively. Figure 7–2 charts the structure of an actual program on this subject called *The Nauticus Shipbuilding Company*. In this program, the user plays the role of a shipbuilder. The user is first asked to choose between three different types of ships that need to be built: transatlantic cargo ship, cross-channel ferry, and oceanographic research vessel. The user is then asked to assemble one of these ships by choosing from a variety of components for the hull, propulsion, and superstructure. At the end of the program, the completed ship is evaluated. As it leaves the dock, it floats or it sinks. This approach teaches the same information as the click-and-read hierarchical approach illustrated in Figure 7–1, but it does so in a much more exciting fashion. The answer to getting beyond click-and-read is to involve the user in some way. This is, after all, **interactive** multimedia.

Approaches to Get Beyond Click-and-Read

The following examples are only a few of the many approaches and techniques that can engage the user. The correct approach should emerge from understanding the information to be presented and the intended audience.

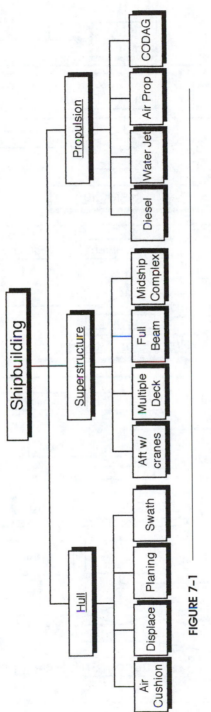

FIGURE 7-1

Structure of a passive information delivery program—click-and-read.

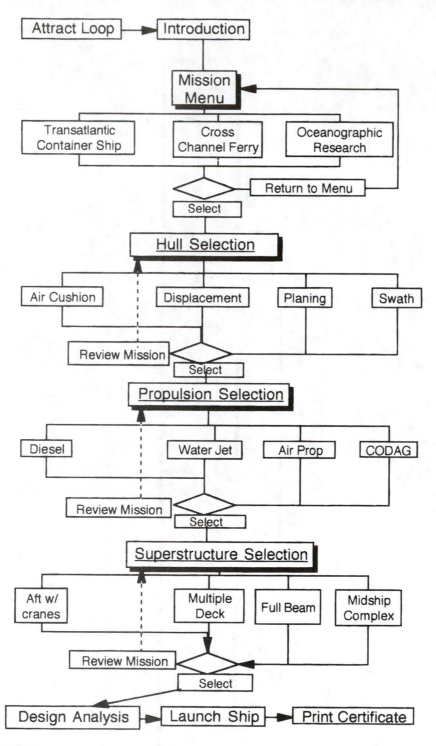

FIGURE 7–2

Structure of active information delivery.

- *Problem solver:* This was the approach *The Nauticus Shipbuilding Company* used. It set up a problem and asked the user to solve it with the information in the program, using the simulation structure. In Houghton Mifflin's *Geology Explorer* Web site, the users are asked to chart the location and magnitude of an earthquake using interactive animation tools. Another exercise in the same program allows users to date the geologic layers of a cross-section of land.

- *Gamer:* In this case the user is a player in a game. Playing this game teaches certain principles. This is somewhat similar to the problem-solver approach, except that it usually operates with more clearly defined game rules. An example from the CD-ROM *Sky High* is the Gravity Lab Game. This game allows users to learn about gravity by discovering what type of ball (basketball, tennis, etc.) can be catapulted through a hoop on each of the planets of our solar system.

- *Reporter:* A number of educational programs, including *Sky High*, allow users to report on their multimedia experience by using a virtual camera and a word processor to write a journal.

- *Explorer:* Here the user explores a physical space in either a complete program or a component of a program. *Into the Cell* allows a virtual voyage into a human cell.

- *Dynamic Information Flow:* Even if the user cannot be engaged interactively for a complete program, at least sections of the program can be developed dynamically. For example, the *Prudential Verani Realty* and *T. Rowe Price* Web sites profiled in Chapters 10 and 11, respectively, both have dynamic information elements such as calculators, tutorials, and customized information that engage the user beyond click-and-read.

INFORMATIONAL MULTIMEDIA GOALS

Informational multimedia programs and Web sites are used in the homes, school, business, and public sites, such as museums. The material covered includes general reference, infotainment, education, interactive magazines and newspapers, sales and marketing, training, public relations, and much more. The good news for the writer trying to grasp the techniques used to create this wide array of informational programming is that most of these productions have one or more of the following major goals:

1. To persuade
2. To entertain
3. To enable transactions
4. To create a sense of community
5. To inform
6. To teach

Of the above goals, the two most fundamental to informational multimedia are the last two: to inform and to teach. These are also the goals that are of the most concern for the writer and that are at the core of most other goals. Because of this, I will only briefly discuss goals 1 through 4 and devote the rest of the chapter to a detailed analysis of how to use interactive multimedia to achieve goals 5 and 6: to inform and to teach.

GOAL #1: TO PERSUADE

Persuasion is a meta-goal that most informational media share. Advertising sells products. Non-fiction book writers try to persuade us to accept their view of the world. And marketing Web sites want to convince us that their company is the best. Because this is such a universal goal, extensive material has already been written about persuasion technique so this topic will not be discussed in detail here. Aristotle was the first to point out the three time tested modes of persuasion to change someone's heart and mind:

- Ethical: If your viewer believes the speaker, they will believe the speech. (Ethos means speaker in Greek). This is the reason that we have to listen to all those highly trained athletes tell us that they love sugary soft drinks.

  A second meaning of ethical is to align your message with the beliefs or ethics of your audience. Many Americans are concerned about the environment. Hence the growth of "green" advertisements that seek to show that a product is as beloved by the little forest creatures as is Snow White.
- Logical: Logical simply means convincing us with facts. Show us why this is a better built tooth brush.
- Emotional: Connect to our emotions. "I am going to be one sexy dude if I wear those blue jeans." This is the approach most used by advertisers.

If you are not familiar with basic persuasion theory, please refer to the article, "Persuasion Theory and Online Advertising" in the Chapter 13 area of the "Chapters" section of this book's CD-ROM.

GOAL #2: TO ENTERTAIN

Entertainment as a goal will be discussed in more detail in the book's Part III, "Writing Interactive Narrative," but one point worth mentioning about entertaining the audience is that all programs must entertain or engage to some degree. Even if a program had the greatest information, it would have limited communication value if it was absolutely boring. A project can be viewed on a continuum, with a plain listing of information at one end, to a program that is pure entertainment at the other end. But most pieces do not exist at either end of this continuum; rather they fall somewhere along the line, embracing elements of both entertainment and information. Where a specific project sits on this continuum is an important consideration for the writer.

GOAL #3: TO ENABLE TRANSACTIONS

The goal "to enable transactions" is important on Web sites that allow users to perform an activity, such as to buy a toy from the etoys Web site or open a bank account online at Fleet.com. In transactional sites, such as these, the writer is still teaching the user information. Many of the principles we will discuss concerning the goal "to teach" will apply to writing for transactional sites. Online transactions and activities do, however, put special demands on the writer who must teach the user about the product and how to perform the transaction in the most efficient way possible. If it takes the user too long to get the information they need to perform the transaction, they simply won't do it. The actual designing of online applications that enable transactions is a topic worthy of detailed study but it is more the responsibility of the interactive architect and the technical architect than it is the job of the writer.

GOAL #4: TO CREATE A SENSE OF COMMUNITY

Many information Web sites try to create a sense of community among their users. For example, the education Web site SmartPlanet (www.smartplanet.com) encourages users to communicate with each other via online chat, message boards, and online courses. These types of techniques can make a user feel as if they belong to group of like minded individuals. Physical communities, such as towns or cities, can use similar techniques on their Web sites to get their citizens involved and make them feel a part of their community. Although this is a valid goal and useful techniques, they do not really demand the skill of the writer except to perhaps suggest such techniques be used as part of the larger information architecture of the site. Much of the information actually written for such sites involves informing the user about their community, its values, and common assumptions.

GOAL #5: TO INFORM

A writer whose goal is to inform wants to provide users with access to a large body of information in a reference work, such as an encyclopedia. The viewers need not and usually are not expected to access all of the information. Instead, they simply take what they need. The information is usually presented clearly and is structured into discreet units with limited manipulation of the material by the writer.

The database is the most common form of a program whose main goal is to provide access to a large body of information. General reference works, such as *Grolier's Multimedia Encyclopedia* and *Britannica Online*, and more focused references, such as *Microsoft Cinemania*, are based on databases. The multimedia database also has many uses in business. For example, real estate companies often have databases of homes for sale. Much of the *Prudential Verani Realty* Web site profiled in Chapter 10 is based on their database of properties. The T. Rowe Price database of mutual fund information is the basis of many of the key features of their Web site (Chapter 11).

Approaches: Creating the Accessible Database

The major challenge with a database is to organize the information in a way that allows users to easily access the information that they want. There are a number of ways to do this.

Grouping by Categories   The simplest way is to group by categories, that is, putting all the same types of items together. For example, *Cinemania* groups movie listings, biographies, awards, and media. The media category includes the subgroups of movie stills, portraits, dialogue, music, and film clips.

Content categories are the most obvious grouping, but material can be organized according to numerous criteria, such as place, time, or theme. For example, *Cinemania* could have a feature that allows searching by place so a user could search for all the material that originated in New York. By time, a search could include all material before 1930. By theme, it could include all material involved with crime.

Even more useful is to combine categories into what is called a complex query. Combine the movie criterion with the place criterion and get all the movies made in New York. Add the time criterion and get all the movies made in New York before 1930. Add the crime theme criterion and get all the movies made in New York before 1930 that deal with crime.

The limitation of this approach is that the categories that the writer comes up with may not be the ones that the user would come up with. The ideal program would help users create their own categories and customize the database to their use.

Concept Maps   Concept maps are a way to visualize categories in a database according to a visual image or map. The museum and journey approach are fairly common. The museum approach allows users to enter a virtual museum, enter exhibit rooms in their area of interest, and view exhibits about a particular subject. The journey allows users to travel along a certain sequence.

A danger with concept maps is combining incompatible maps. An early draft of the program *Sky High* attempted to combine the temporal map of journeying along a time line with the spatial map of the stars and planets. These two different types of maps did not work smoothly together and had to be abandoned. (See Chapter 15, "Educational Multimedia Case Study: *Sky High*," for a full discussion of this issue.)

Customized and Personalized Information   Another excellent approach is to presort the database and only present the user the information that they need or want. To do this, the Web site or other multimedia program has to first collect the user's information preferences and/or needs. There are two basic ways this can be done: customization and personalization.

Customization involves the user consciously inputting their preferences into the computer program. This is usually done by filling out a form or clicking answers on a questionnaire. Once the user's preferences are noted, then just the information that interests them can be presented. For example, on the T. Rowe Price site (see Chapter 11), users can define what mutual funds they want data on. Next time they log on to the site, only those funds will be presented. Learning programs can also be customized by allowing the user to choose which sections they want to study and in what order.

Personalization's main difference from customization is that the user generally does not provide conscious input about their preferences. Instead, the computer program learns the user's preferences by previous activity on the program or Web site. Personalization is most commonly used in transactional Web sites that are trying to match their products with the user. The best known example is the online retailer Amazon.com that will track the books and other items you bought in the past and recommend new purchases based on your previous activity. Amazon.com will also try to guess your preferences by associating you with other customers. If you bought books about angels, and several other customers who bought books about angels also bought books about devils, then Amazon.com might suggest some devil books to you on your next visit. Personalization can also be used on learning programs that can track the user's progress through the program and adapt the type and difficulty of material it will present based on the user's previous performance.

Guides and Agents   One of the most promising approaches for making a database accessible is by creating guides or agents to lead users through the material. These guides could be software creations that are part of the program. For example, *The Mayo Clinic Family Health Book* CD-ROM includes an on-screen character who introduces material and helps to guide users in the direction that they want. This type of a guide is limited by the material that was written for the screen character to present, but there has been much research into how to create truly intelligent agents who could be told by the user what information he or she needed, and then the user could go get a cup of coffee while the helper searched the world and delivered the information to the user's desktop computer. From repeated interactions, such an agent could continue to refine their knowledge of the user's preferences. Software agents are also being used for other purposes, such as providing recommendations for products, automated negotiations and business processes, and even as on-screen computer assistants.

Avoiding Cognitive Overload by Controlling Complexity

Guides, agents, and customized information are some ways to keep users who are browsing a vast database or several databases from getting confused by the diversity and complexity of the unsequenced material they encounter, but cognitive overload is still a problem. Browsing a database is quite a different experience from reading a textbook, where the information is carefully explained and structured to build understanding of an overall topic gradually. In a database, just the opposite can occur. Topics of varying degrees of difficulty can be encountered and only partially understood by the student. "A failure to control this complexity can lead to cognitive overload and failure to learn" (Ambron and Hooper 127).

Cognitive load can be reduced in a number of ways; for example:

- Reduce the number of choices available on the screen at any one time: "seven plus or minus two" is optimal (Ambron and Hooper 128).

- Reduce the level of difficulty available to the student at any different time. Students must have viewed crucial introductory material before they are allowed to access advanced concepts.

- Build a note-taking function into the program so students can track their progress and note partially understood concepts. (Note-taking can include text and pictures.)

- Give students the opportunity to "mark" a section of the program that they can return to later.

- Build in a clear orientation so students can understand where they are and that the various pieces of information are connected. Navigation maps and consistent interface design help with this.

GOAL #6: TO TEACH

A database provides access to a wide body of information. Exactly what information the user accesses and learns is up to the individual. In a teaching program, however, the information may be more narrowly defined and the writer has a clearer goal of what information he or she wants the user to take away from the program.

The Integrated Media Group's *Video Producer* is a good example of a teaching program at the college level. Its goal is to teach the basics of video production. It is carefully structured to do this with mini-lectures, examples, reviews, and quizzes. Fidelity Investments' training program for retirement counselors is similarly focused on teaching a skill. Houghton Mifflin's *Geology Explorer* Web site teaches key concepts about geology.

Instructional theory is a complicated subject that must be studied in depth if one is to become an instructional designer, but it is important to be at least familiar with some of the basic concepts of instructional design before writing educational or training programs.

Interactive Multimedia Instruction as Interpersonal Instruction

Some experts in interactive instruction claim that effective interactive instruction should include the characteristics of interpersonal instruction: immediacy of response, nonsequential access to information, adaptability, feedback, options, bidirectional communication, and interruptibility (Schwier and Misanchuk 175–176).

Immediacy of Response In practical terms, this means that an action the learner takes should get a response immediately. It is psychologically important for the learner to feel connected. For example, when a student clicks on an answer in a quiz, he or she should get some sort of response even if it is just a sound. Similarly, if there is going to be a wait after a student clicks an icon to access a large file, something should be happening on the screen—preferably something more interesting and tied to the program than an hourglass or a watch. Wait-state and other responses should be in tune with the program. Rodney's *Wonder Window*, a humorous children's educational CD-ROM, has funny wait-state text messages, such as "Please wait, Rodney is putting on clean underwear," and visual images, such as the heads on the character icons spinning around or their hair curling.

Feedback Immediacy of response does not mean complex feedback to every action. Deciding what kind of feedback to give and when to give it to the learner is a difficult question. There is no consensus on this subject. There is even disagreement on simple types of feedback. For example, some writers provide only a minimal response, such as "Correct," to correctly answered test questions, and reserve complex feedback for questions answered incorrectly. Others include detailed feedback for correct answers as well, to reinforce the message and to guard against students' guessing the right answers and not learning the material.

Bidirectional Communication Clearly related to immediacy of response and feedback is bidirectional communication and interruptibility. A well-designed learning program gives the user ample opportunity to communicate with the program as well as for the program to communicate with the user. This includes letting the learner communicate through various methods, including typing text, manipulating images, and sound. This is essential if maximum learning is going to happen for the maximum number of students, because studies have proved that we all learn in different ways— some by watching, others by doing, and yet others by analyzing. Thus, it is important to present the message in a variety of approaches.

Interruptibility   Students should be able to interrupt the program at any point and go in the direction that is useful for them. They should, for example, be able to return easily to earlier material for review. If they feel comfortable with the material, they should be able to jump ahead to a more advanced part of the program.

Programs that do not allow this movement can be frustrating. *Video Producer*, an otherwise excellent education program on video production, requires that students complete a series of quizzes on video production techniques before they are allowed to create a video in the program's studio. This defeats the purpose of interactive multimedia and incorporates the drawback of linear media and classroom instruction where all levels of students must progress through the material in the same way.

Inclusion of standard navigation tools can also improve interruptibility. Many programs respond to standard quit commands, such as command Q on the Macintosh. When users quit, they should be able to leave a bookmark at the spot they left and return to it when they start again without having to start at the beginning.

Help   Excellent help programs are now included in basic productivity programs, such as word processors, but a surprising number of educational programs or complex Web sites do not provide a constant helping hand. Help features are particularly important with Web applications, such as opening a bank account online. As in the case of wait-state messages, a writer who can make the access to help more interesting and in tune with the particular program than a help button will contribute to the program's effectiveness. It is important to build the help function into the interface design from the beginning as well as into the writer's schedule. Writing help pages can be extremely time-consuming.

Personalizing Instruction: Nonsequential Access to Information, Adaptability, and Options   Multimedia's ability to access information in the order that the user finds most useful allows a writer to personalize or customize a program and make it adaptable to the user. Many programs allow users to customize the program at the beginning by filling out a user profile based on such criteria as educational level, job, and familiarity with the subject. Once entered into the computer, this profile might cause the program to take the user down a completely different path, or just alter the text on certain screens, or offer different product suggestions.

Personalization can also occur without the user's conscious involvement. Transactional Web sites, such as Amazon.com, track what products you have purchased and use this activity to determine what products to show you in the future. Whatever the approach, personalizing the program continues beyond the beginning by tracking the user's progress and adapting to his or her needs. For example, a learner who consistently has difficulties in a certain area might be directed to special remedial sections geared to that particular problem. The program might also alter the way it presents the instructional material in the rest of the lesson. If the student learned best from the video segments, the video might be increased and text minimized.

A simple way to customize a multimedia piece is to allow students to choose the level of difficulty and thus advance at their own rate. Another adaptation is the degree of control allowed the student over the learning material. Some studies have suggested that weaker students can benefit from more structure (Schwier and Misanchuk 186).

The way subject matter is approached also customizes a program. Someone learning marketing should be able to choose various contexts designed into the program in which to practice their new skills, such as marketing a virtual baseball team, video store, or rock group.

LEARNING TO LEARN: EDUCATING TOOL-MAKERS

In addition to teaching a specific skill or subject matter, multimedia is also very successful at teaching students how to learn. A generation ago, the standard structure for most elementary school classrooms was a teacher standing in front of a sea of students at desks and delivering knowledge from his or her information-packed brain to those of the empty-headed students.

A visit to most classrooms today would find a different structure. The sea of desks is gone. Students are grouped in fours or fives around smaller tables and are engaged in activities. The teacher moves about the room, facilitating their learning. This different structure reflects current learning theory, which rejects the concept of empty heads waiting to be filled and replaces it with the goal of teaching students how to learn. Some theorists have used the metaphor of the tool-maker—that is, teaching students how to create the learning tools that will serve them throughout life (Reddy 284–324).

A big reason for this major change is the rapid explosion in knowledge. A hundred years ago, the body of knowledge was relatively stable. Individuals could learn a trade and successfully perform that trade until retirement. Today, however, information is expanding so rapidly that education has become a lifelong pursuit. Students have no assurance that the information they are learning will be valid in a few years or even that the careers they are training for will exist after graduation. To thrive in this type of a world, students must be excellent learners and have a full bag of learning tools to take with them for the rest of their lives.

TEACHING TOOL-MAKERS WITH INTERACTIVITY: PLAYING AS IF

One of the best ways to develop these tools—to learn how to learn—is through hands-on learning, an opportunity to interact with the subject under study. One way to do this is through interactive multimedia programs. However, as Edith Ackerman of the MIT Media Lab points out, "we should not assume that 'hands-on' activities alone will make for a meaningful experience of constructive learning. . . . Any activity remains essentially undirected and noncontrollable, blind, and meaningless, if it is just acted out without any evaluation of its consequences" (Ackerman 1–3).

Approaches to evaluating these consequences include reliable feedback and giving the learner the ability to reconstruct the experience. There should be some way to reconstruct and replay the learning experience in a safe environment, because the major way learners incorporate new material is not through the experience itself but through the ability to recreate the material in some fashion, thus making it their own. In short, "Interactivity is important, not because it allows the direct manipulation of real objects, but because it fosters the construction of models or artifacts, in which an intriguing idea (thought and feeling) can be run or played out 'for good' in a make-believe world" (Ackerman 6).

In an interactive multimedia program, this construction of models can range from trying out different marketing techniques learned by managing a virtual candy store or building an entire city in the simulation *SimCity 3000*. Such game elements allow the students to explore "what" will happen "if" they try various options. And as Ackerman points out, "Scientific inquiry, as much as other forms of cognitive investigation, indeed requires playing 'what if'" (Ackerman 6).

REFERENCES

Ackermann, Edith. "Tools for Constructive Learning: Rethinking Interactivity." Cambridge, MA: MIT Media Lab, October 1993.

Ambron, Sueann, and Kristina Hooper, eds. *Learning with Interactive Multimedia: Developing and Using Multimedia Tools in Education.* Redmond, WA: Microsoft Press, 1990.

Reddy, M. "The Conduit Metaphor: A Case of Frame Conflict in Our Language about Language." In Andrew Ortony, ed., *Metaphor and Thought.* Cambridge: Cambridge University Press, 1979.

Schwier, Richard A., and Earl R. Misanchuk. *Interactive Multimedia Instruction.* Englewood Cliffs, NJ: Educational Technology, 1993.

C H A P T E R   8

INFORMATIONAL MULTIMEDIA AND WEB ARCHITECTURE

CHAPTER OVERVIEW

There are two key aspects of high-level interactive architecture:

- the overall structure and grouping of information
- the navigation connecting these different information groups

Multimedia programs and Web sites have a wide variety of possible structures and navigation. Rarely do these approaches exist in a pure form. Most projects have some combination. A key question the writer must ask when developing a piece is which approach will best achieve the communication goals. As discussed in Chapter 3, "High-Level Design, Management, and Technical Skills Useful to the Interactive Writer," information architecture is often planned with flowcharts. Every possible interactive architecture is not listed here, merely those that are most commonly used by the writer and designer of nonnarrative, informational multimedia.

LINEAR STRUCTURE AND NAVIGATION

Defined: Linear structure can be compared to a desert highway with no crossroads. It is the structure of most motion pictures and television programs.

Use: Linear structure makes it possible to integrate into multimedia some of the standard linear informational structures, such as the problem-solution structure and the dialectical structure. The problem-solution structure is used by setting up a problem linearly and then asking the user to solve it interactively. Dialectical structure, a favorite of the TV news magazine *60 Minutes*, sets up a dialogue between two different points of view. First we hear from the Army general who wants to spend billions on a bomber; then we hear from the peace activist who doesn't want to spend any more money on new weapons. This A/B, love/hate pattern is repeated until a conclusion emerges or we can draw our own conclusion. A simpler use of linear structure in interactive media is the presentation of key information that should not be interrupted. This is often used for introductory material. The *Geology Explorer* Web site begins each major section in this way.

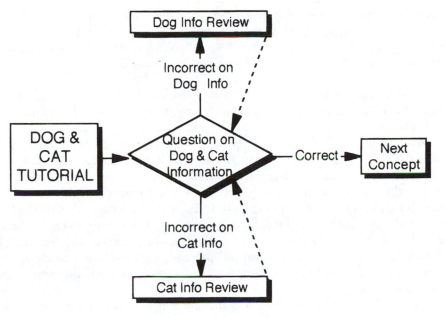

FIGURE 8-1

Linear structure with scene branching.

LINEAR STRUCTURE WITH SCENE BRANCHING
NAVIGATION

Defined: This structure can be compared to the desert highway that has a few detours. (See Figure 8–1.) The detours, however, always return the traveler to the same highway. This is basically a linear structure with a few limited choices as to how certain scenes will play out.

Use: This is sometimes used in training pieces that are explaining a step-by-step concept by following a linear structure. There is often an option of detouring from the step-by-step instruction for a review of the concept or for additional material, but after the detour, the user is returned to the page that he or she had left. The Work-plus.com Web site does this in the section of the site where it explains to the user how to use the company's product. The basic step-by-step instruction is brief, but users have the options to link to the help pages in each section for additional background material.

HIERARCHICAL BRANCHING

Defined: This approach could be compared to going to a mall searching for an Italian cookbook. At the first fork in the mall, you can choose left for the department store, straight ahead for the bookshop, or right for the electronic shop. You want a cookbook, so you choose straight and go to the bookshop. Now you must choose between nonfiction, fiction, and magazines. You choose nonfiction, which includes many choices, ranging from biography to cookbooks to zoology. You choose cookbooks. The cookbook section has French cookbooks, Indian cookbooks, and Italian cookbooks. You choose Italian and, phew, you are finally done.

Use: Hierarchical branching in a multimedia program works exactly this way with a hierarchy of ever-narrowing choices, except your finger does the clicking instead of your heels.

Although this is one of the most popular structures on the Web, it has several potential pitfalls. One is branching explosion, which means creating too many user options. Too many options are created because increasing the number of decision points or the number of choices at each decision point means that the total number of possible choices increases exponentially. In Figure 7–1 on page 63, near the beginning of the previous chapter, the options quickly jump from three, to twelve, and, by adding one more level, to forty-eight. The amount of material quickly expands to a volume difficult for a writer to create and prohibitive to produce. Branching explosion is kept under control by limiting options and creatively reusing the same program components.

Another danger with hierarchical branching is that if there are too many levels of information, the user can get lost and find it difficult to make connections with material on the same level. There is also a practical limitation to the number of choices at any one branch (some studies say that five to seven choices is the most people can easily comprehend). Hierarchical branching is an effective way to narrow informational choices, but it is pure click-and-read and not very exciting.

SINGLE-LEVEL LINKING

Defined: As opposed to hierarchical branching, which looks like a well-organized mall, single-level branching is like wandering into a chaotic flea market. At a flea market you can go any number of places and talk to anyone in any order.

Use: There is no hierarchy in this approach. Usually the user is presented with a problem and given a number of possible resources for solving this problem. In the interactive documentary *A Right to Die: The Case of Dax Cowart*, Dax Cowart has a serious illness. He wants to refuse treatment and die. His doctors and others feel differently. The user of this program can access video interviews, text, and other material about this case in order to answer the question, Does Cowart have the right to choose his death? (The irony of this piece is that Dax was not allowed to choose his death; the therapy was successful, and he went on to live a happy life.) Although single-level linking structure is useful, it is fairly rare on a complete program because it must be limited to a focused topic with limited options. If there are too many options, then a hierarchical structure or another approach has to be used to organize the material.

Single-level linking is more common in small parts of programs. An area of the *Geology Explorer* Web site examines the formation of a cross-section of land. Within each part of the program, students have the option of looking at pages dealing with a description of a layer, an animation showing the process of layer formation, an explanation of the geologic event that caused the layer to be formed, or a quiz. Because it is useful for the student to compare all these elements, they have the option of accessing and reviewing this material in any order.

PARALLEL PATH OR MULTI-PATH ARCHITECTURE

Defined: This approach is borrowed from interactive narrative where one of the main structures is parallel path stories. See Figure 19–4 on page 226 in the middle of Chapter 19, "Elements of Interactive Narrative." In a parallel paths story, the writer lays out three or more possible versions of the same basic story. Depending on players' choices as they move through the game, they move back and forth through the different versions. This will be explained in more detail in the narrative section of the book. When applied to an informational program, this approach creates three or more distinct paths the user can travel through a specific body of information. In the physical world this could be compared to a traveler having three or more possible distinct routes that would lead towards the same destination.

Use: The most effective use of this approach is with online transactions or other activities where the user is trying to accomplish a specific goal. One example would be users who wanted to open a bank account online at a bank Web site. The challenge for the writer is that these users are a heterogeneous group. Some are Web savvy; others are newbies. Some know a lot about banking products; others need a lot of explanation.

To accommodate this variety of users, the writer can prepare multiple information paths through the online account opening application. This can be achieved through good interface design, such as putting the essential information and activities on the left side of the page and putting the secondary product information on the right side of page, perhaps in a box to indicate that it is secondary. Lastly, help using the application itself could be available from a drop down menu on every page. Another approach would be to allow users to customize the transaction by choosing their knowledge and skill level at the beginning of the process.

With designs, such as these, the Web savvy user who knows banking products can move quickly down one path performing only the essential activities. The Web savvy user who needs product information could take a slower path moving to the product information and then to the essential activities. The user most in need of help could move through the help feature, to the product information, and finally the essential transactional activities.

WORLDS STRUCTURE AND NAVIGATION

Defined: This structure (also called virtual structure) is similar to the single-level structure but more complex. In this case our metaphorical traveler is dropped into a complex world to explore. The worlds structure organizes the options available to the viewer not in a linear fashion or in a hierarchy but in a graphic spatial representation. *Myst* is the most famous example of a worlds structure, where the viewer can explore an island and discover prescribed situations and locations. An advantage of this approach to complex information is that it is less easy to get lost than with a hierarchical structure.

Use: This structure is most useful if there is a large body of information that can be incorporated in a location. It does not have to be a physical location that we normally visit. The museum interactive piece *Into the Cell* allows viewers to take a fantastic voyage into a living cell. A writer approaches a project like this by first deciding on a list of locations in the virtual world that he or she is creating, then determining what will happen in each location, and finally how the user will be able to discover these events. A flowchart is not that useful here. More useful is a graphical illustration of the world, a list of the locations, and descriptions of the events that will occur in each location.

SIMULATION

Defined: In a simulation, the user does not merely visit a world and discover what is there; rather, the user creates (or destroys) a world from a series of components that have been built into the system.

Use: This is great for communicating a body of information that is best learned by doing. It can be a single skill, such as flying a jet in *Flight Unlimited,* or as complex as building a city, as in *SimCity 3000.* In this program, the user is given the power to build a city by altering the landscape, adding parks, schools, railroads, power plants, and other components, but it must be done within budget and the user must cope with disasters, such as flood, fire, and alien invasion.

The writers Brian Sawyer and John Vourlis suggest that the best way to write a simulation is to start with the "most basic categories: 'Characters' and 'Locations,' then break these down into sub-categories, and so on . . . After laying out the categories, the next step is to fill in the details of each object: 1) its attributes and 2) its rules of behavior" (101).

For example, in the ship-building simulation, *The Nauticus Shipbuilding Company,* the attributes of the air cushion hull are that it is capable of high speeds, needs flat water conditions, and has a flat deck that is easy to load. Its behavior, if chosen for the oceanographic research vessel, is that it will sink because it can't withstand the rough seas off New England.

Attributes and Behavior of the Hulls in *The Nauticus Shipbuilding Company* **Simulation***

ATTRIBUTES	BEHAVIOR OF HULLS IF USED FOR OCEANOGRAPHIC RESEARCH VESSEL
Air Cushion: • Flat hull rides on cushion of air • Capable of high speeds • Needs flat water conditions • Flat, rectangular deck easy to load	Nonfunctional • Can't withstand rough seas

ATTRIBUTES	BEHAVIOR OF HULLS IF USED FOR OCEANOGRAPHIC RESEARCH VESSEL
Planing Hull: • V-shaped hull capable of high speeds • Performs best in flat water conditions • High stress levels on hull	Functional • Capable of high speeds • Not very stable in rough seas • Limited work and living space
Displacement Hull: • Deep, rounded hull very stable in all conditions • Very large cargo capacity • Stable platform for large propulsion systems • Needs very large propulsion system	Functional • Stable in rough seas • Plenty of work and living space • Deep draft limits access to shore areas
SWATH (Small Waterplane Area Twin Hull): • Two submerged hulls very stable • Flat deck provides good work area	Optimal • Very stable in rough seas • Plenty of protected work and living space • Shallower draft provides access to shore areas

MULTISITE BRANCHING

CD-ROMs and museum kiosks are closed systems. The user has access to the program material in that system and nothing more. On the World Wide Web and other networks, however, it is possible to link from words or images on one site to related information on other sites all over the world.

The Web allows the possibility of linking all of the above structures in one unlimited search for information. A user might start at one site that is hierarchical, link to another site with a linear video, and yet another that involves him or her in a simulation. A graph of this would look like a mad combination of all of the examples above. With multisite branching, the individual creator has the resources of the world to present his or her information, but the writer gives up much of the control in so doing.

Multisite branching involves researching other sites that have links that would amplify the information on your site. For example, the city of San Diego's Web site allows users to link to the Planet Earth Home Page—Welcome to California. This site allows a link to Other California Resources, which includes a link to Going Places— United States National Parks. Once the user gets to another site, however, the writer of the original Web site (San Diego) has no control over what information the user will access at the new site or if he or she will ever return to the original Web site. In this example, does information about U.S. National Parks achieve the goals of the designers of the San Diego site?

CONCLUSION

This chapter concludes the introductory material. Beginning with the next chapter, major informational multimedia programs and Web sites will be examined in depth to better understand how the principles we have been exploring so far are applied on actual projects.

REFERENCE

Sawyer, Brian, and John Vourlis. "Screenwriting Structures for New Media." *Creative Screenwriting* 2 (Summer 1995): 95–103.

C H A P T E R 9

INTRODUCTION TO THE INFORMATIONAL MULTIMEDIA AND WEB SITE CASE STUDIES

The case studies in the chapters that follow demonstrate how various goals were achieved and challenges were met in specific multimedia programs and Web sites:

- *Prudential Verani Realty Web Site:* a detailed profile of the writing of this site, from proposal to meta tags. Verani is one of the largest realtors in New England.
- *T. Rowe Price Web Site:* the investment firm T. Rowe Price offers interactive information for new and seasoned investors. This chapter also includes a description of the different types of commercial Web sites.
- Britannica.Com and *The Harlem Renaissance:* an analysis of Web site portals and writing the online feature story.
- *ZDU Online Ad Campaign:* a World Wide Web advertising campaign produced by ZDNet to promote its online course site ZDU (later renamed Smart Planet).
- *The Nauticus Shipbuilding Company:* a museum kiosk shipbuilding simulation located at Nauticus, National Maritime Center, Norfolk, Virginia.
- *Sky High:* an elementary school CD-ROM on the subject of flight and space.
- *Clinical Support Staff Interactive Certification Program: Vital Signs:* an interactive video disc training program for medical assistants at a health maintenance organization (HMO) on the process of taking medical vital signs: temperature, pulse, respiration, and blood pressure.

An understanding of how the writers of these programs dealt with informational multimedia issues will give you insight into how to deal with similar issues when they arise in your work. Each case study answers the following questions:

- Program Description and Background. Is the program a typical example of its genre, or is it unusual? Who commissioned, developed, and wrote the program? What was the preproduction process?
- Goals. What were the writers and designers' goals in creating this project? What information or experience were they trying to communicate?

- Challenges. Which goals were particularly difficult to achieve? What approaches were successful in achieving these goals and which were discarded?

- Response to the Project. Did the program achieve its goals? Was it a critical and/or commercial success?

The case studies are documented with script examples, screen shots, and flowcharts. Additional script samples and other material are available for many of the programs on the *Writing for Multimedia and the Web* CD-ROM.

NOTE: Because all the case studies follow the above structure, the Chapter Overview section that has been appearing at the beginning of previous chapters will not appear on the case studies. It will be replaced by a descriptive summary of each case.

C H A P T E R   1 0

WRITING A MARKETING WEB SITE FROM PROPOSAL TO META TAGS: PRUDENTIAL VERANI REALTY

Summary

Name of Production: *Prudential Verani Realty* Web Site
  (http://www.pruverani.com)
Writer: Timothy Garrand
Developers: InterWrite
Audience: Commercial and Residential Real Estate Customers, General Public
Medium: World Wide Web
Location: Where Web is Viewed
Subject: Real Estate
Goals: Inform, teach
Architecture: Branching, hierarchical branching, dynamic database generated

The text samples, flowcharts, and illustrations used in this chapter are courtesy of Prudential Verani Realty. © 1999 Prudential Verani Realty.

SCOPE OF THIS CHAPTER

This chapter studies all the different types of writing that can be required to develop a commercial Web site, with an explanation of the goals of each document and some tips for achieving those goals. Although a writer's efforts are sometimes limited to the content of a site, the writer may be also called upon to write the initial proposals, planning documents, maintenance instructions, and online marketing writing, such as meta tags. The writer playing these roles needs to understand organizational tools, such as flowcharting software; how writing affects the site's online marketing efforts; and the capabilities of the latest Web technology to communicate information effectively. This chapter is different from the later case studies that will focus primarily on writing the project's content.

PROGRAM DESCRIPTION AND BACKGROUND

PROGRAM DESCRIPTION

The *Prudential Verani Realty* Web site is a marketing and content Web site designed for Prudential Verani Realty, one of the largest real estate companies in New England. The goals of the site are to:

- Attract buyers of commercial and residential real estate
- Attract real estate sellers to list their properties with Prudential Verani
- Attract customers for other Verani services, such as relocation and mortgages
- Present a positive image for the Prudential Verani company
- Recruit new agents to join the company
- Present useful real estate information

The site includes extensive searchable information about Verani properties, descriptions of Verani services, general real estate information, and numerous interactive tools, such as calculators, checklists, maps, and E-mail updates. The site consists of more than 300 HTML pages, a number of Active Server Pages and an extensive database of real estate properties. (Active Server Pages or ASP is a programming language that can be used to make Web pages more interactive and functional.)

PRODUCTION BACKGROUND

Prudential Verani Realty approached my company, InterWrite, to develop the second generation of their Web site. The first, limited version of their site had been done some years earlier and had to be completely redone with all new information architecture, graphics, content, and programming. I served as the writer, information architect, and project manager of the site. I brought in Steve Street who led the InterNoded team for graphic and HTML design, and Ken Jones of Essayons Enterprises for programming and technical development. Laurie Strysko did the photographs. The Prudential Verani Realty executives on the project were Suzanne Burns and Giovanni Verani.

PLANNING THE PRUDENTIAL VERANI REALTY WEB SITE

One of the keys to a successful largescale Web site is adequate planning. Adequate planning insures that a Web site achieves its goal and communicates its intended message for the least possible cost. A clear plan on paper allows a client to discuss options and make revisions for far less cost than it does to make revisions on a completed site.

SCOPING A PROJECT: GOALS, TOOLS, AND PRICE

The first stage of developing the site was to better define the project. This is accomplished through researching similar sites, meeting with the client, and digesting all of the client's existing marketing material. Some of the key questions that have to be answered and discussed with the client are:

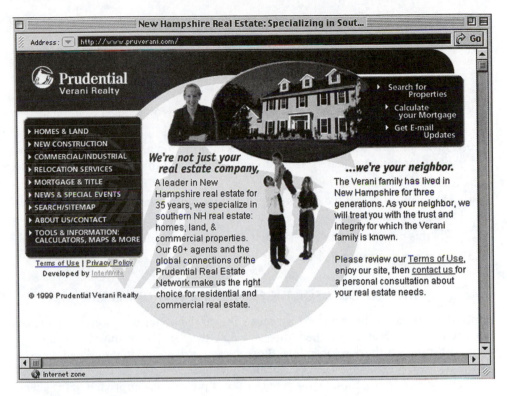

FIGURE 10-1

The Home Page for Prudential Verani Realty. (The original color image for this screen shot is available on the *Writing for Multimedia and the Web* CD-ROM.)

1. What are the client's goals for this site? For example, is the primary purpose informational, marketing, content, or transactional—selling products online?

2. Who is the audience for this site? What are their demographics? What information about the product are they most interested in? What information do they already have? How sophisticated are they with using the Web? How advanced are their browser and modem? What are the key use cases? (Use cases are the most common ways visitors will use the site.)

3. What is the client's wish list? What elements does the client think would be great for the site? Why would these elements be effective in achieving the client's goals? Can the client rate the wish list items in order of importance?

4. Who are the client's competitors? What are their Web sites like? What techniques do they use?

5. Where will the site be hosted? What are the technical capabilities of the hosting service or the client if they are doing the hosting? What platform will the hosting service be using?

6. What are the elements in existing company material that the client likes or that seem particularly effective? What resources already exists, such as pictures or a database of information? Is this material suitable for the Web site?

7. What are the branding issues? Are there guidelines for a specific way material needs to be presented?

8. Is a Web site the correct medium to present the material, achieve the client's goals, and reach the intended audience? Would a disc-based interactive program be better, or even a video or a brochure?

9. What form does the intended information take? Is it numbers and statistics? Video? Graphics? Text?

10. How often and how extensively does this information need to be updated? Does the client have adequate staff to do updating or will this require a maintenance contract?

11. Are there ways that we can present this information that are dynamic and customizable for the user?

12. Will this project need to pay for itself, for example by incorporating advertising?

13. What are the ways this site can be marketed to drive traffic to the site?

THE PROPOSAL FOR THE PRUDENTIAL VERANI WEB SITE

Once the project has been defined by answering all the above questions, and a rough idea of costs has been established, then it is time to write the proposal. For the *Prudential Verani* site, the developer, InterWrite, created a proposal that outlined the goals of the site, two possible approaches to achieving those goals, and the approximate costs of each of these approaches. (Most proposals only present one approach to the client.)

The purpose of proposal writing is to present options to the client clearly, succinctly, and appealingly. This should not be a hard-sell document, but it should point out the advantages of the work being suggested. Note the modular approach in the proposal to the design and pricing of the project. This allowed the clients to delete or combine elements in a way that created the site and budget they desired. This is only one approach to proposal writing. There are many other approaches. Some major companies request so many specific topics to be addressed that proposals can be forty to fifty pages long. Note also that the stage listed below as "The First Step" is often called "Discovery" or "Requirements."

Section of Prudential Verani Web Site Proposal

```
Goals of an Improved Web Site

1. Better attract and serve customers (buyers)
2. Better attract and serve clients (sellers)
3. Sell properties more effectively
4. Help agents and staff make the most effective use of
   their time
5. Improve cooperation with business partners


The First Step

The first step to revise the Verani site is to clearly
define the message, content, functionality, and
navigation. This material will be presented in outlines
```

and flowcharts of the proposed site. Once this step is completed, we can develop a precise budget. Until then, the amounts below are estimates.

The cost to develop the outline, flowcharts, and budget would be: $XXXX–$XXXX.

Web Site Revision Options I've presented two approaches to revising your site in the document that follows.

- Option 1: Achieves the most important goals for your site at a moderate cost.
- Option 2: Achieves all the goals that we discussed for your site at a higher cost.

Both of these options have been broken into sections so we can delete and combine elements to achieve exactly the Web site and budget you desire.

Option #1: Revision to Achieve Most Important Goals

SUGGESTED REVISION (To protect the client's privacy, all dollar amounts have been blocked out.)	ESTIMATED COST
Expand Content: The Real Estate and Relocation Information Source for New Hampshire Your current site tells the user about your company and your properties. An alternative is also to make your site an information resource for sellers and buyers of real estate. This would greatly increase traffic to your site. Users would come to your site for information. This well-presented information would demonstrate that you are a well-run, knowledgeable company. This would encourage users to use you when they are considering buying or selling a home. The site would also of course continue to fulfill its current functions of presenting your properties and company. Types of information that could be included are: • Mortgage calculator • School reports • Town reports • Relocation information • List of home inspectors • Interactive tutorials on how to buy a property This material would be presented in such a way that the user makes a positive connection with your agency. For example, after a site visitor uses our mortgage calculator to determine his/her maximum mortgage amount, then we would offer to show the visitor Verani properties in that price range.	$XXXX

Graphic and HTML Redesign of Site This includes a complete graphic redesign of the site, including redesigning the home page, secondary pages, headers, buttons, original graphics, and integration of graphics into HTML. The goal is to make the site a more upscale, friendly place, demonstrating that Prudential Verani: • has the resources to sell your property most effectively • has the knowledge and resources to make your home search efficient and successful • has a friendly, professional staff that would be a pleasure to work with	$XXXX

NOTE: This is only part of the proposal. In the full proposal, many additional elements are outlined in the table and the total budget is estimated. The proposal also includes a second, more expensive revision option and an approximate production schedule for completing the project.

SCOPE OF WORK/REVISION PLAN

The above proposal was discussed with key members of the Prudential Verani team and eventually options were eliminated and the scope of work of the project was clearly defined. This scope is an important document because it can be the basis of your contractual agreement with the client. The writing needs to be very clear and unambiguous. There is no need for salesmanship here. Do not promise anything you cannot deliver, and make it clear what work is not your responsibility. Many of the elements in the scope of work/revision plan have been refined and simplified from the original proposal.

REVISION PLAN/SCOPE OF WORK FOR THE PRUDENTIAL VERANI WEB SITE

1. Production Planning and Content Definition

The first stage of designing the Web site is to clearly define the site in an outline and flowchart. The flowchart will consist of a complete graphical plan of the site, illustrating every internal page in the site and each page's place in the overall site architecture. A first draft of the outline and flowchart will be presented to key Verani staff for comments. Based on these comments, a second draft will be created that will also be submitted for comments.

   Once the tasks and content are clearly defined, then we can produce a detailed and final budget, production plan/timeline, and payment schedule.

Production Planning Costs: $XXXX Payment for production planning will be in three stages:

- $XXXX to initiate the project
- $XXXX due at completion of first draft outline and chart
- Balance of costs for production planning due at sign-off for final draft chart, outline, budget, and production schedule. Costs for the outline/charts will be a minimum of $XXXX but no more than $XXXX.

2. Web Site Creation

Once the production planning is complete, the second stage of the process is to produce the Web site. The tasks contracted for include the following.

Graphic and HTML Redesign of Site This includes a complete graphic redesign of the site, including redesigning the home page, secondary pages, headers, buttons, original graphics, and integration of graphics into HTML. The goal is to make the site a more upscale, friendly place, demonstrating that Prudential Verani:

- has the resources to sell your property effectively
- has the knowledge and resources to make your home search efficient and successful
- has a friendly, professional staff that would be a pleasure to work with

Improve the Content about Your Company and Properties The current site presents your properties, company, and agents. We will create new material and build on the existing material to make this presentation more effective. For example, we will improve the graphic design of the results page for the properties database search. This page will also include links to other relevant information on the site. Another improvement would be to create custom templates for the New Construction section, making this section easily updateable.

In addition, we will add new material about the company that is not on the current site, such as a new mortgage and title section. We will also increase the functionality of the site, such as adding a site-wide search and an easily updateable Special Events page for announcing open houses or special meetings.

NOTE: This is a fragment of the scope of work/revision plan. The complete scope continues similarly to the above, clearly defining every element that will be created for the site. The last part of the scope below defines the services and production schedule.

3. Services Included

InterWrite Design or its subcontractors will complete all of the tasks agreed upon in the final outline. All payment will be made to InterWrite Design, who will be responsible for payment to all subcontractors and for subcontractors completing their work. Prudential Verani agrees to pay InterWrite Design within 30 days of the agreed upon dates in the payment plan. Payment will be made at the completion of major stages of the project. This payment plan will be developed after completion of the production planning and outlines, described in Step 1 at the beginning of this document.

The final product will be a fully functioning and tested Web site placed on the server of your choice. The final Web site will be owned and copyrighted by Prudential Verani.

After the Web site is completed, Prudential Verani will be responsible for the regular upkeep of the site unless additional contracts are made with InterWrite Design.

4. Approximate Time Frame

- This time frame can be finalized after completing the final outlines. At this point, this is a rough estimate, subject to change.
- Keeping this time frame requires a speedy turnaround (2–3 days) of drafts for comment from Prudential Verani. With longer turnaround times, InterWrite Design cannot keep this schedule.

Project Start	December 7
Final outlines/charts completed	December 31
First Drafts of Content and Graphics	January 29
Complete First Draft of Site Launched	February 19
Final Site Launched	March 1
Online Marketing Completed	March 8

FLOWCHART/SITEMAP

Using the scope of work as a guide, continuing discussions with the client lead to the development of a flowchart or sitemap of the site. The flowchart should indicate every page of the site. The goal is for the flowchart to be a clear visualization of site structure. See Chapter 3, "High-Level Design, Management, and Technical Skills Useful to the Interactive Writer," for a detailed discussion of flowcharting and flowchart software. As discussed in Chapter 3, there are a number of techniques that help make the flowchart a more useful tool, including:

1. Give every page of the site a unique number and name.
2. For ease of printing and presentation, run the chart vertically as in Figure 10–3 instead of horizontally.
3. Simplify where you can. If there will be multiple sections that will be designed in the same way, it is OK to say that in a note. No need to draw out all the boxes for repetitive pages.
4. It can make it easier to see the main sections of the Web site by writing those pages in bold with drop shadows.
5. Indicate cross-links (links to pages within the site that are already on the chart) and external links (links to other Web sites) as text only.
6. Visually indicate pages that will have special functions. For example, pages that will have interactive elements or that will be generated dynamically from a database.

OUTLINE

As discussed in Chapter 3, "High-Level Design, Management, and Technical Skills Useful to the Interactive Writer," the flowchart illustrates the overall navigation, structure, and size of the site; the outline provides more details about the actual content and functionality of the individual pages. The flowchart and outline that follow are most effective when used together. The client consults the chart for overall structure, then reads the outline for the details.

The structure of each page on the outline below is fairly simple. The outline should be adjusted to match the specific project. The elements include:

- Title: The page title, which should be the same as what is on the flowchart.
- Image: Describes possible images for the page.
- Text: Describes onscreen text.
- Links: Includes all the links on this page from text within the page and from the graphical navigation bar.

KEY

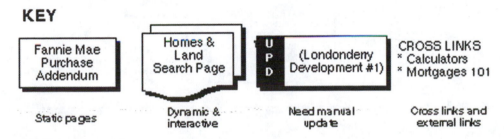

FIGURE 10–2

Symbol key for *Prudential Verani* Web site flowchart/sitemap.

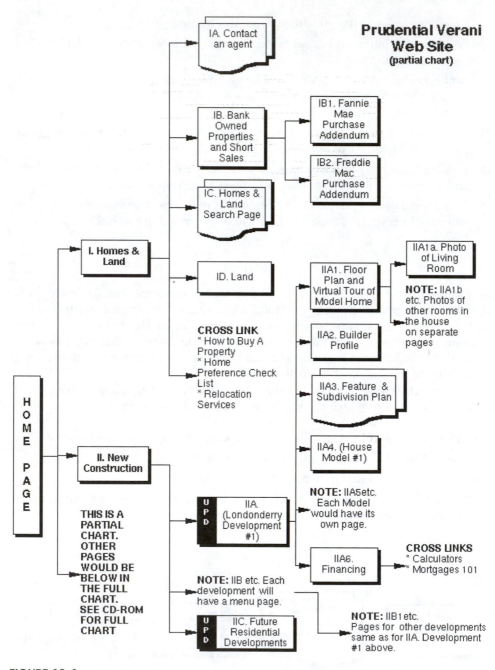

FIGURE 10–3

Partial flowchart/sitemap for the *Prudential Verani* Web site.

- Navigation bar: The specific buttons that will have to be created for the navigation bar.
- Functionality: This describes what the user can do on this page besides click-and-read. For example, can they search for properties or calculate their mortgage.

Partial Outline of the Prudential Verani Web Site

Home Page

Title: Prudential Verani Realty

The Real Estate and Relocation Resource for Southern NH

IMAGE: Images which demonstrate that Verani is a professional, friendly place. Possible images: Prudential logo, friendly Verani staff, Verani office, people enjoying a beautiful home. Might have other images on page to lead user to some of our key features, such as a calculator image for the tools and an E-mail icon for our custom E-mail notification service.

TEXT: Explain that we are part of Prudential, one of the largest corporations in the world, but also a family-owned company with strong roots in Southern NH. We have the resources to sell your property effectively and/or make your home search efficient and successful. Also should introduce some of the key features of the site, such as our searches, custom E-mail notification tools, extensive information resources, etc. Near the bottom of the page should be a short disclaimer stating that we have made every effort to make the information on this site accurate but are not liable for any errors or omissions; please see our Terms of Use Policy.

LINKS: Homes and Land, New Construction, Commercial and Industrial, Relocation Services, Verani Mortgage and Title, Real Estate Information and Resources, News and Special Events, Search/Site Map, About Us/Contact.
   Might also have a link from a calculator image to the tools and calculator section. In text on the bottom of the page and every page will be links to Terms of Use, Privacy Statements, and a WebMaster E-mail link.

NAVIGATION BAR: Homes and Land, New Construction, Commercial and Industrial, Relocation Services, Verani Mortgage and Title, Real Estate Information and Resources, News and Special Events, Search/Site Map, About Us/Contact.

I. Homes and Land

TITLE: Homes and Land

IMAGE: Small image of attractive house. This could be the same picture all the time, or a regularly changing featured house.

TEXT: Briefly explain the range of properties we offer and the area we cover. Direct the user to the search page and other services that will help them in their moving and home buying, such as Relocation Services, the How to Buy a Property Section, Home Preference Check List/Questionnaire, and New Construction.

LINKS: Home, Search, Contact, Relocation Services, the How to Buy a Property Section, Home Preference Check List/Questionnaire, and New Construction.

NAVIGATION BAR: Home, Search, Contact.

IA. Contact an Agent

TITLE: Contact Us

IMAGE: Photo of Friendly agent.

TEXT: Phone numbers, addresses, and E-mails for all offices, plus a form that user can fill out and submit so that we can contact them.

LINKS: Home Page, Search, Contact, Homes and Land.

NAVIGATION BAR: Home Page, Search, Contact, Homes and Land.

FUNCTIONALITY: Users can fill out a form with their address and E-mail, click the type of information they want, write a short note, and submit it to us. Message will go to different people at Prudential Verani, depending on what type of information the user requests.

NOTE: This is a partial outline. See the Chapter 10 area in the Chapters section of the *Writing for Multimedia and the Web* CD-ROM for a full outline.

WRITING THE WEB SITE

Once the outline and site flowchart have been thoroughly discussed with and approved by the client, a detailed budget and scope of work will be created. (Because this final scope of work is similar to the preliminary scope discussed earlier in this chapter, and because production budgeting is outside the parameters of this book, these documents will not be discussed here.) With an approved outline and final scope of work/revision plan, the content for the Web site can now be written.

ONLINE WRITING STYLE TIPS

As discussed in Chapter 2, "Writing for Many Media," strong writing for the Web and multimedia follows many of the principals of good journalism, including:

- Strong lead sentences that summarize content
- Inverted pyramid style: put most important content first
- Simple sentence construction
- Concrete words: nouns and verbs, avoid adjectives and adverbs
- Active not passive voice verbs

As also discussed in Chapter 2, "Writing for Many Media," there are also a number of writing techniques that are specific to writing for the computer screen, including using:

- highlighted keywords
- meaningful subheadings (not "clever" ones)
- bulleted lists
- one idea per paragraph
- half the word count (or less) than conventional writing
  (Nielsen, *The Alertbox: How Users Read on the Web*)

These concepts are particularly true on the first couple of levels of a Web site or multimedia program where the user is trying to find the information they want. Once they have located their information deeper in the site, users may be content to read longer text material.

These general style techniques apply to most online writing, but specific types of pages make unique demands on the writer. Examples of special types of pages on the *Prudential Verani* Web site include:

- Home page
- Section menu/introduction pages
- Static content pages
- Interactive and dynamic content pages

Each of these page types will be discussed in detail in the remainder of this chapter, including how to write pages so that a site will show up well when users search for the site's topic in search engines and directories.

SEARCH ENGINES AND KEYWORDS

A unique aspect of writing for the Web is the need to consider search engines. In most cases, search engines such as Lycos, and directories such as Yahoo, are the primary way that users will find your site. When users go to Lycos and type in keywords related to your site, such as "New Hampshire real estate," you want your site to appear in the top ten to twenty search engine results. To achieve this, you need to pay attention to keywords.

The challenge is to decide which keywords to use on your site. For the first draft of your site, you need to use your own intuition as to what terms users would be likely to type into a search engine box to find your site. Clients can also be a big help. They know their business better than you do. Because repetition is an important factor in search-engine ranking, you need to focus on a few keywords and repeat them judiciously throughout the home page. For the Verani site, the primary keywords are: New Hampshire real estate, NH real estate, Southern New Hampshire real estate, and southern NH real estate. As in this example, it is usually wiser to use keyword phrases of two or more words. Single word keywords or even common short phrases, such as "real estate" are not specific enough to a allow a user who is making a focused search to pull up your site on the first page or two of the search results.

Your work with keywords is not completed once you finish the site and submit it to search engines. Evaluating and modifying your choice of keywords is an ongoing process to better your search engine placement. Two software tools can help with this process and allow you to better refine your keywords. After you have submitted your site to the search engines, and the site begins showing up in the search engine indexes, you can use hit analysis software, such as WebTrends (http://www.webtrends.com/), to monitor who comes to your site and what search words they use. Once you have determined the most common search words being used to find your site, you can rewrite your site to include more of them.

The other useful tool in this process is search-engine position-analysis software, which will search specific keywords on the major search engines and report your ranking for that specific term. For example, when searching Alta-Vista for "New Hampshire real estate," the *Prudential Verani* site comes up third in the search results. You can do without the search position software by doing multiple searches of your keywords in the major search engines, but it will take a while. Useful position agent software includes: SubmitIt!'s Position Agent (http://www.submit-it.com) and Web-Position (http://www.firstplacesoftware.com/).

This chapter will have considerable discussion about how to write your Web site to improve search engine placement, but adjusting the site's text is not the only way to improve search engine and directory rankings. For other nonwriting tips on marketing your Web site, check out the reference material on SubmitIt! (http://www.submit-it.com) and Search Engine Watch (http://www.searchenginewatch.com/). Also, if your client has sufficient resources, they might consider a search engine positioning company. These companies have special techniques to boost your search engine rankings. Some search engines will also improve your ranking for a fee.

THE HOME PAGE

The home page is the most important page of a Web site. (See Figure 10–1 for a screenshot of the home page.) If this page does not accomplish its goals, then the user may go no further and the site can fail. There is a heavy burden on the home page. It must:

1. Hook the user's interest.
2. Communicate the basic message and tone of the site.
3. Introduce key site elements and lure the user deeper into the site.
4. Provide the correct keywords and frequency of keywords for good search engine placement.
5. Address legal issues.

The writer shares some of the above duties with the graphic and interface design-ers, but good writing is a major component of the success of any home page. It is important for the writer to work with the graphic designer when creating the page so that the designer's images support and expand on the writer's content.

The Title

Word for word, the title is probably the most important text on your home page. The page title and the main heading are frequently confused. The page title is not the heading that appears immediately above the text. On the *Prudential Verani* home page (Figure 10–1), the main heading is "We're not just your real estate company . . . we're your neighbor." The title on the *Verani* page appears in the bar at the very top of the browser: "New Hampshire Real Estate: Specializing in Southern NH Homes, Land, and Commercial Properties."

The functions of the title are to:

1. Identify an open Web page.
2. Provide key site information to search engines' spiders. (Spiders are software pro-grams that search Web sites and collect information for search engine ranking.)
3. Identify the site in search engine and directory lists.
4. Identify the site in bookmark lists.

Of these functions, the bottom three are by far the most important. For many search engines, the title is one of the most important elements for determining how your site will rank when someone searches for one of your keywords.

The title in the first draft of the home page,

```
"Welcome to Prudential Verani Realty,"
```

identifies the business and is a common sort of title on the Web. However, this title made a poor showing in search engine tests. The second draft title is much more descriptive of the Prudential Verani services. It also contains many keywords that will help determine search engine placement. The second draft title is:

```
New Hampshire Real Estate: Specializing in Southern NH
Real Estate, Homes, Land, and Commercial Properties.
```

Longer titles, such as this, may not show in their entirety in all browsers and search engine results, but the entire title will be indexed for keywords, which will boost your search engine ranking.

Do not write keywords in your title that do not relate to your site. Also, do not write a long list of keywords, especially repetitive words in the title. Browsers are getting better at determining spam (attempts to fool the search engine) to gain good search engine placement. If a search engine detects spam, it may penalize your site by dropping it lower on the list or eliminating it from its index altogether. So make sure that your title makes sense grammatically and in terms of the content of your site. It takes clever writing to create a site that gets strong search engine placement and is still a good read for the user.

In addition to improving your search engine ranking, another key function of your title is to identify your Web site in search engine and directory lists. Remember that, unlike the title of a newspaper story, a Web site title often must stand alone in a search engine or directory list. So be sure that your title is effective on its own. Don't use a teaser or trick title that has little independent meaning. Stick with something that is clear and descriptive of your site.

The Main Menu

The main menu on the home page is the clickable list of the main sections of the site. Its key functions are to:

1. Provide a brief outline of the site, giving the user a sense of what lies within.
2. Serve as a main navigational tool

The titles in the main menu should be descriptive and brief. Many designers also believe that they should be limited in number. Other designers, however, like to give their sites a portal look with dozens of links. This approach requires careful text design, but it can still overwhelm the user who is looking for quick information.

The first draft menu titles on this site are:

- `Residential`
- `New Construction`
- `Commercial/Industrial`
- `Relocation Services`
- `Mortgage and Title`
- `News and Special Events`
- `Search/Sitemap`
- `About Us/Contact`
- `Resources`

The only change with the second draft was to use more descriptive language for two of the titles: "Residential" was changed to "Homes and Land"; "Resources" was changed to "Tools and Information: Calculators, Maps, and More."

If a menu is made up of text links, it can also provide a good source of keywords to boost search engine placement. Unfortunately, in many cases a graphic menu is more visually attractive. You can compensate for the use of a graphic menu by using Alt Image tags, HTML, which describe the content of the picture. But only a few search engines read these tags. Another alternative is to repeat your graphic menu links on the bottom of the page as text links. This not only helps search engine placement, but is also useful to the visually impaired who have special machines that can read text but not graphics. (See "Writing Accessible Multimedia" in the Background section of the *Writing for Multimedia and the Web* CD-ROM.)

Links to Exciting Elements

In addition to the main menu links on the home page, it is also a good idea to have links to any areas of your site that the user might find particularly exciting or interactive. The goal is to:

1. Lure the user deeper into your site.

2. Get the user interacting with your site. If you can get a user doing things on your site besides reading, you have taken a good first step to getting them to explore the site. Some designers call this making the site "sticky."
On this site the links to exciting elements include:

   - `Search for Properties`
   - `Calculate your Mortgage`
   - `Get E-mail Updates`

As you can see, these links are brief, descriptive, and written in terms of actions. They address some of a user's key interests for visiting a real estate site, and they encourage the user to do something. There were no changes between the first and second drafts.

Slogans/Headings

A slogan can help express the tone of the site. If the slogan has keywords, is in text, and is written as a heading, it can also boost search engine placement. Some search engines give greater importance to words surrounded by HTML heading tags. (See the Background section of the *Writing for Multimedia and the Web* CD-ROM for an introduction to HTML.) As is the case with menus, as discussed above, a slogan or heading may look better as a graphic, and you may choose to forego the search engine advantage to improve the visual look of the page.

The slogan for this page is:

```
We're not just your real estate company...we're your
neighbor.
```

Each of the two parts of the slogan is centered over the paragraph that relates to it.

Body Text

The body text is the main text on the page. Its functions are to:

1. Hook the user by explaining why this is the site you want to explore for your real estate needs.

2. Introduce the type of material that is in the site.

3. Boost the search engine rating by including keywords.

4. Get the user to make contact.

5. Strengthen the legal protection for the company.

The first draft body text below satisfies many of our requirements for good Web writing.

- Brief: The user can see the entire home page without scrolling.
- Strong lead sentence that summarizes content.

- Inverted pyramid style: put most important content first. The integrity of the Verani family is secondary to the size, experience, and capabilities of their company.

- Concrete words: uses nouns and verbs, avoiding adjectives and adverbs. There is little fluff here. The user is not told that Verani is the best company around. Instead, the company is described in very concrete terms: the number of agents, years of experience, sales figures, and affiliations. This information shows rather than tells the user that this is a hot company.

- The word "contact" in the last sentence is a link to a contact information page encouraging the user to get in touch.

```
FIRST DRAFT: More than 60 agents, 35 years of
experience, $100 million in sales, and the global
connections of the Prudential Real Estate Network make
us the right choice to help you buy or sell
residential and commercial properties.
     The Verani family has lived in New Hampshire for
three generations. As your neighbor, we will treat you
with the trust and integrity for which the Verani
family is known.
     Enjoy our site, then contact us for a personal
consultation about your real estate needs.
```

The problem with this first draft was that in tests with search engines, this text produced poor search engine rankings for the site. This is important because the body text is used by virtually all search engines to rank your site. The first paragraph was rewritten to include more keywords and keyword repetition. The challenge was to incorporate more keywords while continuing to make the site engaging to the user. The ideal page from a search engine's point of view is a page without tables or frames, limited graphics, and lots of text. Such a page may get a site a high ranking in a search engine, but once the user gets to this unattractive, text-heavy page, they will probably not click beyond the home page.

```
SECOND DRAFT: A leader in New Hampshire real estate for
35 years, we specialize in southern NH real estate:
homes, land, and commercial properties. Our 60+ agents
and the global connections of the Prudential Real
Estate Network make us the right choice for residential
and commercial real estate.
```

The one other change, which was on advice from the company lawyer, was to add a link to the terms of use statement in the body text:

```
SECOND DRAFT: Please review our Terms of Use, enjoy our
site, then contact us for a personal consultation about
your real estate needs.
```

The Terms of Use is an important legal document that can help reduce the site owner's liability. Every commercial site should have one. But don't worry, this is not one more job for the writer. A lawyer must write the Terms of Use. When you are on the Web, click the "Terms of Use" link at the bottom of the Prudential Verani home page to see what such a document looks like.

Bottom Text Links

Text links at the bottom of the home page are typically used for legal and business purposes, such as links to Terms of Use or the WebMaster. It is also the place where you will usually place the name of the site developer.

For the second draft, the writer added a text menu of key site links to aid navigation and to incorporate additional keywords for search engine placement. Do not just put a list of keywords in tiny or invisible text at the bottom of the page or the search engine will punish you for trying to spam them. A text menu at the bottom of the page is, however, a legitimate addition to your home page.

Complete First and Second Draft Home Page Text

After the previous discussion about writing the home page, review the first and second drafts of the home page text to get an overall understanding of the impact of the changes. Changes are in bold.

First Draft Home Page Text	*Second Draft Home Page Text* (Changes are in bold)
TITLE: Welcome to Prudential Verani Realty	TITLE: **New Hampshire Real Estate: Specializing in Southern NH Real Estate, Homes, Land, and Commercial Properties**
SECTION MENU:	SECTION MENU:
Residential	**Homes and Land**
New construction	New construction
Commercial/industrial	Commercial/industrial
Relocation Services	Relocation Services
Mortgage and Title	Mortgage and Title
News and Special Events	News and Special Events
Search/sitemap	Search/Sitemap
About Us/Contact	About Us/Contact
Resources	**Tools and Information: Calculators, Maps, and More**
LINKS TO EXCITING ELEMENTS:	LINKS TO EXCITING ELEMENTS:
• Search for Properties	• Search for Properties
• Calculate your Mortgage	• Calculate your Mortgage
• Get E-mail Updates	• Get E-mail Updates
SLOGANS/HEADINGS: We're not just your real estate company . . . we're your neighbor.	SLOGANS/HEADINGS: We're not just your real estate company . . . we're your neighbor.
BODY TEXT: More than 60 agents, 35 years of experience, $100 million in sales, and the global connections of the Prudential Real Estate Network make us the right choice to help you buy or sell residential and commercial properties.	BODY TEXT: **A leader in New Hampshire real estate for 35 years, we specialize in southern NH real estate: homes, land, and commercial**

```
The Verani family has lived
in New Hampshire for three
generations. As your neighbor,
we will treat you with
the trust and integrity for
which the Verani family is
known.
Enjoy our site, then contact
us for a personal
consultation about your
real estate needs.
BOTTOM TEXT LINKS:
• Terms of Use
• Privacy Policy
• Developed by InterWrite
```

```
properties. Our 60+ agents
and the global connections
of the Prudential Real
Estate Network make us the
right choice for
residential and commercial
real estate.
The Verani family has lived
in New Hampshire for three
generations. As your
neighbor, we will treat you
with the trust and
integrity for which the
Verani family is known.
Please review our Terms of
Use, enjoy our site, then
contact us for a personal
consultation about your
real estate needs.
BOTTOM TEXT LINKS:
• Terms of Use
• Privacy Policy
• Developed by InterWrite
• New Hampshire Homes and
  Land
• New Hampshire New
  Construction
• New Hampshire
  Commercial/Industrial
  Real Estate
• Relocation Services
• Mortgage and Title
• Real Estate Tools and
  Information: Maps,
  Calculators, and more
• Contact
```

Home Page Meta Tags

Meta tags are HTML tags that enclose special text at the top of your Web page. Unlike the page title, the text between meta tags never appears on the Web page that is displayed on your user's computer screen. The main purpose of meta tag text is to improve your page's ranking with search engines. As with the page title, you need to access the HTML code of your page to write meta tags. In most cases, the production people will do this for you. See the background section of the *Writing for Multimedia and the Web* CD-ROM for an explanation of HTML. You can also view the meta tags and the HTML source code for a Web page simply by opening the View menu of your browser and clicking Source.

The meta tags of key concern to the writer are the Keyword and the Description meta tags. These tags can affect the way certain search engines:

1. Rank your site for specific keyword searches
2. Describe your site in search results

It is important to note that not all search engines read META tags so don't rely on them as your primary search engine strategy. But for the search engines that do use them, well-written META tags can make a difference.

Description Meta Tag   The description meta tag describes your site. This tag is indexed by some search engines for keywords that will affect your search engine ranking, and some search engines also use this meta tag as the description of your site that will appear in the list of search engine results when a user searches for one of your keywords.

It is important to have a strong first sentence that summarizes your site and convinces the user to click on your link in the search engine results. One reason for this is that the amount of text search engines will display for a description range from approximately 130 to 400 characters. So in many search engines, the first sentence may be all that is displayed for the description. Another reason for the importance of the first sentence is that users are in a rush. They are quickly scanning the search engine results to find the information that they want. So be sure to quickly and clearly tell them who you are and why you are worth clicking on.

The following example clearly states that Prudential Verani is a successful real estate agency. This statement is backed up by the concrete figure of their annual sales. The second sentence explains what type of real estate they sell. Additional paragraphs are also added because they add additional material for the search engine to index, and the longer description may show up in some search engine results.

```
<meta name="Description"
    content="Prudential Verani is one of the largest and
most successful real estate agencies in New Hampshire
with $100 million in annual sales. We can help you buy
and sell homes, land, and commercial property.
    We have served the real estate needs of New
Hampshire and northern Massachusetts for more than 35
years under the ownership of the Verani family. We know
the area, and as your neighbor, we will treat you with
the trust and integrity for which the Verani family is
known.
    Our emphasis on customer service, commitment to
employee training, affiliation with the Prudential Real
Estate network, and utilization of the latest
technological resources give us a competitive edge in
all our real estate dealings.
    We are the real estate information resource for New
Hampshire. Our Relocation Services division can supply
school reports, town reports, and free moving
publications. Our 300+ page Web site is packed with
interactive tools and information to help you make
informed real estate decisions."
```

Keyword Meta Tag   The keyword meta tag lists keywords that a user might type in a search box to find your site. This tag is indexed by some search engines for keywords that will affect your search engine ranking. See the discussion about choosing your keywords under "Search Engines and Keywords" earlier in this chapter. Some keyword tips:

1. You may list up to a thousand characters in your keyword meta tag.

2. Put your most important keywords first.

3. Concentrate on two or more word phrases.

4. Enter your keywords all in lowercase, because in most search engines, even if the user searches in uppercase, the search engine will match that search with lowercase keywords.

5. As was discussed earlier with titles, do not list the same word multiple times or you may trigger the search engine's spam detector and your keywords—and maybe even your site—will not be indexed. It is, however, OK to list different phrases that include some of the same words, such as "new hampshire real estate" and "southern new hampshire real estate."

6. Think of as many synonyms and variations on your keyword as you can so you can catch as many searches as possible, such as using "new hampshire" and "n.h."

7. If there are common misspelling of your most important keywords, it is also not a bad idea to include a few of them.

8. Put commas between each of your keywords.

9. Review your keyword choices with your client. They know their business better than you do.

```
<meta name="KEYWORDS"
    content="new hampshire real estate, nh real estate,
southern new hampshire real estate, southern nh real
estate, southern nh realtors, relocation services, nh
homes for sale, new hampshire, nh, southern new
hampshire, southern n.h., property listings, new
construction, real estate financing, land development,
manchester new hampshire, commercial locations, n.h.,
massachusetts, homes, houses, residential, commercial,
realty, prudential, prudential verani realty,
relocation, nh realtors, verani, mortgage, property,
properties, housing, mortgage calculators, mortgages,
land, real estate careers, manchester nh, londonderry,
salem, nashua, kingston, derry, interstate 93, i-93,
bank owned, reo, short sale, subdivisions, rural,
lease, school reports, town reports, agents, real
estate agents, real estate maps, radon, lead, windham,
raymond, bedford, pelham, exeter, plaistow, skiing,
employee assistance, portsmouth, municipal permitting,
bank-owned, pru review"
```

Alt Tags

Alt tags are similar to meta tags in that they are part of the HTML of your site that the user does not see on the Web page. The alt tags describe the images on your site in text. The following example shows the alt tag for the first navigation button on the home page. The alt tag is located immediately after the image source tag, which tells the browser where to find the image that will be displayed on your page.

```
img src="homepix/navhomes.gif"
alt="New Hampshire Homes and Land"
```

The function of the alt tag is to:

1. Boost search engine rankings.
2. Describe your images for surfers who have their images turned off.
3. Describe your images for the visually impaired, who use text readers to access your site.

Alt tags should provide a clear, succinct description of your images. This includes navigation buttons. Because some search engines use alt tags to boost your search engine rankings, it is advisable to work keywords into your alt tags if you can do so without distorting the content. In the example above, the actual navigation button says "Homes and Land," but the alt tag is "New Hampshire Homes and Land" to create a more effective keyword.

Another reason for descriptive alt tags is that some search engines create the description of your site that appears on the search engine results from all the text on your page, including the alt tags. If you are using an HTML editor, such as FrontPage, it may automatically enter alt tags for every image. Be sure to edit them and delete the ones that have no relevance to the content. For example, if you have a decorative bar on top of your menu, your editor might give this bar the alt tag of "Navbar top." A search engine might use this text in the description of your site, which will be useless for the user.

MAIN SECTION MENU/INTRODUCTION PAGES

If you have a large site with sections of unique content, then you will need to write an introductory page for each section of the site. The primary function of these pages is to:

1. Explain what is in the section
2. Lure the user to click deeper into the site
3. Provide local navigation to complement the global navigation for the entire site
4. Improve search engine rankings

There are three main parts of a well-written section introduction page:

- The body text
- Local navigation
- Global navigation

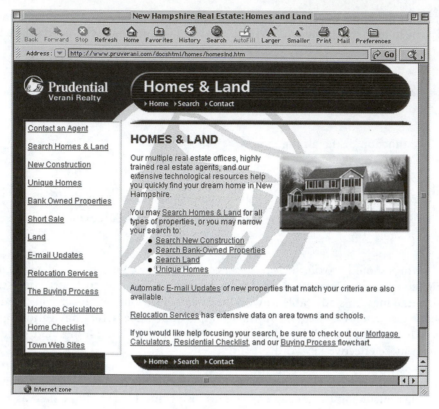

FIGURE 10–4

Homes and Land Section Introduction Page.

Figure 10–4 is the introduction page for the Homes and Land section of the Web site. This example shows the global navigation on the top of the page (a graphic "navbar" on the actual site), the local navigation in a text menu on the left, and the body text on the right. Global navigation links relate to the site as a whole. Local navigation links relate primarily to this section. Underlined text indicates a link. To see this actual page, go to the *Prudential Verani* home page (http://www.pruverani.com) and click the Homes and Land link in the main menu.

Homes and Land Section Introduction Page

Navigation
A surprisingly large number of Web sites make the error of using global navigation throughout the site to the exclusion of local navigation. This error loses an excellent opportunity to encourage a user to explore deeper into the site. In the Homes and Land example, global navigation allows the user to go to the home page and from there access the menu for the main sections of the site. Global navigation also allows the user to go to a search page that has a site-wide search and a sitemap.

With global navigation dealt with simply and cleanly in a navigation bar at the top of the page, the main menu area on the left can be used for local navigation. This menu concentrates on listing the main pages and activities of the site related to homes and land. This introduces the elements of this section and hopefully lures the user deeper into the site. The writing challenge here is the same as it was writing the main menu on the home page. The menu items need to be succinct, descriptive, and engaging.

Body Text

The body text of the section introduction page fulfills many of the same functions as the menu. The body text is peppered with links to other sections of the site, but it also includes brief explanations of why the user might be interested in these links. This provides redundant navigation to accommodate different users. Some users of a site never read the body text. They just jump to the menu to find what they want. Other users want a little more help and read the body text for guidance. A writer needs to accommodate as many types of users as possible.

The body text also has unique functions not shared by the menu. The introductory sentence explains in concrete terms why Prudential Verani can serve your Homes and Land needs. The text also directs the user to the personalized search service. If site visitors want to, they may focus their search to specific types of properties: new construction, bank-owned, or land. The style of the text follows the guidelines established at the beginning of this chapter under "Online Writing Style Tips": clear, concrete, simple construction, bullets, and highlighting key terms.

Meta Tags and Title

Like the actual home page, you should pay close attention to the section introduction page's title and meta tags. The reason is that most search engines will index all the main pages of your site, and some search engines will display multiple pages from the same site in search engine results. You should focus your meta tags for these section introductory pages to their specific content. For example, for the Homes and Land section main page, the meta tags focused on homes, land, residences, and so on. This may allow this page to appear higher in a search for New Hampshire homes and land than would the home page for the entire site.

STATIC PRINT CONTENT PAGES

If the writer and designers have correctly written the home page and the main section introduction page, then the user will be drawn to the primary content pages of the site. The content pages contain the major information that the site has to offer. For a commercial site, such as the *Prudential Verani* site, the primary function of these pages is to:

1. Present information
2. Lure the user into other parts of the site
3. Get the user to explore the client's products and/or contact the client

The content pages have a local and global navigation system similar to that described for the section introduction pages, except the local navigation links on the content page are of course focused on that particular content. The concept of local navigation was discussed extensively earlier in this chapter in the Main Section Menu/Introduction Pages discussion, so it will not be repeated here. You can view the local navigation links for the following samples on the *Prudential Verani* Web site (http://www.pruverani.com).

Content Page Example

The main challenges presenting complex content on a Web site are to write succinctly and to chunk the content down into bite-sized bits with meaningful headings. (Chunking is a Web term meaning to divide large amounts of content into subcategories and if necessary display these subcategories on separate pages.) Nothing sends Web site visitors running more than a long uninterrupted page of text. The following example is an explanation of mortgages, a topic that could easily fill a book. Notice how the material is broken down into short paragraphs with meaningful subheadings. There are also abundant links to some of the more interactive elements in the site. Lastly, there is a link to the agents' directory to encourage the user to get in touch.

This page does not directly connect to the client's product, in this case real estate, but the pages to which it links do. For example, after users use the mortgage calculator to determine how much property they can afford, there is a line of text on the calculator results page that asks them if they want to search for properties in that price range. This takes them to the search page and the client's product.

MORTGAGES 101

How Much House Can You Afford

Before starting serious house-hunting, it is a good idea to get an estimate of how much house you can afford. Review some of the basic concepts below, then try out our ***How Much House Can You Afford*** and our ***Renting vs. Buying Calculators.***

The Down Payment Most mortgages require a minimum down payment of 5% of the house purchase price ($10,000 dollars on a $200,000 home). If you are a military veteran or a first-time buyer and qualify for a VA or FHA loan, it is possible to pay 3% or no down payment at all.

Debt to Salary Ratio Generally, your housing payment should not exceed 25% to 35% of your gross monthly income, and your total long-term debt should not exceed 38% of your gross monthly income. Long-term debt include school loans, car loans, credit cards, etc.

Total Monthly Payment (PITI) It is important to keep in mind that your monthly housing payment includes more than the loan for the property. It includes principle, interest, taxes, and insurance. In New Hampshire, property taxes can be a large percentage of your costs. Use our ***Mortgage Calculator*** to determine your monthly payment.

Closing Costs In addition to the down payment, there are a number of other expenses when you finalize or close the purchase on your property. These other costs may include: points (fees paid to the lender for lower interest rates), taxes, title insurance, private mortgage insurance (PMI), property appraisal, credit report, homeowners insurance, and real estate taxes. Use our ***Closing Costs Calculator*** to get an estimate of your closing costs.

Types of Mortgage

There are various types of mortgages available:

- Fixed rate mortgages maintain the same interest rate over the life of the loan.
- Adjustable rate mortgages (ARM) adjust their rate according to fluctuations of interest rates in the market.
- FHA and VA mortgages are guaranteed or insured by the federal government. These mortgages often have lower down payments and lower interest rates than standard mortgages. VA loans require the borrower to be a military veteran.

Preapproved and Prequalified

Visiting your mortgage lender early in the house-hunting process is a good idea. After looking at your financial materials, the lender can prequalify you, which means give you an estimate of how much house you may be able to afford. Preapproval takes this one step forward by actually submitting your full loan application. Once this is accepted you know for sure how much you can spend on a house. Preapproval also speeds up the house-buying process when you finally make a decision.

See an Expert

The calculators on this site and the above material are meant to give you general information about mortgages, but you should see a qualified mortgage lender before making any final decisions. There is a ***list of mortgage lenders*** in the directory section of our site. Your ***Prudential Verani agent*** also has other resources for mortgage information, such as the free "Easy Moves" magazine.

GRAPHICAL CONTENT

The writer should examine the content to be communicated and determine if there is a way to present it that would be more effective than straight text. Depending on the capacity of the site, video, audio, or even a graphic chart might be an option.

The example that follows is a portion of a chart that explains all the steps that occur in the buying process. For reasons of space, only the last half of the chart is presented here. Because of the various directions the buying process can follow, this chart provides a more effective way of visualizing this information than would a list

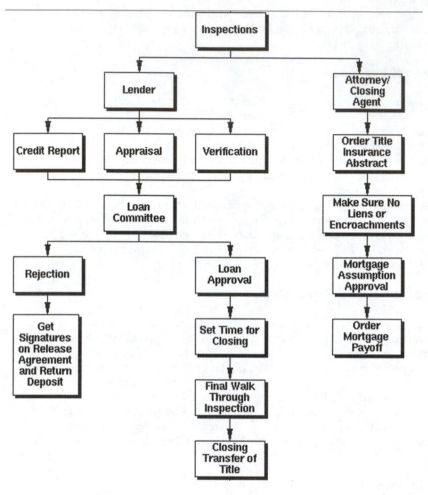

FIGURE 10-5

A portion of the real estate buying process illustrated with a flowchart.

or an essay. The writing challenge here is to break the information into smaller units, chart the process, and write brief, clear symbol titles.

NOTE: An earlier version of this chart was created by Prudential Verani Realty for their print material.

INTERACTIVE, PERSONALIZED CONTENT

Whenever an interactive media project can get the user to interact with the content beyond clicking and reading, and thereby customize the content for that particular user, the user is more likely to feel connected and dig further into the information.

The *Prudential Verani* site has a number of examples of interactive content. Calculators allow the user to compute how much house they can afford, renting versus buying options, closing costs, and mortgages. The homes and land search can be customized to the user's needs through multiple criteria. E-mail updates allow the user to get E-mail notification of houses that meet their criteria as soon as they come on the market. The interactive checklist creates a customized list of user preferences.

The execution of these tools and others owe much of their success to the skills of the site's programmer Ken Jones. But the writer's skills are still required to explain how these tools work and to write the interactive content.

Interactive Content Writing Example 1: Checklists

The custom checklist allows the user to define their dream house by clicking a series of options. When they push "submit" a custom checklist with only their criteria is produced. They can then take this checklist with them as they visit properties for sale.

On the site, this custom checklist has the Prudential Verani name and contact information at the top to encourage the user to get in touch with them. This list also gives the user the option of e-mailing the completed checklist to Prudential Verani and/or getting e-mail updates that match the criteria that they have defined in the checklist.

Writing something like this checklist makes the writer realize that one of the major jobs of the writer is selecting, sorting, and organizing information. Once that is done, then this information needs to be expressed as clearly as possible. This is only a section of the complete checklist.

CUSTOM CHECKLIST FOR YOUR NEW HOME	
DEFINE YOUR IDEAL HOME Create a custom checklist using the form below to: • Focus your priorities for your new home for you and your realtor • Evaluate and track the properties you visit	DIRECTIONS • Select your choices below • Push the "Create Custom Checklist" button at the bottom of the page • Print out one copy of the resulting Custom Checklist for each property you will visit
CRITERIA Type of home What type of home are you looking for?	CHOICE ○ Single family ○ Multifamily ○ Condo/Condex ○ Mobile Home
Price range What is your price range?	○ Under $100,000 ○ $100,000–$125,000 ○ $125,000–$175,000 ○ $175,000–$225,000 ○ $225,000+
Neighborhood What type of neighborhood are you looking for?	○ Urban ○ Subdivision ○ Rural

AFTER THE SITE IS FINISHED

MAINTENANCE INSTRUCTIONS

The last type of writing that is often overlooked but which is much appreciated by clients is a "how to manual" for the site. In many cases, clients expect to do a certain amount of site maintenance themselves. Written instructions can help them stay on track and keep them feeling positively towards the developer. The best designed maintenance system can sometimes be overwhelming without some instructions. A key part of these instructions should be design specifications—describing fonts, colors, and other design elements used on the site.

OUTSTANDING ISSUES

At the completion of a large project there is often the urge to exit as quickly as possible, but the smart developer writes up an outstanding issues proposal similar to the proposal at the beginning of this chapter. This is your chance to remind the client of all the bells and whistles that they could not afford or did not have the time to produce this time around. This memo can also point out additional enhancements to the site that might be needed as the business grows. Be careful not to write this proposal in such a way that you are saying the site you just built is inadequate. Written and presented correctly, this memo can sometime result in additional contracts from the same client.

CONCLUSION

The goal of this chapter was to outline all the different types of writing that goes into the development of an interactive media project from the first proposal to the final exit memo. The example used here was for a medium-sized Web site, but the suggestions above hold true for many types of interactive media projects as well, with larger projects being much more complex.

REFERENCES

Inspiration Flowcharting Software's Web site. http://www.inspiration.com.
SubmitIt!'s Online Marketing Web Site. http://www.submit-it.com.
Nielsen, Jakob. *The Alertbox: Current Issues in Web Usability*.
    http://www.useit.com/alertbox/.
Nielsen, Jakob. *The Alertbox: How Users Read on the Web*.
    http://www.useit.com/alertbox/9710a.html.
Prudential Verani Realty Web Site. http://www.pruverani.com.
Search Engine Watch Web Site. http://www.searchenginewatch.com/.
Web Position's Web Site. http://www.firstplacesoftware.com/.
WebTrends Hit Analysis Software Web Site. http://www.webtrends.com/.

C H A P T E R   1 1

CORPORATE WEB SITE CASE STUDY: *T. ROWE PRICE* WEB SITE

Summary

Name of production: *T. Rowe Price* Web Site (Second Generation)
Writers: Members of the Shareholder Communications Group
Developer: T. Rowe Price Internet Services
Subject: Mutual funds, investment, and retirement planning
Audience: Seasoned investors, first-time investors, anyone interested in mutual
   funds
Medium: World Wide Web
Goals: Inform, teach
Architecture: Branching, hierarchical branching

The images used in this chapter are courtesy of T. Rowe Price Associates, Inc. © 1998, 1999 T. Rowe Price Associates, Inc.

PROGRAM DESCRIPTION AND BACKGROUND

PROGRAM DESCRIPTION

The *T. Rowe Price* Web Site is the online home of T. Rowe Price Services. This site offers extensive information to help investors learn about and invest in mutual funds. The strength of this site is that much of the information is dynamic; the information is either updated frequently or can be personalized for each user. Updates range from quarterly updates, such as Performance Update and the T. Rowe Price Report, to daily updates, such as daily prices on mutual funds.

Other sections of the site can be personalized to the individual investor's needs. These include the mutual fund Watch List, which reports on the funds the user chooses, and the Online Investment Strategy Planner, a tutorial that helps establish the user's approach to investing.

The site also provides tools in the form of calculators, guides, and applications that help investors make informed investment decisions. (See the Chapter 11 section of the *Writing for Multimedia and the Web* CD-ROM for a link to the *T. Rowe Price* site and other sites mentioned in this chapter.)

T. ROWE PRICE AND THE COMMERCIAL WEB SITE

There are five basic categories of Web sites:

1. Personal. Created by individuals to share material about themselves and their interests.
2. Educational. Created by schools, museums, and other educational institutions to provide information.
3. Governmental. Created by government agencies or elected officials as a service to their constituents.
4. Entertainment. Created by publishers, movie studios, TV production companies, and others to provide online entertainment. Online magazines, soap operas, and travel sites, are examples of this category.
5. Commercial. Created by businesses to promote their companies, products, and/or services. T. Rowe Price is a commercial site.

Types of Commercial Web Sites

According to Poppe Tyson agency's Peter Adams, the designer of T. Rowe Price's first-generation Web site, companies create sites for various purposes.

- Transactional site.

The primary purpose is to perform transactions, such as ordering merchandise. All the content in the site revolves around setting up that function. Example: Amazon.com (www.amazon.com) sells books, videos, and much more from their site.

- Consumer site.

This type of site is promotional. It's fun and highly visible but does not usually offer much information. Example: The Absolute Vodka site (www.absolutvodka.com) has various games and graphics with limited hard data about vodka.

- Marcom site (marketing communications).

This approach has lots of information about the company, including material on the company's products and how to contact the company. Example: The Daimler-Chrysler site (www.daimlerchrysler.com) has extensive information on corporate developments as well as sections devoted to Chrysler and Mercedes vehicles.

- Content site.

A content site offers extensive information on the general type of product or service that the company is involved in, such as investment information on the *T. Rowe Price* site, or real estate information on the *Prudential Verani* site, which is profiled in Chapter 10 of this book. The goal of a content site is to draw users to the site because of the strong content and then get them interested in the company's products. Excellent content on a site also demonstrates to users that this company is expert in its field.

A content site differs from a Marcom site in that a content site is generally bigger, has much more content on the general topic (e.g., investment information) offered to users, and has less emphasis on marketing and more on information. This is not to say it can't be used for marketing purposes. It is also possible to transform a content site into a transactional site, such as buying or selling mutual funds. A content site is financially supported by transforming part of it into a transactional site or through online advertising.

Sites have successfully blended elements of the above categories, but one key to a successful site is to be clear about your site's primary focus: transactional, consumer, marketing communications, or content site.

PRODUCTION BACKGROUND

The first generation *T. Rowe Price* site was launched in 1996. In recent years, the site has been substantially revised. For the first generation site, T. Rowe Price commissioned the Poppe Tyson agency to create its Web presence through the online subsidiary poppe.com. The site was created in-house at poppe.com under creative director Peter Adams. Adams, Ken Godfrey, and Matt Freeman wrote some of the material for it, but the content was primarily written by the members of T. Rowe Price's Shareholder Communications Group. Poppe Tyson has since merged with Modem Media to create a major digital marketing communications company called Poppe Tyson Modem Media.

The second generation T. Rowe Price site was created in-house by T. Rowe Price Internet Services with additional content created by members of T. Rowe Price's Shareholder Communications Group. Many elements of the first-generation site were retained. Emmett Higdon, T. Rowe Price Assistant Vice President of Internet Services, said that it is important not to change a site that deals with the general public too quickly and too often. Users don't want to have to completely relearn how a site works every six months. One of the challenges developing a large site is to make changes without losing a large portion of your audience. The changes on the T. Rowe Price site are driven largely by the needs of customers. These needs are tracked through site usage and through special audience focus groups.

PREPRODUCTION PROCESS

Poppe.com's process for writing and designing the first-generation *T. Rowe Price* site is worth looking at as a model for developing content sites. A key part of the approach is to work from the beginning with the entire production team: writers, programmers, art directors, and designers. At poppe.com, developing a Web site is a collaborative process with several stages:

1. Gather content. The team engages in lengthy talks with clients to understand their business and digest existing material on the subject. The goal of this first stage is to understand and identify all the content that will be involved in the site.

2. Define categories and placement of content. The gathered content is spread out on a table before the entire production team, who ask a variety of questions: How would users make sense of all this content? What do they need to know when they get to the Home Page? What general category of information does this site offer? What is the main focus within this category? (The *T. Rowe Price* site category is mutual fund investing with a focus on investment planning and retirement.)

Once the above questions are answered, then the team needs to:

- Group content into categories
- Determine the importance of each category
- Decide on accessibility of categories. How quickly do users need to get this information? Should it be on the Home Page? What information is going to change regularly and what is going to remain static?

3. Organize information below the main categories and decide on the interactive structure. For example, how will categories and subcategories be linked? The team evaluates whether a tree structure, branching, or dynamic flow will be best, and then they flowchart this interactive structure. They start at the home page, then the level 2 pages, then the level 3 pages, and continue to the bottom level. The final form at this stage is flowchart boxes with legends indicating the type of content and whether it is dynamic or static. This flowchart is attached to a marketing creative brief that explains the goal of the site in detail.

4. Writing the content. When the flowchart is approved, the team writes and designs the actual pages, starting from the top down and building section by section.

MEETING THE CHALLENGES OF WRITING AND DEVELOPING THE *T. ROWE PRICE* WEB SITE

The main challenge with this site was to write and organize it intelligently from the user's perspective so that it would be easy to navigate and understand. This was not an easy task because of the breadth and difficulty of the content.

DYNAMIC INFORMATION FLOW AND CUSTOMIZATION

A major element that was retained from the first generation site was the use of dynamic flow of information. The poppe.com team used this approach to make the program easy to navigate and understand. Dynamic flow means letting the users customize pages or choose unique paths through the information, based on interactive questions. This lets users develop custom content around their interests in ways not possible with linear media, such as books or videos. (See the "Chapters" section, Chapter 11 area of the *Writing for Multimedia and the Web* CD-ROM for illustrations of the following examples.)

Dynamic Flow Example #1: User-Designed Information-Watch List
The Watch List is a dynamic flow tool that helps users navigate mutual fund price and performance information quickly and easily. The Watch List is prominently featured on the top right of the home page. (See Figure 11–1.) On the first visit, a user will have to register to create a Watch List. Clicking the underlined word "register" links to the Watch List Registration page, where the user types in his or her name, E-mail address, login ID, and chooses mutual funds from the following:

- Domestic Stock Funds
- Money Market Funds

- Taxable Bond Funds
- Tax-Free Bond Funds
- Variable Annuity Portfolios
- International Stock Funds

If the user chooses the last item, International Stock Funds, then he or she jumps to the list of investment options for the International Stock Funds:

- Emerging Markets Stock
- European Stock
- Global Stock
- International Discovery
- International Growth and Income
- International Stock
- Japan
- Latin America
- New Asia
- Spectrum International

A user who chooses the Japan Fund and Emerging Markets Stock Fund from this list and then submits his/her registration will link to a new screen, which shows these two funds with their current prices. Once a user has established a Watch List, every time this person logs on, he or she will be able to access the information for these two funds instantly instead of having to search a long list of mutual funds. Of course, a Watch List can be altered at any time. This approach is called customization. The users design how the Web page will present the information.

Dynamic Flow Example #2: The Interactive Tutorial: Online Investment Strategy Planner

A different approach to structuring information through dynamic flow is the interactive tutorial. The Online Investment Strategy Planner is reached from the home page by clicking text in the middle of the page that reads "Investment Strategy Planner." This leads to a page of text that explains how the tutorial works and gives the user the choice of continuing with the tutorial by choosing: "Step One: Define your financial goals and time horizons." This step explains possible financial goals and gives the option to select the time horizon to achieve these goals:

- 3–5 years
- 6–10 years
- 11+ Years

On the next page, the user selects the level of risk: Low, Moderate, or High. The final result is a suggested investment strategy showing a mix of stocks and bonds, and with one more click, the user can choose the T. Rowe Price mutual funds geared to implementing this strategy.

TWO-CLICK NAVIGATION

Although the dynamic flow features from the first-generation site have been quite popular with users, they were less happy with the site's hierarchical navigation that required three or four clicks to get to desired information. In response to user demand, navigation was completely redesigned for the second-generation site.

The goal of the navigation redesign was to make important information on the site no more than two clicks away. The designers wanted to achieve this goal without confusing new users. Focus group studies had told the designers that new users prefer static menus, whereas the more experienced users are comfortable with search functions and more dynamic navigation features.

Static Menus

In focus group studies conducted for the Web site revisions, T. Rowe Price learned that new users generally prefer static menus. Unlike a drop-down or popup menu, a static menu is already visible on the page without requiring the user to click to make it appear. The home page (Figure 11–1) has a static menu on the left side with "FIND OUT ABOUT" at the top. This menu provides access to the main sections of the site. For example, a user who clicks on Mutual Funds would come to the main Mutual Funds page as illustrated in Figure 11–2.

From the main Mutual Funds Page, the new user can continue to click the static menus on the left-hand side of the page to find the information that he or she wants. Every page of the site has a static menu on the left-hand side. But compare the static left menus on the Home Page (Figure 11–1) and those on the Mutual Funds page

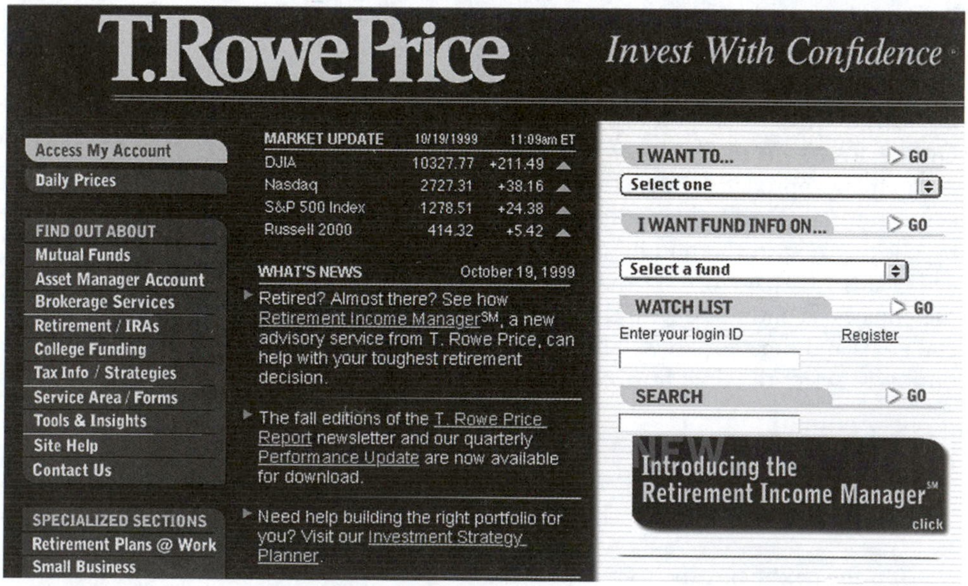

FIGURE 11–1

Home page for the *T. Rowe Price* Web site (see the *Writing for Multimedia and the Web* CD-ROM for the color image).

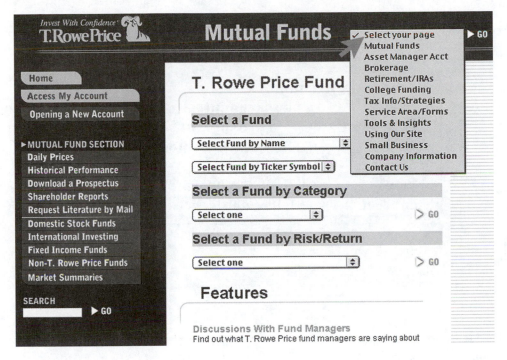

FIGURE 11-2

Main menu for Mutual Funds Section with mouse-clicked drop-down menu.

(Figure 11–2). Note that the menu items on the Mutual Funds page are different from those on the home page. The home page menu is for global, site-wide navigation. The Mutual Funds page menu is for local navigation in the mutual fund area. The local navigation on the Mutual Funds page allows the user to quickly access additional mutual fund information and explore this area in depth. This better accommodates typical user behavior than does having global site-wide links on every page. The user can still access site-wide links from the Mutual Funds page by clicking the Home Page link, which will lead to the home page's menu.

Drop-Down Menus

The static menus work great for the new user, but the experienced user knows where he or she wants to go and wants to get there fast. For this group of users, T. Rowe Price has added the I WANT TO . . . feature on the top right of the home page (Figure 11–1). When the user clicks I WANT TO . . . a menu drops down as illustrated in Figure 11–3. The I WANT TO . . . Drop-Down Menu allows the experienced user to jump immediately to the most commonly used sections of the site.

If you refer to Figure 11–2, which shows the Main Menu for the Mutual Funds Section, you'll notice another drop-down menu on the top of that page, which has been clicked to display it. This drop-down menu is on every page of the site and serves as global navigation. By clicking the links in this menu, the user can go to any page on the site.

FIGURE 11–3

Detail of home page: I WANT TO . . . drop-down menu.

Other Navigational Aids

Anther navigational feature on every page is the search box. Users can enter a term and search the site for whatever information they want. It is important to have a search feature on a site because this is the first place that many experienced users go on a new site. Also included on every page are links to Home and the investor's account. Planned navigational enhancements for the future include treed menus, such as you now find in Windows, and a sitemap that shows all the pages on the site on a single screen. A sitemap is an important element, particularly for new users.

INFORMATION GROUPING

The other major area where users requested a change was in better information grouping, particularly in the area of Mutual Funds and Tools and Services. In the site revision, T. Rowe Price responded by gathering all the mutual fund information into one location, as evidenced in Figure 11–2. From this one page, the user can easily access information on price, performance, management, top holdings, and can download a prospectus or annual report. Once the user selects a specific fund, summaries that are called Fund Fact documents give a quick overview of all the key information for that fund. Lastly, every fund's performance is compared to an industry benchmark in a clear, visual graph.

The tools and services on the site were similarly grouped into one area. From a main Tools and Insights menu page, users can now access all the tools and special services on the site. These include: interactive calculators, worksheets, retirement planning software, and special forms to open a new account. Plans for future services will be a completely redesigned mutual funds trading area.

MANAGING CONTENT ON A CONTENT SITE

One of the challenges of a content site is figuring out how to update a site with lots of dynamic content without the cost of having a whole team of Web experts on staff. Poppe.com solved this problem by creating content interfaces that allow the user to change the content without programming. For example, anyone can add new press releases to the site simply by cutting and pasting copy. An old release can also be put into an accessible archive for future use. Easy updating is a feature most clients request for Web sites.

CONCLUSION: RESPONSE TO THE PROJECT

The site has been very popular. Thousands of users have registered and the site saved T. Rowe Price tens of thousands of dollars over traditional ways of presenting the information (direct mail, salespeople, etc.). This Web site also creates immeasurable value, such as developing awareness of the T. Rowe Price brand.

REFERENCES

Adams, Peter. Telephone interview with the author, March 1996.
Higdon, Emmett. Telephone interview with the author, July 1999.
Modem Media.Poppe Tyson Web site. http://www.modemmedia.poppetyson.com/.
T. Rowe Price Web Site. http://www.troweprice.com.

C H A P T E R   1 2

RESEARCH PORTAL WEB SITE AND THE ONLINE FEATURE STORY: BRITANNICA.COM AND *THE HARLEM RENAISSANCE*

Summary

Name of production: *The Harlem Renaissance* spotlight on Britannica.com
Writers for *The Harlem Renaissance*: Andrew Nelson, Tom Michael
Developer: Encyclopaedia Britannica
Harlem Renaissance Subject: Black history and culture in the 1920s Harlem
    neighborhood of New York City
Audience: Students, general audience
Medium: World Wide Web
Goals: Inform, teach
Architecture: Branching, hierarchical branching

The images used in this chapter are reprinted with permission from *The Harlem Renaissance*. ©
1999 by Encyclopaedia Britannica, Inc.

PROGRAM DESCRIPTION AND BACKGROUND

PROGRAM DESCRIPTION

Britannica.com is a Web site created by Encyclopaedia Britannica, the company that has been known for their book encyclopedias for generations. Britannica.com presents a synthesis of recommended links to other Web sites, articles from Encyclopaedia Britannica's own massive database, and new material, such as a news digest and multimedia features called spotlights. The spotlights are special sections of the Britannica.com site that focus on a specific topic, such as women's history, D-Day, or black history. The purpose of these spotlights is to engage the user by presenting information in a highly visual and interactive manner, as opposed to the more text-based online encyclopedias. The spotlights are produced for Britannica.com and for its predecessor, Encyclopaedia Britannica Online.

The Harlem Renaissance is a spotlight that was designed to encourage interest in black history. Rather than presenting a broad overview of this subject, Britannica Online Editor Tom Michael and writer Andrew Nelson decided to focus on telling the story of a key moment in black history—the Harlem Renaissance. The Harlem Renaissance took place in Harlem, New York in the 1920s. It was a period of astounding black cultural and political activity. The spotlight uses powerful writing, period graphics, and multimedia elements to evoke an era and engage users in the broader study of black history.

(See the Chapter 12 section of the *Writing for Multimedia and the Web* CD-ROM for a link to the sites mentioned in this chapter.)

THE WEB SITE PORTAL AND BRITANNICA.COM

Britannica.com is a type of portal Web site. The goal of a portal Web site is to be the user's entrance or doorway to the Web. A portal's designers want it to be the page that you use as your start page whenever you go online. The portal organizes links to other Web sites into key categories and provides tools to search those sites. The best portals also review all or most of their sites before including them in their database so that you have some guarantee of quality. Some portals, such as realtor.com and ZDNet, review sites and organize links to other sites on a narrow subject, in these cases real estate and high-tech. Other portals, such as Yahoo and Excite, attempt to cover a broad range of content.

In addition to directories of links, major portals also include basic information and tools, such as news, stock quotes, sports scores, chat, E-mail, games, entertainment guides, product reviews, and shopping. A number of portals also have customization features, such as My Yahoo!, that allow the user to custom design the portal page so that it presents the information that they are most interested in.

The major portals attract hundreds of millions of page views a day. Because of this heavy traffic, portals are one of the most sought after sites for advertising and E-commerce. This success has made the portal approach one of the most common designs for new sites attempting to attract mass users. With sites, such as Yahoo! and Excite, already well established in the broad information portal category, new portals have had to come up with fresh angles to make themselves appealing to users.

According to Britannica.com's Executive Director of New Product Development, Peter Meyerhoff, Britannica.com fills a niche somewhere between Yahoo.com and Discovery Channel Online. He labels Britannica's approach to portals as a research or knowledge portal. Britannica.com covers a broad range of content, similar to Yahoo, but Britannica.com also creates and presents it own content. Because of its huge archive of material from years of creating encyclopaedias and other publications, Encyclopaedia Britannica is uniquely qualified to create such a site. For example, a search on Yahoo! for the Harlem Renaissance will produce a list of sites and categories on this topic. You'll also have the option of clicking a link for related news stories. A similar search on Britannica.com will provide more substantial results, including:

- Full-text, crossindexed articles from Encyclopaedia Britannica
- Reviewed and rated Web sites
- Full text magazine articles
- Related books with options for ordering them
- Definitions and pronunciation guides for every word in the Merriam-Webster's Collegiate Dictionary (optional)
- A multimedia feature story related to the topic called a Spotlight. Spotlights, such as *The Harlem Renaissance*, are one of the key ways that Britannica.com distinguishes itself from the other portals. The writing and information design of these spotlights will be the primary focus of the rest of this chapter. Spotlights are featured periodically on Britannica.com, but they are a regular part of Encyclopaedia Britannica Online (www.eb.com). Try the "sample search" to view spotlights.

PRODUCTION BACKGROUND FOR *THE HARLEM RENAISSANCE*

The Harlem Renaissance was originally conceived as a spotlight for Britannica's subscription-based site, Encyclopaedia Britannica Online. This site will continue to exist for institutional users who prefer an advertising-free site. However, *The Harlem Renaissance* was also shown on Britannica.com. *The Harlem Renaissance* was initiated by Peter Meyerhoff and developed by Tom Michael and Andrew Nelson. *The Harlem Renaissance* site was created to promote Britannica's encyclopedias and as a service to customers in schools. Black History Month is important in middle and high schools. Unfortunately, *The Harlem Renaissance* was pulled from all Britannica sites immediately before the publication of this book. Other spotlights can be viewed at www.eb.com.

PREPRODUCTION DEVELOPMENT PROCESS FOR *THE HARLEM RENAISSANCE* SPOTLIGHT

Britannica had previously created *The Encyclopaedia Britannica Guide to Black History*, a popular spotlight that presented an overview of black history. The goal with *The Harlem Renaissance* site was to do something very different: to present a large body of information by focusing on a specific story, similar to a feature story in print journalism. According to online editor Tom Michael, after *The Harlem Renaissance* topic was chosen, the site was developed according to the following steps. This is a useful model for organizing a site that draws from a large database of information.

1) Research topic.
Get an understanding of the history and the mood of the period, looking at books and other available material.

2) Create a master list of articles on the topic.
Search the database of articles Britannica already has as well as obtain needed outside essays. Because of the encyclopedic tone of the existing articles, an overarching essay was needed to bring it all together.

3) Divide articles into categories.
Work with the writer to organize all these articles and link them to the master essay and other navigational devices. Organize these categories and links into a

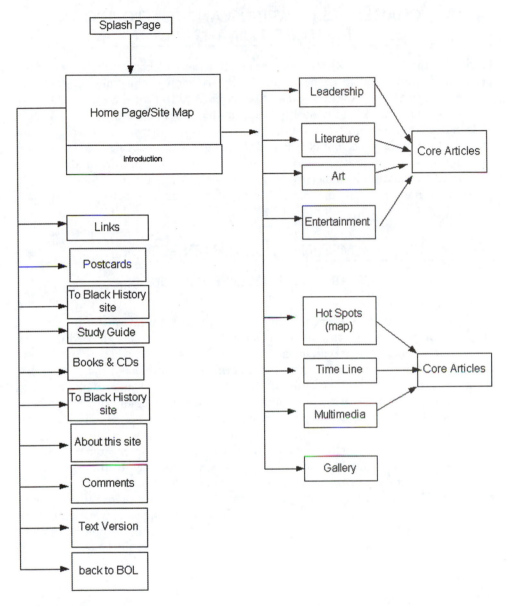

FIGURE 12-1 ────────────────────────────────

Sitemap showing navigation of site.

sitemap, presented with a flowchart (Figure 12–1). Check if any articles need to be updated or rewritten, and decide if new articles are needed, including introductions to the major sections.

4) Identify and locate images.
Identify what images are needed for the site.

5) Finalize the navigation and interface.
This included creating a hot spots map of Harlem and a timeline. Research photos and information for these navigational elements.

CHALLENGES OF WRITING AND DEVELOPING
THE HARLEM RENAISSANCE

Harlem in the 1920s was the site of a major flowering of black culture, but it is a period that many members of the potential audience know nothing about. One of the goals of the site was to create an immersive experience to give users the feeling that they are in Harlem, seeing the sites and hearing the voices of the era. Writer Andrew Nelson said that he tried to create the project as if the user were a tourist visiting Harlem. One of the ways that Nelson and the designers wanted to achieve the feeling of being there was to create a mood that is celebratory and upbeat. Another important part of creating this immersive experience was to develop clear navigation that allowed the users to access the material from a variety of approaches.

MEETING THE CHALLENGES

CREATING AN IMMERSIVE EXPERIENCE

Graphical Pages

Perhaps the most unusual element of this site's design is the rendering of the text and graphics for every page into full-page images (Figure 12–2). This allowed the close integration of the site's text with images of major figures of the era, Harlem locations, and graphics from period books and artwork. The entire page/image was then sepia-toned to add to the period mood. Each main section (Leadership, Literature, Art, and Entertainment) was then subtly tinted a different color for variations on the mood. The effect is to create the feeling that visitors to the site are entering a different era.

Although this approach of making each page into one large graphic achieved its goals of bringing the user into the experience, according to Tom Michael, it created production challenges. The major problem was that it limited the editing of the site. HTML text is easy to change, and small pictures are easy to move about or delete, but because every page was one or two large images, even minor text changes required the entire image do be redone. An additional problem for users on slow modem connections is that the large images load slower than a text and small image page.

Video and Audio

Extensive graphics, video, and audio on the site are another way the designers tried to make the era come to life. A few examples include:

- Fats Waller (on piano) performs the song "The Joint is Jumpin'."
- Tap dancer Bill "Bojangles" Robinson performs his trademark "stair dance," 1932.
- Bessie Smith sings with a backup choir in the film *Saint Louis Blues*, 1929.
- Langston Hughes reads his poem "The Negro Speaks of Rivers," 1921.

There is also an extensive photo gallery of Harlem Renaissance figures and locations.

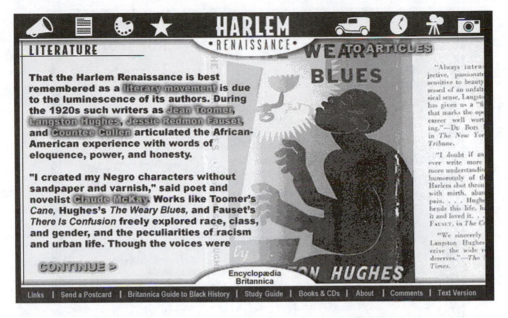

FIGURE 12-2 ————————————————————————————

Introduction to the Literature Section of the site, with cover of *The Weary Blues* by Langston Hughes.

Hot Spots Map

Some of the navigational devices contributed to Nelson's goal of making the user feel like a tourist to the era. The Hot Spots map (Figure 12–3) not only allows the user to get an overview of the location, but it is also a clickable menu. When the name of a location such as The Cotton Club is clicked, a picture and description of the night-club appears.

Writing Style

The visual style of the writing on the site also plays a key role in getting the audience involved. The Entertainment section's first paragraph is a good example:

> The Roaring '20s produced a deafening prosperity. Across the nation saxophones wailed, factories thrummed, Wall Street crowed, and Tommy guns spat in Prohibition inspired firefights. . . . For many, the decade was a party, and it was African American entertainers who set the tone and tempo. (Harlem Renaissance Spotlight)

In addition to visualizing the scene, parts of the paragraph, such as "the decade was a party, and it was African American entertainers who set the tone and tempo," lure users deeper into the site by creating questions in their minds. How was this a party? What did people do? How did African Americans have this much impact?

The site's writer Nelson suggested that another way to get users to click deeper into the site is to use small ads on the Home Page or upper-level pages, advertising or hinting at content deeper in the site. "Whatever you do, make the link to the advertised section clear and easy. I favor hotlinking the graphic itself. People look at that and want to click immediately" (Nelson, E-mail).

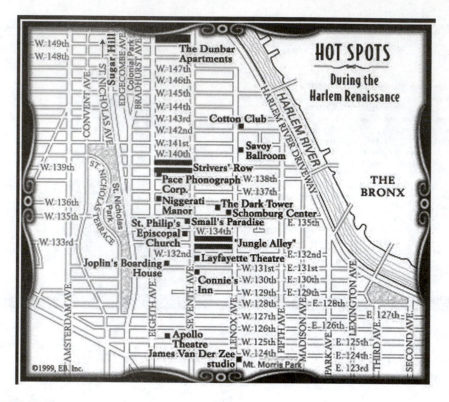

FIGURE 12-3

Harlem Renaissance site's clickable Hot Spots Map.

He also pointed out that to connect with your site users it is important to "write as if you are talking to an individual, not a collective group of anonymous Web surfers. Ask direct questions of them: 'What do you think?' 'Do you agree?'" (Nelson, E-mail).

NAVIGATION: MULTIPLE APPROACHES TO CONTENT

A strength of the navigation on *The Harlem Renaissance* spotlight is that it allows the user to access the information from at least four different perspectives. This is important, because every user approaches the search for information in a different way. A site that relies on just one navigational approach will have many frustrated users. The navigational approaches on Britannica.com include the following

(1) Hierarchical Menus

(a) Main Categories   From the Home Page and any page of the introduction, the user can go to the main menu with one click. On the main menu, the site categories are listed: Leadership, Literature, Art, and Entertainment. Links to these categories are also repeated as icons on the top of every page (see Figure 12–2). Clicking on one of the main menu links or one of the icons, such as Literature, leads to an introductory article that describes the category (see Figure 12–2). From this article, the user can click to the next level of information—specific people and events.

(b) Bibliographies   Users can also jump directly to a list of the core site articles by clicking a "TO ARTICLES" link in the upper right of each introductory essay. From every page of an article, you can click a "TO BIBLIOGRAPHY" link that leads to a descriptive bibliography of key books on the era. Clicking the title of one of these books leads to BarnesandNoble.com where you can purchase the book. A portion of these book sales are returned to Britannica. Thus, this bibliography not only adds depth and convenience to the site for the user, but also adds important revenue to support the site. Writer Andrew Nelson said that online retailing, such as this, will play a much bigger role in the future.

(2) By Location
In addition to the hierarchical menus described above, users can also access information by location. The Hotspots map (see Figure 12–2) allows spatially oriented users to chose a location, such as The Cotton Club, and click on it to get a description and image.

(3) By Time
The Time Line (Figure 12–4) allows users to click on a specific year and get a list of key events for that year. Key people and events in the list can be clicked on to access detailed articles.

FIGURE 12–4

Harlem Renaissance clickable Time Line.

(4) In Context

All of the articles (see Figure 12–2) also provide links within the text through high-lighted words. For example, clicking the highlighted words "Jean Toomer" in the first paragraph of the text on Figure 12–2 leads to an article on that writer.

OTHER SITE ELEMENTS

Send a Postcard

The "Send a Postcard" link at the bottom of every site page leads to a section that allows the user to E-mail picture postcards about the site to friends. This element helps support the tourist-to-the-era approach that the designers were trying to achieve. It is also a free marketing device for the site.

Study Guide

This section of the site (reachable from a link at the bottom of every page) provides activities related to the site. Among other activities, the guide asks students to:

> Imagine that you are staging a 1920s variety show in a Harlem club at which African Americans will be welcomed. Your show will feature writers reading from their books, an art installation, and performances of music, theater, and dance. (Harlem Renaissance Spotlight)

CONCLUSION: RESPONSE TO THE PROJECT

The launch of Britannica.com was, if anything, too successful. The site was shut down for a week because of the high volume of users. Since getting back online, it has become a very popular site on the Web. *The Harlem Renaissance* has also gained equally strong response from its users with comments peppered with adjectives such as superb, magnificent, thorough, and riveting.

REFERENCES

Britannica.com Web Site. http://www.britannica.com

The Harlem Renaissance Web site. No longer available online. To see similar "Spotlights," go to Encyclopaedia Britannica Online and try the "sample search."

Meyerhoff, Peter. Telephone interview with the author, September 1999.

Michael, Thomas. Telephone interview with the author, September 1999.

Nelson, Andrew. Email to the author, October 1999.

Nelson, Andrew. Telephone interview with the author, September 1999.

C H A P T E R 1 3

ONLINE ADVERTISING CASE STUDY: ZDU (SMARTPLANET.COM) CAMPAIGN

Summary

Name of production: ZDU Online Ad Campaign

Writer: John Hargrave

Developer: Media Shower Inc. Developed in conjunction with John Hargrave, ZDNet Editorial Projects Director

Subject: Promoting ZDU (Ziff-Davis University) a Web site that offers online courses

Audience: All Web users, but primarily experienced Web users who might take an online course

Medium: World Wide Web

Presentation location: Where Web is viewed: Home, office, schools

Goals: Persuade

Structure: Linear with interactivity

The images used in this chapter are courtesy of Ziff-Davis Inc. © 1999 Ziff-Davis Inc.

PROGRAM DESCRIPTION AND BACKGROUND

PROGRAM DESCRIPTION

This ZDU online advertising campaign was designed to promote membership in ZDU, an online learning site launched by Ziff-Davis Inc. Ziff-Davis is a leading media and marketing company focused on computing and Internet-related technologies. It publishes computer magazines, such as *PC Week, Mac Week,* and *Computer Shopper.* It also has a number of online ventures, including ZDNet and ZDU. ZDNet is the online network of Ziff-Davis that presents online versions of its magazines, as well as original content about computer technology and information. The ZDU online learning site has recently been expanded and renamed as SmartPlanet. SmartPlanet (ZDU) offers both instructor-led and self-study courses, related products for sale, and an opportunity to interact within the SmartPlanet learning community.

ONLINE ADVERTISING

Online Advertisements Defined

Online advertisements are advertisements placed on the World Wide Web or on commercial online services, such as America Online. For most products and services, the Web is the primary location for ad placement. One of the major forms of online advertisements is the banner. The banner is a small image and text composition that looks like a short billboard. The goal of the banner is to persuade the user to click and go to the Web site where the product or service is offered.

Advantages of Online Advertising

Online advertising has numerous advantages over print and broadcast, among them the following:

• Measurability. Every time a user views or clicks on an online ad, it is recorded. This makes it possible for advertisers to know exactly how many people are viewing their ads, and how many people are following these ads to the desired Web site. It also tells them when interest in an ad is beginning to fade. This is a key advantage over other types of media.

• Rotation. If an ad is beginning to fade, the advertiser can pull it immediately, or the advertiser can choose to rotate new ads into the slot. Advertisers can also adjust the portions of an ad that are not getting attention. This is usually not possible in print or broadcast ads, which are scheduled weeks or months in advance.

• Direct Contact with Customers and Personalization. By simply clicking a button on an ad or on an advertiser's Web site, a customer can E-mail the advertiser, download product information or a sample, or even order a complete product. The advertiser can also track the user's ad viewing and product-buying habits and personalize the ads for that particular user.

• Interactivity. There are myriad possibilities here both for the ad and for the final Web site that the ad leads to. For example, on the Web site, a car buyer could click on different colors for a car that he or she is interested in, or link from the ad to an online auto magazine that has reviews on a certain model. The ad itself can be

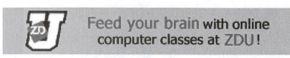

FIGURE 13–1

Third draft of ZDU online advertising banner. (See the "Chapters" section, Chapter 13 area of the *Writing for Multimedia and the Web* CD-ROM for interactive color ads.)

highly interactive, as in the ZDU ad profiled later in this chapter that has animations and multiple pages.

• Cost. It is much cheaper to let the customer find information on a Web site than it is to hire a salesperson. A downloaded or viewable sample costs the advertiser nothing (beyond the basic cost of the Web site). Compare this to the cost of an expensive mailing. It is also cheaper to design an online ad than it is to produce a broadcast commercial or even a spread for print media.

• Unlimited Space. Once an advertiser can get a user to a Web site, then the advertiser can use as much space as needed to present the products. A site can have links to dozens of pages and images within the advertiser's site and links to related sites that might help the user understand the product. This is a far cry from the severe space limitations of a broadcast or print ad.

Limitations

• Modems. Of course, it is not a completely rosy picture. Online technology is rapidly changing, but the slow modem speeds of many users make it difficult to transmit online large files, such as video, sound, and large pictures. This means that to work effectively, files must be kept to a minimum size. The smaller they are, the faster they will appear on the user's screen and the happier the user will be. If users have to wait too long for a screen to load, they will cancel the operation and click elsewhere. Notice the small size of the images in Figure 13–1.

• Click-Through. Another major problem is getting people to click on an ad. Unlike a TV ad, which will run whether or not viewers do anything, the product's Web site will not be seen at all unless the user clicks on the banner. With users becoming more sophisticated, ads are being ignored and the click-through rate continues to go down. Getting users to click will be dealt with in more detail in the analysis of the ZDU advertising campaign later in this chapter.

• Site Owners' Resistance to Interactive Ads. One of the solutions to get better click-through is to make ads more exciting through greater use of multimedia and interactivity. Unfortunately, some site owners are leery of allowing ads with these features on their site because they don't want to cause problems with users with older software and modems. They are also concerned about creating additional demands on their servers.

Measuring an Online Ad's Success: Click-Through

John Hargrave, ZDNet Editorial Projects Director and the designer of the ZDU online advertising campaign, wrote that there are a number of ways that the success of an online advertising campaign can be judged. Sometimes ads, such as the ZDU ad, are trying to get users to register for a product or service. Other ads are simply trying to create brand awareness. However, most advertisers

> look at the clickthrough of an online ad campaign as the ultimate measuring stick of its success . . . ads are tracked using impressions and clickthroughs. Impressions are the number of times the ad has been shown, and clickthroughs are the number of times users have clicked on the ad. (Hargrave, E-mail)

The actual design of the ad and what site the ad is placed on are the two elements that have the greatest impact on clickthrough.

Ad Placement to Improve an Advertisement's Success

To increase an ad's success (in most cases defined as its clickthrough rate), a banner ad is either placed on a popular Web site with similar content to that of the product or service being advertised, or the ad is placed on a site of general interest, such as a Web site portal. Portals, such as Lycos and Yahoo, are described in more detail in Chapter 12, "Research Portal Web Site and the Online Feature Story: Britannica.com and *The Harlem Renaissance*." Portals attempt to make the Web more accessible primarily by organizing links to other Web sites and providing search tools. Portals are a particularly good location for ads due to the following:

- Heavy traffic. A high percentage of all Web users visit portals. The major portals get hundreds of millions of page views a day.

- Personalization. Many portal pages are also able to focus the audience for a product in ways that are impossible for any other type of advertisement. A different ad will appear on the page, depending on what a user is searching. For example, if the user submits a search for "hard drive" on a portal, an ad for a hard drive manufacturer or a computer shopper magazine will appear on the screen, along with a list of Web sites on the topic. If the user typed in a different word to search, such as "music," he or she might see an ad for an online music store or a new CD. Load a search page, such as Lycos or Infoseek, and try it out. Type different search words and see what ads appear. Of course, what ads can appear are limited to the paying ads currently running on a particular search service. Not all browsers and search services function this way, so try a few until you find one that works.

Writing and Design to Improve an Advertisement's Success

John Hargrave points out that there is no "magic bullet," no one trick that will make an advertisement a success. He claims that good ideas, writing, and design are what make great online ads. He does, however, outline the following basic writing and design guidelines for online advertisements.

- Simplicity. Abbie Hoffman once said that the secret of communicating through modern media is finding the one word, image, or phrase that gets your idea across—in other words, oversimplifying to a fault. You must take a complex issue and boil it down to its most one-dimensional component. Nowhere is this more true than in advertising, especially online advertising, where studies show that you have less than half a second to connect with the user before he or she moves on to the rest of the page.

- Interactivity. Interactivity is a subjective term, since all online ads are by definition in some way interactive. I define interactive ads as ads which go "beyond a click." In other words, they do something else besides just take you to the advertiser's site—they let you play a game, they animate when you click them, they play a sound file or video. Interactive ads generally perform better than those that aren't. The drawback is that many sites still do not accept, or offer only limited support for, interactive ads. This is inefficient if you're trying to develop a campaign to be run across many sites.

- That Personal Touch. Personalized advertising is just beginning to take root, whereby you're shown ads which you're likely to be interested in. If your surfing habits indicate you're looking to buy a printer, you'll be shown printer ads. If you like to click on funny ads, you'll be shown more of them. The area that personalized advertising really makes sense at this point is in E-mail. E-mail advertisements (which are usually just text messages sent directly to a person's e-mail box) average three to four times higher clickthrough than banner advertising. They're usually cheaper, and they're much easier to create, because you don't have to worry about designing a graphical ad.

- Real Estate. Generally speaking, the bigger the ad, the bigger the clickthrough. This makes sense—the more in-your-face the ad is, the more you're likely to notice it. Our banner wraps, which literally wrap around the side of the page, are our highest performing ad unit. (Hargrave, E-mail.) (See Figure 13–2.)

The Future of Online Advertising

Online advertisements have evolved rapidly from the early days of the Internet, when ineffective logos and repurposed print ads cluttered Web pages. Just since the last edition of this book, the middle page, formerly a major component of an online advertisement has disappeared (see the "Chapters" section, Chapter 13 area of the *Writing for Multimedia and the Web* CD-ROM for more on middle pages). Today ads are designed with the Web in mind from the beginning. This means designing within the technical limitations of today's online technology. It also means drawing from the persuasive techniques of modern advertising to create an ad that will appeal to the online audience.

FIGURE 13–2

Banner wrap advertisement for ZDNet.

Hargrave believes that online advertising will continue to evolve with increased multimedia, interactivity, and personalization. As bandwidth capacity increases, expect to see the ads that incorporate multimedia, such as audio, video, and deeper interactivity, as the ads that flourish. The ZDU case study in this chapter is a good example of using multimedia in an ad. Interactivity is also being pushed to the limit, with some banner ads offering the user the opportunity to print product information or make secure purchases without ever leaving the banner space. See the Enliven Web site (www.narrative.com) for examples.

Personalization of advertising will also continue to grow in importance as advertisers understand that the Web can be a one-to-one medium and not just a mass medium. This personalization is being made possible for various tools that track how you surf, where you click, and what you buy online. If Levi's can "remember" who you are the next time you see a Levi's ad banner or visit the Levi's site, then Levi's can send you personalized messages, talk about sales you might be interested in, offer you a coupon, or send you a Levi's screensaver, which is of course even more advertising for Levi's (Hargrave, e-mail).

Future online ads will shatter the impression/clickthrough model by offering deeper ways to interact with the ad. The audience for interactive ads will continue to grow explosively with the majority of upper-income American homes already online (Barkow). This growth in audience will translate into an increase in spending on online advertising. Some experts are predicting that Internet ad spending will top $20 billion in less than a decade (Gardner).

PRODUCTION BACKGROUND ON THE ZDU ONLINE ADVERTISING CAMPAIGN

The ad campaign for ZDU was developed by Media Shower Inc. in conjunction with John Hargrave ZDNet Editorial Projects Director. The purpose of this campaign was to draw additional traffic and registrations to the ZDU site.

The development process for this ad is typical of many other online ads:

1. Needs meeting. The creative team meets with the client to identify the client's needs.

2. Creative platform. This is the creative team's basic strategy session when they decide what they are trying to say, identify who the audience is, and come up with possible approaches to present the message.

3. First-round creative. This is the first attempt at creating the ads. The ads are posted on a server. With an online connection, clients can look at them on their own computer anywhere in the world and give their comments.

4. Second-round creative. Based on in-house reaction and client comments on the first-round creative, a second series of ads is created.

5. Third-round creative. This is usually the finished product, although with online ads, the second round is often the final one.

This process is similar to what happens in print and broadcast advertising, but in online ads the entire process can take place in two days or less. The major reasons for this compressed time frame follow:

- Client comments can be instantaneous. As soon as the first round of ads is put on the server, the clients can see them and comment on them. There is no need to gather everyone together for a meeting.

- The ad copy and images can be quickly revised because they are created in digital media.

- Ads can be distributed on the Web instantaneously. There are no magazines to be printed or TV show schedules to deal with. An ad is placed on a server, and it is immediately available to the consumer.

CHALLENGES AND SOLUTIONS WRITING THE ZDU ONLINE AD CAMPAIGN

(The Personal View case study from the first edition of the book is in the Chapter 14 area in the "Chapters" section of the *Writing for Multimedia and the Web* CD-ROM.)

THE CHALLENGES

The goal of this ad campaign was to get Web users to click their way from the banner to ZDU and register for courses. The challenge was finding the most concise way to present a complex service, an online education site, and the value of the free scholarship. This challenge is made more difficult by the small size of the banner. (Note that the name of ZDU has recently been changed to SmartPlanet.)

MEETING THE CHALLENGE: DESIGNING THE BANNER

A number of things can be tried in the banner to catch the viewers' eyes and get them to click. One common approach is the value-added banner, which offers free items, such as downloads of software, or a chance to try a product for free. Another tactic is a teaser: an intriguing line that creates more questions than answers and makes the viewer want more information. The teaser should, however, have some connection to the product. It is generally not a good idea to lure the viewer in with a false teaser, such as saying "Sex, Sex, Sex" on the banner and then try to pitch computer printers. Most users get angry and just click off. The ZDU campaign offered both free items and a teaser.

Because interactive ads get better clickthrough than noninteractive ads, all the ads in this campaign were in some way interactive. There is, however, a fine line between an ad being interactive and taking control of the user's computer. In the case of this ad, once you click on the ad banner, you are going to be shown some images and taken to the SmartPlanet (ZDU) Web site, whether you want to or not. You cannot stop the process, short of forcing your browser to quit. Most advertisers and probably most users feel that once the user clicks on the ad banner, then there is an agreement that the user can be shown something or taken to another site. Some advertisers stretch this a bit further and will grab control of your screen if you just pass your mouse over their ad. Some sites will even pop up ads or second screens that you have not requested at all. Some usability tests have shown that these unrequested ads are hated and clicked off with a vengeance (Nielsen). It is probably good advice to consider your particular target audience's reaction to losing control of their computer before you take over and start popping up random screens and dragging them off to other sites that they did not request.

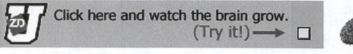

FIGURE 13–3 ————————————————————————————————

First-round creative banner.

The banners for the ZDU ad campaign were developed in three stages: first-round creative, second-round creative, and third-round creative. An additional change was made after the banner was tested online. (See the "Chapters" section, Chapter 13 area of the *Writing for Multimedia and the Web* CD-ROM for color interactive versions of these ads.)

First-Round Creative Banner
In an E-mail and phone interview, John Hargrave outlined the process of creating these ads.

In this first version, the user clicks on the brain and it grows in size, then pauses a few moments before whisking you away to the ZDU site. The client liked the general idea, but wanted to play up the educational concept behind ZDU. He suggested adding something about the "free scholarship" concept—a free trial that ZDU gives out to prospective students.

Second-round creative banner
John Hargrave's team added an alert box that pops up after you click on the banner and before you are taken to the site. The alert box says, "Click OK for a FREE two-week scholarship at ZDU!" The client wanted to change the wording in the alert box, and recommended putting a mortarboard on the brain to further promote the educational angle.

Third-Round Creative Banner
The mortarboard on the "big brain" wouldn't fit within the 468 × 60 pixel screen space allotted to a banner ad, so Hargrave had to make the brain shrink back down so the mortarboard would fit (see Figure 13–1). The new alert box text now reads: "With over 150 online computer courses to choose from, ZDU will expand your mind. Click OK for a FREE two-week scholarship!"

Final Banner After Testing
After some testing on the site, it was found that the ad actually performed better if the ZDU logo wasn't on the first frame. This is probably because of the "curiosity factor," where people are more likely to click when they don't know exactly what the offer is.

THE SMARTPLANET (ZDU) WEB SITE

Once a banner lures the user to a Web site, it is key that the site be designed to hook the user. The SmartPlanet (formerly ZDU) Web site does this by explaining succinctly the site benefits and the free scholarship offer at the top of the Home Page: "Welcome

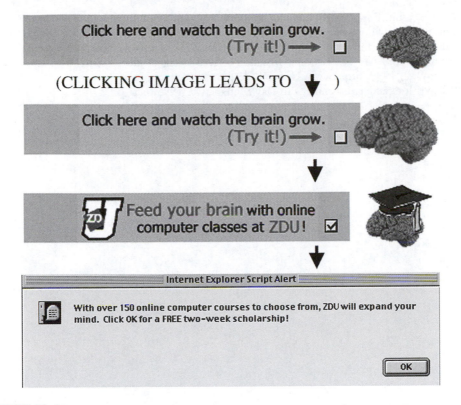

FIGURE 13–4

Final interactive banner and alert box.

to a new world . . . of learning. Pick from 350+ courses covering computers, finance, hobbies, and more. Pursue your interests today!" Just to the right of this text is a graphic with a button labeled, "Join for Free. Learn from the experts, share your ideas with others, and even teach your own courses—ALL FOR FREE!" For a different type of product, the advertiser's Web site could be very complex, offering a wide variety of information about the product, tours of the facility, free items, and so on.

CONCLUSION: RESPONSE TO THE PROJECT

The "Brain Grow" banner was one of the best-performing ads in this series. It received 2 to 2.5 times the site average clickthrough. It had a higher rate of users who registered for the free scholarship than any other campaign in this series.

REFERENCES

Barkow, Tim, ed. "Raw Data." *Wired, 4.07* (July 1996).
Enliven Web site. http://www.narrative.com/.
Gardner, Elizabeth. "Meeting of Big Advertisers Point up Web's Problems." *Internet World.* August 24, 1998. http://www.internetworld.com.

Hargrave, John. E-mail to the author. July 1999.
Hargrave, John. Phone interview with the author. July 1999.
Lindley, Matthew. Interview with the author. Cambridge, MA, November 1995.
Nielsen, Jakob. "The Top Ten New Mistakes of Web Design." *Jacob Nielsen's Alertbox*,
     May 30, 1999. http://www.useit.com/alertbox/990530.html\.
Ziff-Davis Interactive. Brochure. Ziff-Davis Interactive, 1995.

C H A P T E R 1 4

MUSEUM KIOSK CASE STUDY: *THE NAUTICUS SHIPBUILDING COMPANY*

Summary

Name of Production: *The Nauticus Shipbuilding Company*
Writer: Steven Barney
Developers: Tarragon Interactive, Chedd-Angier Production Co.
Audience: General
Medium: Computer hard drive in kiosk setting
Location: Nauticus: National Maritime Center, Norfolk, Virginia
Subject: Shipbuilding
Goals: Entertain, teach
Architecture: Simulation, hierarchical branching

The script samples and illustrations used in this chapter are courtesy of Chedd-Angier Production Company. © 1994 Chedd-Angier Production Company.

PROGRAM DESCRIPTION AND BACKGROUND

PROGRAM DESCRIPTION

The Nauticus Shipbuilding Company is an interactive museum kiosk program that introduces users to basic concepts of shipbuilding. The program is run on a computer's hard drive accessed by users touching images or menu items on the touch-screen monitor. The computer and monitor are housed in a stand-alone kiosk in the museum's main exhibit hall. Near the kiosk is a wall of graphic and text information on shipbuilding that supports the kiosk program. *The Nauticus Shipbuilding Company* is also being used in classrooms as part of the museum's curricular outreach.

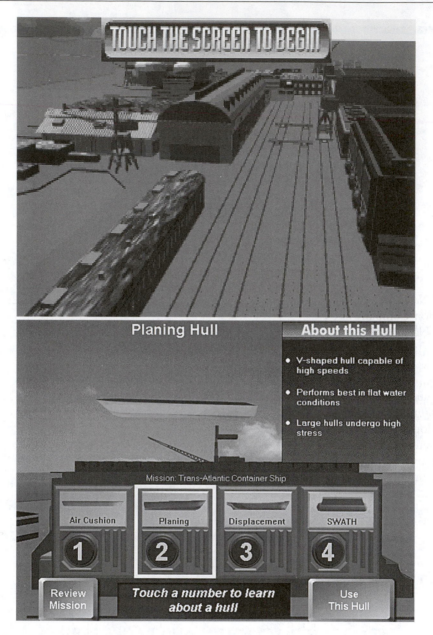

FIGURE 14–1

Top screen: From the attract program for *The Nauticus Shipbuilding Company*. Bottom screen: Where the user chooses hulls. (The original color images for these screen shots and others in the book are available on the *Writing for Multimedia and the Web* CD-ROM in the Chapter 14 area of the "Chapters" section.)

MULTIMEDIA IN MUSEUMS

A single-user kiosk presentation, such as *Nauticus*, is a common way to present multimedia in a museum or other public site. Because of the need to accommodate large groups, multimedia in museums is also presented in a group format, where a number of people control the action on the screen. An example is the National Scouting Museum's Boy Scout Patrol Theater, which allows eight users to take on the role of the individual Boy Scouts portrayed in the multimedia program. (See Boy Scout Patrol area of the "Chapters" section of the *Writing for Multimedia and the Web* CD-ROM.)

In addition to exhibits, many museums also have learning centers, which house a variety of multimedia "edutainment" programs for groups or individuals. Larger museums are active in educational outreach, providing curricular support for schools. The old fossils-on-wheels programs, which brought artifacts to schools, is now being supplemented by multimedia programs such as *Nauticus*, and by online programs from museums, such as the Museum of Science in Boston, the Exploratorium in San Francisco, and the Franklin Institute Science Museum in Philadelphia. (See the Chapter 14 area of the "Chapters" section of the *Writing for Multimedia and the Web* CD-ROM for links to these sites.)

PRODUCTION BACKGROUND

The Nauticus Shipbuilding Company was jointly developed by Chedd-Angier Production Company and Tarragon Interactive for Nauticus: National Maritime Center. The National Maritime Center, located on the Norfolk, Virginia waterfront, offers exhibits, films, and multimedia programs dealing with shipping, the Navy, and the sea.

The Chedd-Angier Production Company is a Boston-based media production company that Nauticus hired to develop a number of the media productions for the museum. Chedd-Angier in turn recruited Tarragon Interactive to develop *The Nauticus Shipbuilding Company* project. At the time of production, Tarragon was a custom developer of multimedia titles for marketing and sales, training, and "infotainment" (museum and CD-ROM titles). Tarragon has since been sold and no longer exists as a separate entity. The writer of this program is Steven Barney, who was president of Tarragon Interactive. He is a designer-programmer with a background in instructional design.

WRITING AND DEVELOPING *THE NAUTICUS SHIPBUILDING COMPANY*

THE DEVELOPMENT PROCESS

On this project, the writer's primary involvement occurs during the first two stages of development: project definition and design/preproduction, but the writer is also often called in during production to make last-minute changes.

The project definition identifies:

- Design objective
- Target audience
- Delivery platform/location

Design/preproduction documents include:

- Proposals. Outlining the program's approach.
- High-level design document. A text-based content treatment and a program navigation flow diagram.

- Scripts. Program navigation flow plus narration, dialogue, screen text, and full description of visuals.

DEVELOPMENT CHALLENGES

Many of the challenges facing the developers of *The Nauticus Shipbuilding Company* are common to media development for museums and other public sites. These challenges are discussed below.

Design Objective

The design objective of *Nauticus* is to provide museum visitors with an interactive environment in which to explore how ships are built for specific missions. This piece uses technical information that must be precisely accurate. The project was reviewed for accuracy by the faculty of MIT's Department of Naval Engineering and members of the National Board of the Society of Naval Architecture and Marine Engineering. The entertainment aspect of this piece was tested through focus groups and by placing a test exhibit at a museum and evaluating viewers' reactions.

Another objective of this program is that users will go through the game and return to play it again. This means that diversity and depth must be designed into the experience, but because of run time, size limitations, and turnaround time (the amount of time it takes someone to complete the program and a new user to begin), this diversity cannot create a huge program. Long turnaround time would mean long lines and frustrated museum visitors.

Target Audience

Developing a program like this for the typical museum audience poses a number of challenges:

- Diversity. Museum audiences include people of all ages, backgrounds, education, and levels of interest in the subject. An exhibit has to have a little something for everyone.
- Short attention spans. Because there are so many exhibits competing for their attention, museum goers generally will not play a program for more than 2 minutes (60–90 seconds is the typical experience time). A program has about 5 seconds to capture a user, but even when captured, many leave after 30 seconds. A complex subject puts demands on the developer to present the material succinctly or to create a piece, such as *Nauticus*, that is so appealing it can lure users into longer than typical play times.

Delivery Platform and Locations

The nature of the delivery platform and location has a significant impact on what is creatively possible. A kiosk program running off a fast hard drive allows the use of video, 3-D graphics, and other features that would be difficult to deliver on media with slower access time. But because most museums are nonprofit organizations, money is often tight, and complex challenges must be met by the writer inexpensively. New museums or new wings of museums tend to be better funded than renovations of existing exhibits.

MEETING THE CHALLENGES

The program's objectives and the challenges must be met by the writer-designer's proposals, high-level design documents, and scripts. There were many revisions of the written material. Here are a few of them.

THE PROPOSAL

The initial proposal is the earliest stage of a project. Compare the proposal with the treatment that follows it and consider what changes were made before reading the analysis.

<pre>
         INTERACTIVE MODULE—#5,7
            SHIP-BUILDING:
</pre>

Objective

<pre>
To simulate modular ship construction at work.
</pre>

Treatment

<pre>
Visitors will use a stylus to draw any kind of ship on
a pressure-sensitive platen. Children might sketch out
a simple shape. Others can create more sophisticated
designs. When the drawing is complete, the user will
push a button. The ship will disappear from the platen
and will then be "built" on the video screen.
    To do this, the program will divide the ship
drawing into modular sections (based on the platen's
grid and predetermined guidelines). These modules will
then be "constructed" on screen, to the accompaniment
of appropriate sound effects, such as hammering,
riveting, and perhaps even the shouts of work crews.
When all the modular sections are complete, they will
be united, forming a replica of the visitor's original
design.
    The video game will be, in effect, a simulation of
the CAD/CAM process, whereby ships are designed on
screen and then built with the aid of computers—in
separate modules.
    If feasible, the computers can be linked to a
printer, and visitors can take home sketches of their
creations.
</pre>

Technique/Method

<pre>
Visitor-activated platen with video monitor.
</pre>

HIGH-LEVEL DESIGN DOCUMENT

After the initial proposal was revised several times and the basic concept refined, the high-level design document, which includes a design objective, creative treatment, and a navigation flowchart, was prepared:

1.0 Design Objective

The objective of the program is to provide museum visitors with a fun, interactive environment to explore how ships are built to accomplish specific missions. Visitors will be able to experiment by building custom ships from a variety of components. Through this experience, visitors will learn to apply the principle of "form follows function" to the process of building ships. Visitors will learn about the major design components of a ship: hull, hold, engine, and special equipment. Visitors will learn how variations in these design components affect a ship's ability to carry out a specific mission.

2.0 Creative Treatment

ATTRACT ROUTINE: When no one is using the program, an attract routine will invite visitors to come explore the program. The attract routine will contain a brief glimpse of one of the mission introductions, picked randomly. This will be followed by a series of snapshots of components being selected, and a ship being built by the program. Text overlays will repeat continuously. Sample text: "Build a Ship to Accomplish a Mission"; "Touch the Screen to Begin."

INTRODUCTION: Immediately upon touching the screen during the attract routine, the visitor is greeted with a brief sequence introducing the program with audio and text. Sample text: "Pick one of the five missions; then go to the shipyard to build your own custom-designed boat. When you are done, see if your boat succeeds in accomplishing the mission." "Let's go to the briefing room to choose a mission."

BRIEFING ROOM: The metaphor of a briefing room will be used to allow the visitor to select from a menu of missions, and then to review each mission. Upon selecting a mission from the menu, the visitor is briefed. Each briefing will consist of a full-screen graphic with text. A one-quarter screen video clip with a talking head keyed over stock footage will introduce the mission. Design criteria for the mission will appear on a checklist. At the conclusion of the briefing, the visitor can either select this mission or return to the mission menu.

Mission 1. North Sea Fire Fighter The North Sea is full of gigantic oil-drilling platforms that use mile-long pipes to drain oil from under the sea floor, then store it in tanks until tankers come to take it to the mainland for processing and distribution to the general public.

Sometimes these platforms catch on fire. Your job is to design a ship that will be able to put out these fires.

The ship must be stable enough to remain near the platform until the fire is put out, and must have pumps powerful enough to drive large amounts of water through its hoses. It must also be able to withstand the rough seas and weather of the North Sea.

Mission 2. Alligator Census Many years ago, the Everglades were viewed as a wasteland, home to millions of potentially disease-spreading mosquitoes. Because of such concerns, the Everglades were drained to create farmland. People now recognize that the Everglades is a beautiful, but fragile ecosystem that was greatly disrupted by the drainage and dredging projects. Many birds and other creatures died as a result. These species are believed to be making a comeback, but the only way to know for sure is to go into the Everglades by boat and count them. The ideal boat for this mission must be quiet so as not to disturb the wildlife, and it should be able to navigate shallow waters and swamp.

Mission 3. Coast Guard Drug Interdiction Undercover police and FBI investigators routinely attempt to infiltrate suspected drug rings and break up shipments of drugs from South America and other countries. They have just ordered a ship from your shipyard that will be able to intercept shipments of drugs coming into Miami, Florida. It must have a high top speed, be able to travel at or near that speed for long distances, and be outfitted with weapons sufficient to threaten and subdue vessels operated by suspected criminals. It should also have a low profile, making it difficult to spot from a distance.

Mission 4. Trans-Pacific Freighter Exports account for an increasingly large portion of our country's economy. Trade with the Far East is expected to double in the near future. Efficient freighters are needed to transport the large flow of goods to and from this important economic region. The design should be cost-efficient, have enough range to travel to Korea, Japan, Singapore, and Taiwan, and be able to carry large quantities of cargo. Speed is a secondary design consideration.

Mission 5. Arctic Ice Breaker The "Land of the Midnight Sun" is an accurate name for the Arctic. Due to the Earth's orbit and tilt, the region experiences six straight months of darkness, followed by six straight months of light. This prolonged darkness contributes to temperatures as low as negative 70 degrees Fahrenheit, more than sufficient to freeze Hudson Bay and the rest of the Arctic Ocean. Ice breakers are needed to clear shipping channels otherwise blocked for months. You must design such an ice breaker to clear a path from Churchill, Canada, to Barrow, Alaska. It must be heavy, as indestructible as possible, and be able to remain at sea for months.

After the user selects a mission, he or she is told: "You have selected a difficult mission. Now let's go to the shipyard where you can design and build your own custom boat to accomplish the mission."

The Shipyard

OPENING ANIMATION: A 3-D animation sequence will give an overview of the shipyard, then zoom in to the point of view of a shipbuilder entering the gates.

After the opening animation, the visitor selects components from a series of menus. The design features for each component are summarized upon selection. After selecting each component, the partially completed boat moves along a track to the next component selection area.

Components

Hulls

Single V:
Efficient, stable, with a large amount of room for supplies, cargo, fuel, and passengers, they make an excellent choice for almost any ship. Single V-shaped hulls are by far the most common.

Double V:
Double V-shaped hulls are far less common than single V's, but they also make a good choice for ships where the main hull not being penetrated is of the utmost importance, such as oil tankers.

Single Flatbottom:
Single flatbottom hulls are used mainly for riverboats and other craft where a shallow draft is important. They are less efficient and stable than other designs, but sometimes a shallow draft is the top consideration.

Hydrofoil:
Hydrofoils are radically different than the other three designs. The boat is fitted with several projections with angled metal plates on the bottom. They lift the boat out of the water when it runs at high speed. This design works only for small boats.

Hold

Cargo:
Cargo holds are used for holding large amounts of goods while on the ship. These range from weapons to cars to food, frequently packaged in the railroad cars which transported them to the harbor.

Passengers:
Passenger space usually consists of many small rooms, of which the interior varies according to type of ship. Cruise lines commonly have rooms to rival the best hotels, where military ships often just have four hammocks.

Ballast:
Ballast is used as a stabilizer for ships with little weight in their hulls. It is usually just a room that has sea water pumped into it.

None:
Small boats infrequently have ballast, as there is not a huge need for it.

Engine

Nuclear:
Nuclear power plants in ships work much like their electricity-generating counterparts on land. Steam is heated passing next to radioactive material, usually U-235. It is then used to push turbines connected to the propellers, giving the ship its power. The shielding around nuclear plants is very heavy, making them efficient only for large ships.

Gas:
Gas power plants are much the same as jet engines, just on a larger scale. Their advantages are high speed and short start-up times, but they are noisy, inefficient for large ships, and require many people to run.

Diesel:
Diesel engines have many of the same characteristics as their counterparts in vans and trucks. They are efficient, low-maintenance engines with an ability to run at low revolutions per minute (RPMs). They are ideal for moving large ships at moderate to low speeds.

Steam:
Steam engines burn oil or gasoline to heat water until it is steam, and then use that to drive turbines.

Special Equipment

Weapons Mounts:
Turrets and mounts with machine guns and small cannon, from .50 caliber to 5 inches.

Cranes, Booms, and Winches:
Equipment for lifting cargo from the decks and holds of ships.

Pumps and Hoses:
Used for spraying water on burning vessels, docks, and other objects in or near the water. Water is drawn from the ocean or river that the boat is in.

Reinforced Hull:
An extra layer of reinforcements to increase hull integrity in certain areas. Useful for ships with a high potential of running into reefs and other obstacles.

Grappling Hooks:
Lines and hooks for latching on to other ships or objects while at sea.

CONCLUSION: After the last component has been selected, a 3-D animation sequence depicts the launching of the vessel. If the design is suitable for the mission, the visitor will see a depiction of the design successfully carrying out the mission. If the design is fundamentally flawed, the vessel will be shown sinking. Some evaluation will be provided as to the ability of the visitor's design to carry out the selected mission. Finally, the visitor will be given the opportunity to print out the design and evaluation.

3.0 Project Schedule

High-Level Design	completed
Research/Scripting	September 1–October 1
Detailed Design Approved	October 1
Prototyping/Initial Graphics Development	October 1–October 31
Initial Graphic Design Approved	November 1
Graphics and Program Production	November 1–December 15
Final Graphics Approved	December 15
Programming/Integration Completed	January 15
Final Delivery	February 1

4.0 Budget

High-Level Design	1 week @	$XXX
Research	2 weeks @	$XXX
	2 weeks @	$XXX

```
Scripting                    2 weeks @      $XXX
Video                        1 week @       $XXX
                             2 weeks @      $XXX
Graphics                    12 weeks @      $XXX
Programming/Integration      6 weeks @      $XXX
QA/Revisions                 2 weeks @      $XXX
Total Budget:                               $XXXX
(Budget dollar amount deleted for this book.)
```

Proposal and Design Document Compared

Comparing the design document's treatment to the proposal shows some striking changes in the evolution of this project. The proposal's initial idea, to have a computer "build" a ship based on a user's rough sketch, was replaced in the treatment by the more structured approach of having the viewer build a ship to achieve a specific mission based on defined ship components. Another key aspect of the treatment is that the user's design is evaluated at the end of the process, and the user is encouraged to play the game again to improve the design.

Although the initial proposal is fun, it illustrates the importance of balancing interactivity with control to teach a specific subject. The proposal provides a rough demonstration of CAD/CAM, but the more controlled approach in the treatment accomplishes much more. It allows users to utilize well-defined principles concerning hulls, engines, and other components to build a ship. The evaluation function suggested in the treatment allows users to learn from their efforts and build on them in repeat plays. With no evaluation function in the proposal, the user does not even know if his or her ship would float.

There are also some practical concerns here. It is important to give the general museum audience a positive experience. The treatment approach of assembling parts means that even a young child can piece together an impressive boat. This may not be true with the proposal approach. What will the CAD/CAM process be able to do with the rough squiggles of a seven year old? There could be a few default ships automatically rendered from unintelligible sketches, but this would not be the ship the user drew, and on repeated plays, he or she could be disappointed if the same ship was produced from different drawings.

Navigation Program/Flow

The creative treatment of the design document lays out the basic content of the production; the navigation/program flowchart defines how that content will be accessed interactively. Compare the flowcharts on the next pages, Figures 14–2 and 14–3, and consider the changes that were made before reading the analysis that follows.

Changes in Navigation/Program Flow

Different flowcharts serve different functions. Some, such as the one shown in Figure 14–2, lay out the possible navigation flow early in a project. Because this chart will be read by clients who may not be sophisticated in multimedia navigation, there is an advantage to keeping it as simple as possible. Detail is limited, particularly in the component section, where the multiple choices under each component are reduced to one broad category.

The second chart comes when the program is more defined. At this point, it is possible to chart all the paths in the project. A chart like this is useful to a

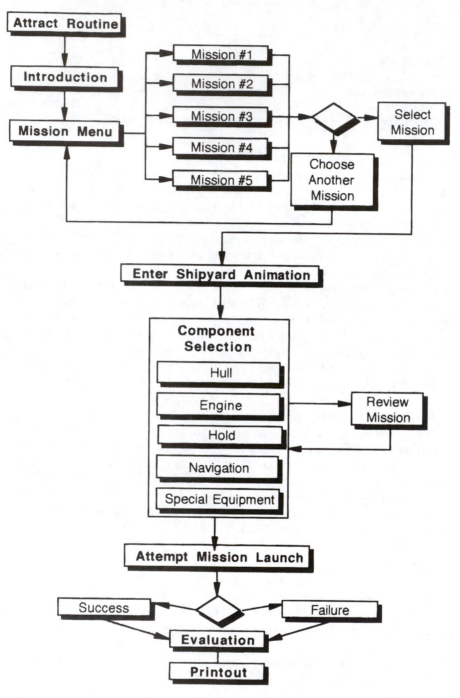

FIGURE 14-2

First draft navigation/program flow.

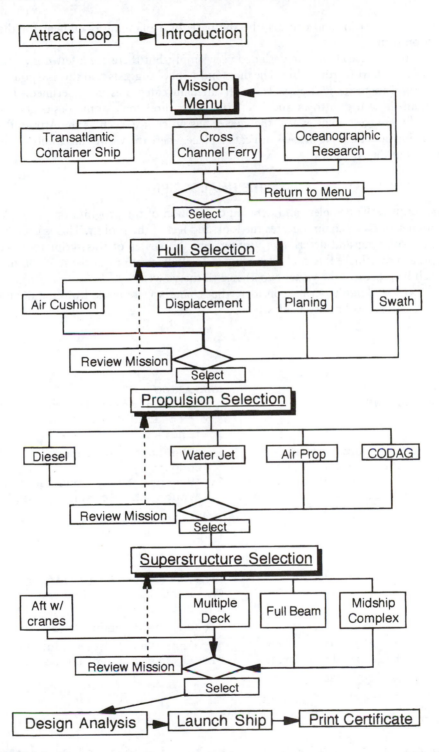

FIGURE 14–3

Final draft navigation/program flow.

sophisticated client and can also be the basis of a planning document for the production team.

Both of these charts are designed very simply, but there are a few conventions in the second chart worth noting. The diamond symbol suggests that this is a point where the user can make a choice. The text in main categories is underlined. The first program flow uses arrows and lines to suggest directions. Some designers also use arrows to suggest a link where the viewer has no choice, such as the Attract Routine to the Introduction. No arrows indicate a place where the viewer has multiple choices, such as in the Missions.

THE FINAL SCRIPT

The script is the complete and detailed description of the program on paper. A well-written script also communicates the look and feel of the project. This is usually done with formatting and descriptive writing, but the writer of this script took a novel approach to achieve this goal. He included small illustrations of the ship components, which help present the visual experience to the viewer.

After reading the script, consider what changes were made from the design document before reading the analysis.

SCENE	NARRATION
ATTRACT ROUTINE	(Note: The following text banners are repeated throughout the attract routine:)
When no one is using the program, an attract routine will invite visitors to come explore the program.	1. "The Nauticus Shipbuilding Company"
	2. "Urgent: Naval Architect Needed"
	3. "Touch the Screen to Begin"
Attract Routine steps	
1. Flyover of shipyard in 3-D.	
2. Cut to rotation of planing hull.	"The Nauticus Shipbuilding Company— the most highly advanced shipbuilding facility in the world."
	"Touch the Screen to Begin"
3. Cut to assembly area with planing hull rolling in.	"Urgent: Naval Architect Needed."
	"Touch the Screen to Begin"
4. Cut to launch area, showing ship launch.	
INTRODUCTION	
Immediately upon touching the screen in the attract routine.	Background sound of helicopter rotors.
Flyover of shipyard in 3-D.	

Cut to helicopter descending and landing on heliport.

"Welcome to the Nauticus Shipbuilding Company.Thanks for being our visiting naval architect on such short notice. The Nauticus Shipbuilding Company is the most highly advanced shipbuilding facility in the world. We can custom-build many different types of ships. Each ship we build is unique and is designed to efficiently meet our client's nautical mission requirements."

"Let's go to our Design Center to see what ships are on order."

Cut to POV [point-of-view] animation leaving the heliport, past office building to Design Center.

Loudspeaker VO: "Naval architect on premises. Ready production facilities."

DESIGN CENTER

Doors of Design Center open, wipe to view of the briefing room.

"We currently have a backlog of orders for 3 ships":
1. "a trans-Atlantic container ship which will sail out of Norfolk."
2. "a ferry that will transport passengers and cars between England and France."
3. "an oceanographic research vessel that will operate off the coast of New England."
"Touch an order to learn more about its mission and design requirements."

TRANS-ATLANTIC CONTAINER SHIP:

Map animating the route between Norfolk and several European ports.

"A large shipping company has asked us to design and build a ship which can safely and economically transport large amounts of cargo between their home port, right here in Norfolk,Virginia, and several European ports. The ship:
—must be able to withstand the rough seas of the Atlantic
—have a very large cargo hold with container-handling facilities
—be moderately fast
—have a long cruising range."

Dynamically build mission checklist.	Container Ship Checklist 1. Ability to withstand rough seas of Atlantic 2. Large cargo hold with container-handling facilities 3. Moderately fast 4. Long cruising range
Visitor is prompted to build the ship or review another mission.	"Press the flashing panel to build a ship for this mission or select another order."

PASSENGER AND CAR FERRY:

Map animating the route between Dover and Calais	"An English ferry operator has asked us to design and build a ship which can quickly cross the English Channel between Dover, England, and Calais, France. The ideal design: —will be very fast, have a cargo capacity for 200 passengers and 50 cars —be easy to load —be able to navigate shallow, crowded harbors."
Dynamically build mission checklist.	Ferry Requirements: 1. Very fast 2. Cargo capacity for 200 passengers and 50 cars 3. Easy to load 4. Able to navigate shallow, crowded harbors
Visitor is prompted to build the ship or review another mission.	"Press the flashing panel to build a ship for this mission or select another order."

OCEANOGRAPHIC RESEARCH VESSEL:

Show map animating area of research.	"A marine research institute requires a new flagship for its exploration of the ocean floor. The ship should: —be a safe platform for working with complex equipment —be able to withstand rough seas —have good performance at all speeds —have accommodations for extended research work at sea
Dynamically build mission checklist.	Research Ship Requirements: 1. Safe platform for working with complex equipment 2. Able to withstand rough seas

Visitor is prompted to build the ship or review another mission.

3. Good performance at all speeds
4. Accommodations for extended research work at sea

"Press the flashing panel to build a ship for this mission, or select another order."

ORDER SELECTED

After selecting an order to build, scene cuts to POV animation leaving the Design Center, past building to hull subassembly area.

"You'll need to make 3 major design decisions to build the ship, all affecting the ship's performance and ability to carry out its mission. You must choose:
—a hull shape
—a propulsion system, and
—a superstructure."

CHOOSE A HULL SHAPE

Hull subassembly area, 4 compartments are shown.

After a compartment is selected, 3-D hull appears above the subassembly area and rotates around 360 degrees in *y*-axis, then 360 degrees in *x*-axis. As hull is rotated, text describing characteristics appears on data screen.

Loudspeaker VO: "Hull type being selected."

"Touch a number to learn about a hull."

After learning about the characteristics for a particular hull, the visitor is prompted to use this hull or examine one of the others.

"Use this hull or press another number."

Air Cushion:
—flat hull rides on cushion of air
—capable of high speeds
—needs flat water conditions
—flat, rectangular deck easy to load

Planing Hull:
—V-shaped hull capable of high speeds
—performs best in flat water conditions
—high stress levels on hull

Displacement Hull:
—deep, rounded hull very stable in all conditions
—very large cargo capacity

After selecting a hull to use, cut to Design Assembly screen, animation of hull rollout.

Cut to POV animation moving to propulsion subassembly area.

—stable platform for large propulsion systems
—needs very large propulsion system
SWATH (Small Waterplane Area Twin Hull)
—2 submerged hulls very stable
—flat deck provides good work area

Loudspeaker VO:
"Planing hull being moved into position."

Background sound of motors whirring and machinery clanging.
"Next, you'll need to choose a propulsion system.

PICK A PROPULSION SYSTEM

Propulsion subassembly area, 4 compartments are shown.

After a compartment is selected, 3-D propulsion system appears above the subassembly area and rotates around 360 degrees in y-axis. As propulsion system is rotated, text describing characteristics appears on on data screen.

Loudspeaker VO:
"Propulsion system being selected."

"Touch a number to learn about a propulsion system."

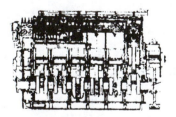

Diesel
—best performance at lower speeds
—fuel efficient
—infrequent maintenance

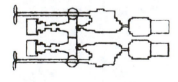

CODAG (Combination Diesel and Gas)
—good performance at all speeds
—improves maneuverability
—frequent maintenance

Water Jet
—low to moderate power
—high speed for right hull
—few underwater projections

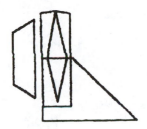

Air Prop
—low to moderate power
—high speed for right hull
—no underwater projections
—affected by bad wind conditions

After learning about the characteristics for a particular propulsion system, the visitor is prompted to use this propulsion system or examine one of the others.

"Use this propulsion system or press another number."

After selecting a propulsion system to use, cut to Design Assembly screen, animation of propulsion system being dropped into selected hull.

Loudspeaker VO: "Air Prop propulsion system being moved into position."

Cut to POV animation moving to superstructure subassembly area.

Background sound of motors whirring and machinery clanging. "Next, you'll need to choose a superstructure."

CHOOSE A SUPERSTRUCTURE

Superstructure subassembly area, 4 compartments are shown.

Loudspeaker VO:
"Superstructure being selected."
"Touch a number to learn about a superstructure."

After a compartment is selected, a 3-D superstructure appears above the subassembly area and rotates around 360 degrees in y-axis. As superstructure is rotated, text describing characteristics appears on data screen.

After learning about the characteristics for a particular superstructure, the visitor is prompted to use this superstructure or examine one of the others.

"Use this superstructure or press another number."

After selecting a superstructure to use, cut to Design Assembly screen,

Loudspeaker VO: "Multiple Deck superstructure being moved into position."

animation of superstructure being lowered onto selected hull.

Bridge with Cranes
—shipboard crane system for container handling
—high bridge provides good visibility

Multiple Deck
—forward bridge provides excellent visibility
—sleek structure reduces wind drag

Full-Beam Bridge
—very high bridge house provides excellent visibility
—work spaces and accommodations close together

Complex Amidships
—compact and integrated work area
—good deck space fore and aft

DESIGN ANALYSIS

Animation of completed designs rotating 360 degrees in *y*-axis.

"Completed design ready for inspection and evaluation."
1 of 3 possible completed design outcomes:
"Very good! You have chosen an optimal design!"
"You have chosen a functional design."
"You have chosen a nonfunctional design."

Animation of hull choice rotating 360 degrees in *y*-axis.

1 of 3 possible hull outcomes:
"Hull Choice: Optimal"
"Hull Choice: Functional"
"Hull Choice: Nonfunctional"
followed by mission-specific feedback for chosen component (see Feedback below).

Animation of propulsion system choice rotating 360 degrees in *y*-axis.

1 of 3 possible propulsion system outcomes:
"Propulsion System Choice: Optimal"
"Propulsion System Choice: Functional"
"Propulsion System Choice: Nonfunctional"

Animation of superstructure choice rotating 360 degrees in *y*-axis.

This is followed by mission-specific feedback for chosen component (see Feedback below).

1 of 3 possible superstructure outcomes: "Superstructure Choice: Optimal" "Superstructure Choice: Functional" "Superstructure Choice: Nonfunctional" followed by mission-specific feedback for chosen component (see Feedback below).

User is prompted to touch graphic of champagne bottle.

"Press the champagne bottle to launch your ship."

After button press or 5 seconds, animation of completed design being launched.

"Ship being launched."

If design was optimal, user is prompted to touch graphic of certificate to receive his/her printout of Optimal Design Certificate.

"Press the button to print your Optimal Design Certificate!"

DESIGN ANALYSIS FEEDBACK

Selected Mission:
Trans-Atlantic Container Ship

Hulls:

Air Cushion

"Hull Choice: Nonfunctional
—Can't withstand rough seas of Atlantic
—Can't support heavy bridge and crane system
—Cargo capacity too small"

Planing

"Hull Choice: Nonfunctional
—Can't support heavy bridge and crane system
—Cargo capacity too small"

Displacement

"Hull Choice: Optimal
—Very stable in rough seas
—Very large cargo capacity"

SWATH

"Hull Choice: Nonfunctional
—Cargo capacity too small"

Propulsion System:

Diesel

"Propulsion System Choice: Optimal
—Fuel efficient

	—Performs well at low to moderate speeds —Infrequent maintenance"
Air Prop	"Propulsion System Choice: Nonfunctional —Not powerful enough —Needs flat water conditions"
Water Jet	"Propulsion System Choice: Nonfunctional —Not powerful enough —Needs flat water conditions"
CODAG	"Propulsion System Choice: Functional —Performs well at many speeds —High maintenance —Gas turbine features not necessary"

Superstructure:

Bridge with Cranes	"Superstructure Choice: Optimal —Cranes allow easy handling of containers —High bridge provides excellent visibility"
Multiple Deck	"Superstructure Choice: Nonfunctional —No way to handle containers"
Full-Beam Bridge	"Superstructure Choice: Nonfunctional -No way to handle containers"
Complex Amidships	"Superstructure Choice: Nonfunctional —No way to handle containers"

Selected Mission:

Cross-Channel Ferry

Hulls:

Air Cushion	"Hull Choice: Optimal —Capable of high speeds —Shallow draft allows easy access to harbors —Rectangular deck perfect for loading cars"
SWATH	"Hull Choice: Nonfunctional —Requires large propulsion system for speed

—Deck shape makes car loading
  difficult"

Displacement

"Hull Choice: Nonfunctional
—Requires very large propulsion
  system for speed
—Deep draft limits access to
  harbors"

Planing

"Hull Choice: Nonfunctional
—Requires very large propulsion
  system for speed"

Propulsion System:

Diesel

"Propulsion System Choice:
Nonfunctional
—Performs best at lower speeds
—Hull projections increase draft"

Air Prop

"Propulsion System Choice:
Functional
—Needs large power plant
—Affected by bad wind conditions"

Water Jet

"Propulsion System Choice: Optimal
—Good for high speeds
—No hull projections keep draft
  shallow"

CODAG

"Propulsion System Choice:
Nonfunctional
—Hull projections increase draft
—Diesel features not necessary"

Superstructure:

Bridge with Cranes

"Superstructure Choice:
Nonfunctional
—Cranes not necessary for cars and
  passengers
—Reduces deck space for cars"

Multiple Deck

"Superstructure Choice:
Optimal
—Multiple levels perfect for cars
  and passengers
—Forward bridge good for high
  speeds"

Full-Beam Bridge

"Superstructure Choice:
Nonfunctional
—Can't handle lots of passengers
  comfortably"

Complex Amidships

"Superstructure Choice:
Nonfunctional
—Can't handle lots of passengers
  comfortably
—Reduces deck space for cars"

Selected Mission:

Oceanographic Research Vessel

Hulls:

Air Cushion

"Hull Choice: Nonfunctional
—Can't withstand rough seas"

Planing

"Hull Choice: Functional
—Capable of high speeds
—Not very stable in rough seas
—Limited work and living space"

Displacement

"Hull Choice: Functional
—Stable in rough seas
—Plenty of work and living space
—Deep draft limits access to shore areas"

SWATH

"Hull Choice: Optimal
—Very stable in rough seas
—Plenty of protected work and living space
—Shallower draft provides access to shore areas"

Propulsion System:

Diesel

"Propulsion System Choice: Functional
—Fuel efficient
—Infrequent maintenance
—Performs best at low speeds"

Air Prop

"Propulsion System Choice: Nonfunctional
—Not powerful enough
—Needs flat water conditions
—Affected by bad wind conditions"

Water Jet

"Propulsion System Choice: Nonfunctional
—Not powerful enough
—Needs flat water conditions"

CODAG

"Propulsion System Choice: Optimal
—Good performance at all speeds
—Makes hull more maneuverable"

Superstructure:

Bridge with Cranes

"Superstructure Choice: Nonfunctional
—Container handling system not necessary"

Multiple Deck	"Superstructure Choice: Nonfunctional —No work space on deck"
Full-Beam Bridge	"Superstructure Choice: Nonfunctional —Too big for appropriate hull —Too far aft"
Complex Amidships	"Superstructure Choice: Optimal —Good work space on deck —Well-integrated space for labs"

Script and Design Document Treatment Compared

There were a number of substantial elements changed from the design document's creative treatment to the final script. These changes illustrate solid interactive writing principles.

Attract Routine   Attract routines play when no one is using the kiosk. Clearly they are very important as bait to lure or attract the players. Without a strong attract routine, a kiosk program is ineffective because no one will play it.

Treatment: The attract routine in the treatment suggests showing one of the program's ships being built and the text: "Build a Ship to Accomplish a Mission."

Script: The script starts with a 3-D animation flyover of the shipyard and the text: "The Nauticus Shipbuilding Company—the most highly advanced shipbuilding facility in the world. Urgent: Naval Architect Needed."

The script changes give a much better introduction to the program by using the shipyard flyover, a standard cinematic establishing shot of the location. The location is extensive and impressive (see Figure 14–1). The script's text also helps build the simulation and the excitement of the program. We are now dealing with the most advanced shipbuilding company in the world. Players are also asked to assume the role of architect and become a part of The Nauticus Shipbuilding Company—and they are needed urgently!

Briefing Room   Treatment: The treatment includes a video clip of a talking head of the shipyard president keyed over stock footage to explain the mission.

Script: The script eliminates the video talking head and the stock footage, replacing this material with more graphic elements, such as maps showing where the ship would travel.

There are several good reasons for this change. One is that the video talking head and documentary footage in a world of 3-D animation creates a conflict in style, one of the effects of which is to point out the artificiality of the animation. By eliminating this conflict, the program has stylistic consistency, and it is raised up one level of abstraction. The user can now more easily enter this fantasy world where he or she is the only real person.

The graphic elements, such as the maps, also ground the user visually in the mission, as opposed to being told about it by the talking head. Finally, the talking head video expanded the number of elements on screen, creating clutter and confusion for the viewer.

Missions   Treatment: The treatment has five missions, ranging from North Sea Fire Fighter to Arctic Ice Breaker.

Script: The script has three missions: Transatlantic Container Ship, Cross-Channel Ferry, and Oceanographic Research Vessel.

The script reduces the number and changes the types of missions. Three factors motivated these changes:

1. The budget and running time of the program.
2. The particular missions that best presented a wide view of naval architecture.
3. The missions that best suited the game design. The ideal missions had to present shipbuilding problems where the answers weren't obvious but not impossible. The information had to allow clues that could be subtle.

Components   Treatment: The treatment's ship components include hulls, hold, engine, and special equipment.

Script: The script's ship components include hulls, propulsion, and super-structure.

The special equipment was combined into the superstructure, and the hold was eliminated to reduce one variable in building the ship. It is important that the overall experience be as short as possible and still be effective. This has an impact on production cost and the time that the user would have to interact with the program.

Evaluation of Design   The script increased the amount of evaluation of the ship design at the end of the program. The goal here was to encourage the user to go back and try the process again. This is ultimately a more successful learning approach than a one-shot deal where the user gets it right or wrong. The chance to try, fail, and redo something without penalty is an important learning feature of interactive multimedia.

CONCLUSION: RESPONSE TO THE PROJECT

The response to *The Nauticus Shipbuilding Company* has been positive in both the museum and in classroom use. It makes strong use of the simulation model and hierarchical structure to accomplish its goals of teaching a subject to a general audience in an entertaining fashion.

REFERENCE

Barney, Steven. Interview with the author. Watertown, MA, September 1995.

CHAPTER 15

EDUCATIONAL MULTIMEDIA CASE STUDY: *SKY HIGH*

Summary

Name of production: *Sky High*
Writers: Maria O'Meara, Ruth Nadel, Ron McAdow, and Beth Chapman
Developer: D. C. Heath and Company
Subject: Space and flight
Audience: Elementary school children
Medium: CD-ROM
Presentation location: Schools
Coals: Inform, teach, entertain
Architecture: Hierarchical branching, worlds, simulation

The script samples and images used in this chapter are from *Discoveries: Sky High* CD-ROM in Heath Literacy by Alvermann, et al. ©1995 D. C. Heath and Company. Reprinted by Permission of Houghton Mifflin Company. All Rights Reserved.

PROGRAM DESCRIPTION AND BACKGROUND

PROGRAM DESCRIPTION

Sky High is a CD-ROM aimed at an elementary school audience on the subject of manned flight and space exploration. Its main interface is a 360-degree panoramic landscape built along a time line from antiquity to the present. Only a portion of the landscape is visible on the screen at one time. The user accesses the hidden parts of the landscape by moving the mouse to one edge of the screen. This causes more of the landscape to appear as the viewer travels forward or backward in time.

At the bottom of the screen is a time line of dates. Above the dates are screen images and text. These hot spots can be clicked with the mouse to reveal an animation, text, video, and/or graphic on an aspect of flight during that time period. Some

FIGURE 15-1 ————————————————————————————————————

Medieval and Renaissance panel of main interface with Dragon, Brother Eilmer, and King Arthur's Castle.

hot spots in a panel are grouped into explorable spaces, such as King Arthur's Castle, Leonardo DaVinci's Workshop, the Wright Brothers' House, and the Visitor's Center. Each of these spaces can be entered by clicking.

Inside these spaces are many more hot spots to click on for more information, such as a photo of the Wright Brothers, a trophy, or "books" on various aspects of flight. There are also games and quizzes in several of these spaces. The students can take notes and snap screen shots for their on-screen journal, which pops up by clicking "Your Journal" in the bottom right of the main interface. (See Figure 15–1.)

MULTIMEDIA IN SCHOOLS

CD-ROMs are a major way that multimedia is used in schools. Some titles, such as *Sky High*, are produced primarily for the classroom; other programs, such as *SimCity* and *Carmen Sandiego* are designed for the school and the home. For larger groups, multimedia is often presented with a computer projection system that allows teachers to instruct an entire class in a fashion far superior to "chalk talk."

There are also numerous Web sites geared for children and elementary school teachers, including: EdWeb, Cisco Educational Archives, A&E Classroom, Ask ERIC, and Busy Teacher's K-12 WebSite, which features a collection of resources for teachers presented in alphabetical order. (Links to these sites and others are included under this chapter in the "Chapters" section on the *Writing for Multimedia and the Web* CD-ROM.)

PRODUCTION BACKGROUND

Sky High was developed by the Educational Technologies Department at D. C. Heath and Company, a major publisher of textbooks for the primary grades through college. Soon after this piece was produced, D. C. Heath was purchased by publisher Houghton Mifflin Company, the current distributor of *Sky High*.

Sky High is part of the Discoveries Series of CD-ROMs that also includes *In the Desert*, *Into the Forest*, and *The Nature Connection*. The Discoveries project was developed as part of Heath Literacy, D. C. Heath's theme-based elementary reading program. The goal of the project was to support the idea that literacy is more than the ability to read. It is the ability to connect ideas that come through a variety of media—sounds and visuals as well as text. In addition, the feeling was that children should be in charge of their learning as much as possible, making choices about what to study in greater depth.

Students can explore the Discoveries CD-ROMs independently or use them to support work on projects involving collaboration and communication with others. Each CD in the series reflects one theme covered in the literacy program. *Sky High* is built around a third-grade theme of space and flight. The plan was that the CDs could be sold and used with Heath literacy, or they could be sold separately to be used alone or with other subject areas. They are also designed to accommodate a wider range of grades than the original target market (Astudillo). The project manager on the series was Deborah Astudillo, and the director of educational technologies was Roland Ochsenbein. The writers were Maria O'Meara, Ruth Nadel, Ron McAdow, and Beth Chapman.

CHALLENGES WRITING AND DEVELOPING *SKY HIGH*

The key challenges in writing and developing *Sky High* were these:

- Organizing and making accessible a large database of loosely related material.
- Reaching a broad elementary school audience.
- Writing to archival material versus creating the content.

ORGANIZING A LARGE DATABASE OF LOOSELY RELATED MATERIAL

Unlike the example in Chapter 14, "Museum Kiosk Case Study: *The Nauticus Shipbuilding Company*," which was tightly focused, *Sky High* covers a wide subject area: manned flight and space exploration. Whereas *Nauticus* is designed to be played in a few minutes, *Sky High* contains hours of material on the subject that can be browsed or searched in the books of the virtual library. This vast amount of information could potentially cause organizational problems for the development team and access problems for the user, who could get lost in such a large database of material.

SCRIPT FORMAT

In a project of this magnitude, the writers and other team members need to use various tools to keep material organized. The script format itself is important. This project used tables in Microsoft Word to separate and label the different types of material.

Sky High's media (text, graphics, video, etc.) are accessed by clicking hot spots, which are grouped on the monitor screen according to a time frame called a panel, such as "Panel IV—Early Aviation." The hot spots in a panel can be further grouped into a location that can be clicked on and entered, such as the Wright Brothers' House.

In the script, the location of the media is first introduced in standard screenplay fashion in single-column format. Then the individual hot spots and their media in that location are explained in a three-column coded format. (The following three-column example does not follow immediately after the description in the script.)

PANEL IV-EARLY AVIATION

IV A. Wright Brothers Close-Up

A Victorian-style house on the panorama opens to a Wright brothers close-up. Note bike leaning on fence outside. This is a nice touch.

Once inside, Katherine, the Wright brothers' sister, narrates. The walls are covered with wallpaper. There are ferns on plant stands and other Victorian doodads. Photos on the walls and in frames standing on the tables highlight family members, the Wrights as children and adults, and a shot of the bike shop.

VISUAL	NARR/SYNC	MUSIC/SFX
Animation **[BUZZ.QT.ANM]** ANIMATED BUZZARDS Lace curtains in window, clicking on window activates buzzards outside to circle.	**Narration** **[BUZZ.QT.NARR]** KATH NARR Wilbur and Orville studied soaring buzzards and observed how they turned by moving their wings.	**Music** **[BUZZ.QT.SFX]** SFX MUSIC Music, subtle underscoring LIBRARY LINK 01.3 HOW THINGS FLY—GLIDING

The first column lists the clickable hot spot. It is written in caps. In this case, the hot spot that can be clicked is an animation of buzzards outside the window of the house.

The buzzard hot spot gets its own code name: BUZZ.QT.ANM. The first word identifies the buzzard image; QT stands for Quick Time, the digital video format used to present the animation; and ANM means it is an animation as opposed to a STL (still picture) or VID (video). The number at the bottom (1.2) indicates that it has a link to Book 1, topic 2 in the Visitor's Center library. The viewer can click on this library link and get more information about gliding.

The second column follows a similar coding procedure, letting us know that this is connected to the BUZZ image and that this is voice-over narration (NARR) as opposed to synchronized sound (SYNC). Synchronized sound usually refers to a sound that appears to be produced by the image on screen, such as a person talking on camera. The next line also lets us know that KATH (Katherine Wright) is the narrator.

The code at the top of the third column labels MUSIC or SFX (sound effects), any sound other than music or speech. This column also clearly defines the link for more information, which in this case is to the "book" in the on-screen "library" titled HOW THINGS FLY. The specific section is GLIDING.

SCREEN FORMAT FOR CARDS AND BOOK PAGES: TECHNICAL LIMITS ON THE WRITER

Each animation in the panorama calls up a card with more information in the form of a video and text, which links to a library "book." The large amount of material in this project necessitated the use of four standard screen formats for these cards:

Format 1: Picture or video on top of the page, with title and text below.

Format 2: Picture or video on top of the page with text below.

Format 3: Text.

Format 4: Text at the top and still picture at bottom.

These standard formats facilitated production because the graphic designers and programmers did not have to design a new screen for every page. The consistency of screen interface also helped the viewer access the material. The viewer could quickly learn that each page had its own rules—for example, no hot spots on all-text screens, and hot spots in certain places on other screens.

Format 1 always had to be first in a sequence because it carries the title panel. The other formats could follow in any order.

These formats created a restriction for the writers, who had to write to one of the specific formats and be sure to flag in the script which format was being used. The writers were limited to the specific number of lines available on each card. This meant writing in journalistic, inverted-pyramid style, with the least important information at the bottom so that it could be trimmed if necessary.

Another limitation on the writer was text that was bitmapped and displayed as an image. This allowed more control over the text's visualization, but as the following example shows, the writers had to write the text in the correct font size and the exact number of lines. This also helped to flag the text as artwork for the production team.

Text	Narration
`[CD.TXT.SPUT]`	`[CD.SPUT.NARR]`
When the Russians sent Sputnik into orbit, it was the first time humans had ever sent anything into outer space. People around the world were surprised. They thought that America would do it first.	When the Russians sent Sputnik into orbit, it was the first time humans had ever sent anything into outer space. People around the world were surprised. They thought that America would do it first.

`Information Card Text (F1)` **[CD.ART.SPUT]:**

When the Russians sent Sputnik into orbit, it was the first time humans had ever sent anything into outer space. People around the world were surprised. They thought that America would do it first.

MAKING THE DATABASE ACCESSIBLE TO USERS

Once the writing process was organized, ways had to be found to make this large database of loosely related material accessible to users. This was accomplished through focusing the scope of the project, using concept maps, and moving beyond click-and-read in a number of ways, including simulations, games, and explorable spaces.

Focusing the Scope of the Project

The project was made more accessible to users by focusing the content and limiting the technical complexity of the program. Originally the series was going to hook into the Internet. It was also going to include the capacity for drawing pictures and recording voice. Eventually, all of these approaches were abandoned as too elaborate and expensive. Instead, it was decided to concentrate on presenting content in the most engaging way possible.

The next decision was to narrow the very broad topics of flight and space to flight firsts: the first person to fly a plane, the first person to fly across the Atlantic, the first man on the moon, and so on. The treatment of space focused on a visit to each planet and a history of its discovery and exploration.

Organizing with a Concept Map

Concept maps are a way to organize the material in a database according to a visual image or map. The museum or journey approaches are fairly common. The basic interface of *Sky High*, which tracks the development of flight from antiquity to the present, is a time-journey concept map.

A danger with concept maps is combining incompatible maps. For example, in *Sky High*, one of the original ideas was to be able to pan up from the earthbound time line to see the stars and planets in the sky. This idea had to be abandoned because the panorama journey is time-based, and the stars and planets would have been space-based. The problem would have been ensuring that the right element in the sky was in the right place in relationship to the time line. For example, if a user was in the 1960s time frame and studying the moon landing, he or she should be able to pan up to the sky and see the moon. But when the user is in 1903 and looking at the Georges Méliès film *A Trip to the Moon*, he or she should also be able to pan up to the sky and see the moon. But the moon can't be in two places: above 1903 and 1969.

Because of this conflict as well as technical limitations, the spatial concept map of the sky was dropped from the main panorama interface and instead included as a planetarium in the Visitor's Center, an explorable building on the map that can be clicked on and entered.

Organizing the Material with Explorable Spaces

The Visitor's Center or planetarium is just one example of an explorable space in this program. An explorable space uses the worlds structure. The interface for this structure is a space that the user can enter and explore, such as a room, a house, or even an entire world. Information related to that space can be accessed by clicking on hot spots, such as photographs on the wall, trophies on a table, or books on a shelf.

Some of the explorable spaces in this project include King Arthur's Castle, which contains medieval flight information; Leonardo DaVinci's Workshop, which contains his drawings and writings; the Wright Brothers' House, which has material about their contribution to flight; and the Visitor's Center, which includes a library, observatory, and trivia games. The Visitor's Center can be entered at any time through its image, which is always located at the edge of the screen between the present and the past, or through its menu bar icon.

Following is a portion of the Wright Brothers' House sequence, a good example of an explorable space. Note the effort to make the media as engaging as possible, such as camera movements and zooms on still pictures, highlighting parts of a plane as the parts are mentioned in the narration, and including entertaining animations, such as the doodle drawing of a kite. Within this "house" the information is also organized into a subcategory with a scrapbook metaphor that can be viewed like a real book.

Wright Brothers' House Sequence

IV A. WRIGHT BROTHERS CLOSE-UP

```
A Victorian-style house on the panorama opens to a
close-up of a room. Note bike leaning on fence outside.
This is a nice touch.
    Once inside, Katherine narrates. The walls are
covered with wallpaper. There are ferns on plant stands
and other Victorian doodads. Photos on the walls and in
frames standing on the tables highlight family members,
the Wrights as children and adults, and a shot of the
bike shop. (Samples from the room sequence follow.)
```

VISUAL	NARR/SYNC	MUSIC/SFX
Video **[BIKE.QT.VID]** IV A. WALL PHOTO #6 VIDEO-EXT. SHOT OF BIKE SHOP Zoom into front door, slowly dissolve to inside. INT. BIKE SHOP Wilbur working. Still from Wright Collection	Narration **[BIKE.QT.NARR]** KATH NARR Back then bikes were all the rage. Wilbur and Orville started out riding bikes, and then repairing them. . . . Soon they were making bikes and selling them.	SFX **[BIKE.QT.SFX]** Machine noise in shop grows louder as we enter. MUSIC SFX, exterior birds, wind
Still **[GRAD.QT.STL]** IV A. WALL PHOTO #7 KATHERINE graduation still from Wright Collection	Narration **[GRAD.QT.NARR]** KATH NARR There I am, Katherine Wright. In this picture, I was graduating from Oberlin College. I was the only child in the family who went to college. Orville was so wrapped up in his printing business, he never went. Wilbur stayed home to care for Mama, when she was dying of tuberculosis. After Mama died, I came home and took care of the family.	MUSIC? **[GRAD.QT.SFX]**
Animation **[BUZZ.QT.ANM]** ANIMATED BUZZARDS Lace curtains in window, clicking window activates buzzards outside to circle [1.3]	Narration **[BUZZ.QT.NARR]** KATH NARR Wilbur and Orville studied soaring buzzards and observed how they turned by moving their wings.	MUSIC? **[BUZZ.QT.SFX]** SFX MUSIC Music, subtle underscoring LIBRARY LINK 01.3 HOW THINGS FLY-SOARING
Animation **[TOYH.QT.ANM]** IV A. TOY HELICOPTER	Narration **[TOYH.QT. NARR]** KATH NARR That's a toy	SFX **[TOYH.QT.SFX]** Rubber band helicopter sound

VISUAL	NARR/SYNC	MUSIC/SFX
spins when activated	helicopter Orville made after he and Wilbur wore out the toy one Papa had given them.	

Photo Album on Coffee Table

A photo album lies on a coffee table. Clicking opens it. Each page has a voice-over which is activated when clicked. Katherine's voice-over narrates a brief history of her brothers' yearly trips to Kitty Hawk. Viewer may page backwards or forwards. STILLS, Wright Collection.

PAGE 5 & 6 (of photo album).

VISUAL	NARR/SYNC	MUSIC/SFX
Art **[ALBM.QT.ART]** (combine pp. 44 and 126 "See Them Flying") ART Basic diagram of a flying machine, with words "wings," "engine," "rudder" written next to appropriate piece HIGHLIGHT the wings HIGHLIGHT engine HIGHLIGHT rudder	Narration **[ALBM.QT.NARR]** Orville and Wilbur decided that a flying machine would need three things. Wings, to lift it into the air—an engine to move it through the air—and a rudder to steer it.	SFX **[ALBM.QT.SFX]** SFX air, whoosh SFX 12 hp engine SFX turning rudder, creak noise

PAGE 7, (L) SKETCH/KITE.

VISUAL	NARR/SYNC	MUSIC/SFX
Art **[ALBM.QT.ART]** SKETCH Drawing of kite, biplane with 5 ft. wingspan, show in proportion to a brother, doodle style, make sure to put cap & bow tie on him. Maybe have doodle with two brothers flying it, kids watching?	Narration **[ALBM.QT.NARR]** To test their theories, my brothers built a huge kite. Every child in the neighborhood showed up to watch them fly it! Delighted at their ability to control the kite, Wilbur and Orville set to work immediately on a glider big enough to carry a person.	SFX **[ALBM.QT.SFX]** SFX Wind, laughter, children's voices

Organizing the Material with a Book Metaphor

The last part of the above example uses a photo album as a way to organize the material. Books are a handy metaphor to organize information. *Sky High* uses this metaphor again in the library of the Visitor's Center with books on a variety of topics. To read a "book," the user clicks on the book, and it comes off the shelf; more clicking turns the pages. Following is a page from the library's working table of contents to show how the material is organized and labeled. To sample the contents of one of the books, read the space shuttle example at the end of this chapter.

SKY HIGH LABELED LIBRARY TABLE OF CONTENTS

[BK.HOW]	How Things Fly
[FLAP]	Flapping (QT)
[GLID]	Gliding (QT)
[HOVR]	Hovering (QT)
[JPRO]	Jet Propulsion (ANIMATION)
[BK.MOON]	The Moon
[ORBT]	Orbit-ANIMATION
[PHAZ]	Phases-ANIMATION (Day, Month)
[ECLP]	Eclipses-ANIMATION
[BK.WHY]	The Book of Why about the Sky
[RAIN]	What Makes Clouds? (ANIMATION)
[TBNN]	Why Is There Thunder and Lightning? (ANIMATION)
[RBOW]	Why Are There Rainbows? (ANIMATION)
[BK.FFLY]	Famous Fliers
[WBRO]	The Wright Brothers (QT)
[LIND]	Charles Lindbergh (QT)
[EAR]	Amelia Earhart (QT)
[BESS]	Famous Person (QT)
[BK. GAZE]	Stargazers
[ANGZ]	Ancient Stargazers (STOCK/QT)
[COP]	Copernicus (STOCK/QT)
[GAP]	Celia Gaposhkin (STOCK/QT)
[NOVA]	Stephen Hawking (STOCK/QT)

Simulation as a Way to Present Material

Most of the above approaches simply organize the material into categories that can be explored in an interesting way through a concept map or a book. There are other ways to present material, however, that are more interactive. Perhaps the most engaging is the simulation approach, which was demonstrated in depth in *The Nauticus Shipbuilding Company* case study in Chapter 14. A simulation structure, however, does not have to be used for an entire piece. As in the next example, it can also be used as part of a larger piece that follows another structure.

"Ye Olde Gravity Lab" is a simulation that can be played by clicking on a castle and entering King Arthur's Court. Ye Olde Gravity Lab is meant to teach principles of gravity by showing what would happen if you catapulted various sizes of balls at a bull's-eye while on different planets or the Earth's moon. Following is the scripted content of the Court followed by a description of the "Ye Olde Gravity Lab" simulation.

PANEL II: MEDIEVAL AND RENAISSANCE TIMES

CLOSE-UP: KING ARTHUR'S COURT-600 A.D.

Click on the castle and go inside!

VISUAL	NARR/SYNC	MUSIC/SFX
Animation **[PHAZ.QT.ANM]** Castle—On the wall, an ancient looking calendar with moving phases of the moon	Narration **[PHAZ.QT.NARR]**	SFX **[PHAZ.QT.SFX]** [BK 2.2]
VISUAL	**NARR/SYNC**	**MUSIC/SFX**
Video **[ECLP.QT.VID]** CASTLE VIDEO— Méliès FOOTAGE, from "The Astronomer's Dream" will probably need to be speeded up a little (ARCHIVE FILMS)	Narration **[ECLP.QT.NARR]**	Music **[ECLP.QT.MUS]** Music [BK 02.3]
Animation **[CATP.QT.ANM]** Castle—Ye Olde Gravity Lab—enter lab and play animated game catapulting different balls. Take catapult to the moon, Mars, and Jupiter to see differences.	Narration **[CATP.QT.NARR]**	Music **[CATP.QT.MUS]**

Ye Olde Gravity Laboratory

When you click on the castle in the panorama, you see a close-up of a wall inside the castle. There are three hot spots on this wall, leading to a moon, to an eclipse, and to Ye Olde Gravity Lab. If you click on the catapult, you enter the laboratory.

The laboratory fills the screen except for the Discoveries control bar on the bottom. The initial laboratory screen contains the following elements:

• Catapult—base with hinge, arm with basket for ball, and compression spring to power the "throw." The base and hinge can be part of the background art, but the arm + basket + spring is separate artwork. In order to do the animation with the arm + basket we need five different positions between the starting position and the ending position. There is a release mechanism, such as a string that you "pull" to fire the catapult.

- Target supported by post or tripod.
- Balls (with labels): Ping-Pong, golf, baseball, and bowling. Each ball is a separate piece of artwork, and each has a labeled resting place that is part of the background art.
- A control panel with radio buttons for four places: Jupiter, Earth, Mercury, Earth's Moon, and an Exit Lab button. These buttons can be painted into the background art BUT there must be an alternate version of each gravity button that is highlighted (radio button on).
- Prompter's booth. The guy who changes the place backgrounds is in this booth. Although you don't see him do it, he also grabs thrown balls as they roll in front of him.
- An Exit Lab button.
- A curtain or other wall covering that appears to be behind the control panel. On the curtain is an instructions box:

Ye Olde Gravity Lab Welcomes You
Click to Choose a Place

When you click a place button, a voice says:
"So, you want Jupiter."
"Okay, here's Earth."
"All right, you get Mercury."
"Here's the moon."
A hand reaches from the prompter's booth to the top of the screen and pulls down a backdrop representing the place requested.

- Jupiter sign: "Jupiter. Twice the gravity of Earth."
- Earth sign: "Earth."
- Mercury sign: "Mercury. One-third the gravity of Earth."
- Moon sign: "Moon. One-sixth the gravity of Earth."

SFX: "WHAPWHAPWHAPT" as backdrop unrolls.

The instructions box says: "Drag a ball to the end of the catapult." When the catapult is loaded, the instructions box says: "To fire the catapult, pull the string."

There are seventeen different throwing possibilities, one for each combination of ball and gravity, plus one for an unloaded catapult. If the ball flies over the target, you hear a SFX "WHOOSH." If it hits the target but misses the bull's-eye!, you hear SFX "THUMP," then as it bounces on the floor you hear

SFX "BOUNCE." If it hits the bull you hear a loud
bell. If the bowling ball goes directly to the floor
you hear SFX "CRASH." If the catapult is fired without
being loaded, you hear SFX "THWANGGGGG."

After a throw, there is a two-second delay; then
the program resets. The place does not change, but the
balls return to their starting points and the catapult
is drawn back into ready position (SFX "SPRING
COMPRESS"). The directions box says "Load the catapult
or change the place."

At any time you can click a different place. A hand
from the prompter's booth pushes up the old background
(SFX "WHIROOP"), then pulls down the new one while you
hear its narration. The instructions box returns to
"Drag a ball to the end of the catapult." You can
change the gravity or exit at any time. Clicking the
Exit Lab button takes you back to the close-up through
which you entered. As you exit, the guy sticks his
head out of the prompter's booth and looks at you.

If you click on the prompter's booth, the "guy"
peers around at you and says "Huh."

Quizzes as a Way to Present Material

Another way to present material is through quizzes, as in the next example. Notice
that there is feedback for every answer and amusing sound effects aimed at the young
audience.

QUESTION 14 [CD.QZ.CSNA 1-BG.PAN]

VISUAL	NARR/SYNC	MUSIC/SFX
Question 14 **[CD.QZ.CSNA.1]** Charles Lindbergh named his plane The Spirit of . . . St. Louis. Ammonia. New York.	Narration **[CSNA.1.Q.NARR]** Charles Lindbergh named his plane The Spirit of . . . St. Louis. Ammonia. New York.	
Answer **[CSNA.1.A]** St. Louis		SFX **[CSNA.1.Q.SFX]** Right answer SFX
Distracter 1 **[CSNA.1.D1]** ammonia.	Narration **[CSNA.1.D1.NARR]**	SFX **[CSNA.1.D2.SFX]** Whew! No!
Distracter 2 **[CSNA.1.D2]** New York.	Narration **[CSNA.1.D1.NARR]**	SFX **[CSNA.1.D2.SFX]** loud honking car

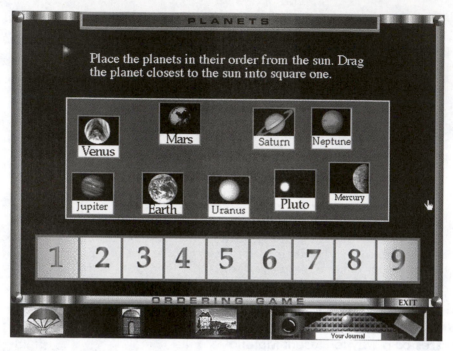

FIGURE 15–2

Ordering game.

Matching Games as a Way to Present Material

Matching games, which use images that viewers can move with the mouse, are another way to get the user to interact with the material. *Sky High* used two basic types of matching games:

- Put things in the right sequence—for example, place planets in order, starting from the closest to the sun (see Figure 15–2).
- Place in the proper group—for example, choose all elements that fly straight up, such as a hummingbird, helicopter, and hot air balloon, or drag planets that have moons into the boxes.

REACHING A BROAD PRIMARY SCHOOL AUDIENCE

In addition to the key challenge of *Sky High*, which was organizing and making accessible a large database of material, the writers also had to maximize the program's use by making the material appealing to a broad primary school audience.

This was done by:

- Using the many media in this program to make the basic information comprehensible to a wide age group.
- Including entertaining elements.
- Expanding the basic subject material to make the program multidisciplinary.

Using the Many Media to Make the Information Comprehensible to a Wide Age Group

Although the *Sky High* CD was aimed primarily at third-graders, multimedia can appeal to a wide audience, because the same information can be communicated in multiple ways and can be replayed by the user. This feature helps both younger children and students with disabilities. For example, on this CD, students have the option of having text read out loud. They can take notes and snap screen shots for their on-screen journal for later review and questions for the teacher. In general, the images also provide a context to understand information. Because of this multimodal communication, the finished CD-ROM has a wide appeal, ranging from grades 1 through 8.

Presenting information in an entertaining way or simply choosing entertaining material is also important with a school-age audience. This can be done in a number of ways:

- Feedback: There's a trivia game in the Visitor's Center in which the user's correct answers are rewarded with different animations of a flying stunt, such as a barnstormer on the wings of a biplane.

- Text and audio quotes: It's important to keep an eye out for quotations that might especially appeal to children. This vivid description of life at Kitty Hawk by Orville Wright has gotten chuckles in the classroom:

VISUAL (Super Quote Still)	NARR/SYNC	MUSIC/SFX
TEXT [CSNA.QT.VID] There was no escape [from the mosquitoes.] The sand and grass and trees and hills and everything was fairly covered with them. They chewed us clear through our underwear and socks. Lumps began swelling up all over my body like hen's eggs. Your brother, Orville	NARR TEXT ORVILLE There was no escape [from the mosquitoes.] The sand and grass and trees and hills and everything was fairly covered with them. They chewed us clear through our underwear and socks. Lumps began swelling up all over my body like hen's eggs. Your brother, Orville	SFX Buzzing mosquitoes

- Audio. The buzz of mosquitoes sound effect in the above script sample is an example of how audio can be used to enliven information.
- Pop culture material. Using material from pop culture can also be effective. For example, a *Flash Gordon* video illustrates some early ideas about vertical flight, and a clip from the TV series *Lost in Space* portrays visions of space travel.

Expanding the Basic Subject Material to Make the Program Multidisciplinary

The audience for this program was broadened by expanding the subject matter beyond pure science issues concerning flight. An example is the inclusion of the story of Bessie Coleman, the first black person to earn a pilot's license. Because of racism, no one in the United States would teach her how to fly. There was, however, less prejudice in France, so she learned French, got her pilot's license, and later returned to the United States and started her own air shows.

Important popular culture material was also included, such as *A Trip to the Moon*, by Georges Méliès. This is a significant work in film history and the first movie about a trip to the moon. It was made the same year the Wright brothers made their flight. General historical context is also available to the *Sky High* user. Clicking on the date on the bottom of the time line reveals a description of other events happening at that time.

WRITING TO ARCHIVAL MATERIAL VERSUS CREATING THE CONTENT

Writing a broad database project, such as this one, means using primarily archival material to present information. Writers can approach this challenge by acquainting themselves with existing archival material and then developing their concepts based on this information, or they can form a general concept of what they want to say, then find (or have a researcher find) the photo, video, quotation, or other element that will best present their idea.

In either case, writers are always adjusting their original conceptions to the archival material that is available. It is important for writers not to become too rigid about their original ideas because sometimes they must abandon them when available media supports a totally different approach.

Below are the first and second drafts of the Space Shuttle section from the "book" in *Sky High*'s Visitor's Center titled "Space Firsts." The original concept in the first draft was to present a serious piece about repairing the Hubble telescope. Unfortunately, the footage received from NASA was about the shuttle crew eating breakfast! The sequence had to be completely rewritten to accommodate the new footage. See what you think of the results.

SPACE SHUTTLE: FIRST DRAFT

VISUAL	NARR/SYNC	MUSIC/SFX
VIDEO [CSNA.QT.VID] NASA, shots of space shuttle #1 TAKE OFF	NARR VIDEO [CSNA.QT.NARR] The crew of this space shuttle went up to repair the Hubble, a powerful space telescope.	SFX take off
#2 Hubble being repaired	The crew worked hard to fix the Hubble.	

VISUAL	NARR/SYNC	MUSIC/SFX
#3 Hubble being repaired	Many people watched them on TV.	Mix in wild sound of astronauts & ground control
#4 Crew leaving Hubble	Now the Hubble can bring us pictures and information about the stars so we can learn more about how our universe was formed. The shuttle comes back ready to go on another mission.	
#5 Shuttle landing		SFX shuttle landing

SPACE SHUTTLE: SECOND DRAFT

VISUAL	NARR/SYNC	MUSIC/SFX
VIDEO **[SHOT.QT.VID]** #1 SPACE SHUTTLE TAKE OFF	**NARR VIDEO** **[SHUT.QT.NARR]** A day in the life of a space shuttle crew member is a lot like yours.	**MUSIC** Skater's Waltz
#2 Floating astronaut putting on pants. #3 Banana spins into mouth #4 POV floating through tunnel	You get up in the morning . . . get dressed . . . have a little breakfast . . . and find your way to school or work.	
#5 3 astronauts stacked up doing push-ups, then flying toward camera #6 ECU hand holding candy, then letting go. #7 Wide shot, woman eating M & Ms that are floating in air	Now you're ready to get down to business. Time for some exercise! Feeling a little hungry? Then it's time for a snack . . .	
VIDEO **[SHUT.QT.VID]** #8 EXT. Astronauts working outside	**NARR** Now for some outdoor activities . . . Of course, everyone has	**MUSIC** Skater's Waltz

Continues

VISUAL	NARR/SYNC	MUSIC/SFX
shuttle, floating in space. #9 INT. Astronauts in bunk area, writing, notebooks floating all over. #10 ECU red globs breaking apart.	homework to do . . . and some experiments to finish.	
#11 Long shot of earth in distance. #12 Astronauts asleep in bunk, arms floating around. #13 EXT. Shuttle going through space.	Then it's time to kick back and just watch the world go by. It's been a long day. Time to get some rest. Goodnight.	

CONCLUSION: RESPONSE TO THE PROJECT

The project is popular in the classroom. In some cases, it is hard to tear students away to give a classmate a chance to play—testament to the skillful way this development team took a large body of loosely related information and fashioned it into an informative and engaging multimedia program.

REFERENCES

Astudillo, Deborah. Interview with the author, Lexington, MA, November 1995.
James, W. R. "Multimedia Goes to School." *Digital Video*, V3 (November 1995).
McAdow, Ron. Fax to the author. November 3, 1995.
O'Meara, Maria. Interviews with the author. Brookline, MA, November 1995.

C H A P T E R   1 6

TRAINING CASE STUDY:
VITAL SIGNS

Summary

Name of production: *Clinical Support Staff Interactive Certification Program: Vital Signs*

Writers: Instructional designer, John Cosner; writer, Fred Bauer

Developer: MediaViz Productions

Audience: Trainee medical assistants at a health maintenance organization

Medium: Interactive video disc

Presentation location: Place of employment

Subject: The process of taking medical vital signs: temperature, pulse, respiration, and blood pressure

Goals: Teach

Architecture: Linear, hierarchical branching, simulations

The script samples and images used in this chapter are courtesy of Harvard Community Health Plan. © 1995 Harvard Community Health Plan.

PROGRAM DESCRIPTION AND BACKGROUND

Clinical Support Staff Interactive Certification Program: Vital Signs is a training program designed to teach trainee medical assistants at Harvard Community Health Plan (HCHP), a Boston-based health maintenance organization, how to take vital signs—temperature, pulse, respiration, blood pressure—and, for the OB/GYN assistants, urine analysis. Figure 16–1 shows the program's interface. The main image area is in the center frame, text to the right, and buttons on top of the page that take the student to each section of the program: thermometer = temperature; heart = pulse; lungs = respiration; manometer = blood pressure; and dip stick = urine analysis.

   Vital Signs presents a classic example of straightforward, effective, computer-based training. One of the ways it differs from the two previous case studies is that its goal is to teach a specific skill to a clearly defined audience. Properly learning this skill has life-and-death importance. Because of this, entertainment value is stressed far

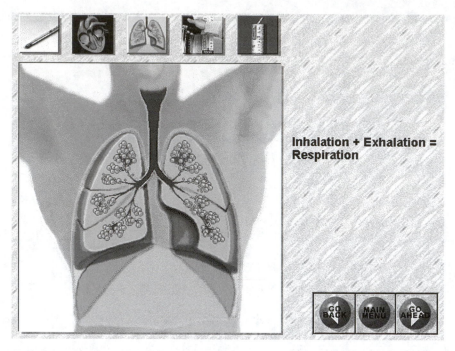

Inhalation + Exhalation = Respiration

FIGURE 16-1

The main interface for *Vital Signs*.

less than it is in the kiosk for the general public, *The Nauticus Shipbuilding Company*, and the sequencing of the information is far more structured and precise than it is in *Sky High*, which provides general information about a broad subject.

MULTIMEDIA TRAINING PROGRAMS

Training programs are the bread and butter of many small and medium-sized production companies. Training is a multibillion dollar business, because in order to keep current, employers must constantly train and retrain employees. Training includes the traditional classroom, print material, and linear media, such as film and video. However, computer-based multimedia and Web training is becoming an increasingly popular part of this mix because it has been proven to be faster, cheaper, and more effective in many cases than other types of training.

Vital Signs was developed in traditional CBT (computer-based training) tutorial style: present the topic, test, and retest. This is a highly effective and common approach in CBT. Some CBT can, however, use more elaborate metaphors and simulations, such as creating a story or a game that the user plays to learn the material, or a discovery program where learners explore their environment.

Vital Signs is a disc-based training program that teaches a specific topic to all students the same way. Some other approaches to training include:

- Customization/Personalization. This training material is focused precisely to the user's needs. This is accomplished by smart programs that adjust based on the user's learning pattern and/or by requiring more information about the user at the start of the program, either through registration or pretest.

- Online Training. Online training is training delivered over a network, such as a company intranet or the World Wide Web. This approach to delivery has become increasingly popular because of its cross-platform flexibility, ease of update, inexpensive distribution, and user familiarity with Web browsers.

- Just-in-Time Training. The formal name for JIT training is employee performance support system (EPSS). Instead of presenting entire programs, just-in-time (JIT) training presents small snippets of information when they are needed. With this approach, an employee with a question about a particular process can jump on the computer and get immediate help. This is similar to help programs in some applications, such as Wizards in Microsoft Office.

PRODUCTION BACKGROUND

Why the Client Produced This Program in Multimedia

Vital Signs was commissioned by Harvard Community Health Plan, a New England-based staff model HMO. A staff model HMO has its own health centers staffed by its own medical personnel, who see only patients who belong to that HMO. Since the production of *Vital Signs*, Harvard Community Health Plan merged and has been renamed as Harvard Pilgrim Health Care, but because HCHP was the original producer of the program that name will be used in this chapter.

The *Vital Signs* training program was aimed toward HCHP medical assistants, who help the physicians and other clinicians by greeting patients, bringing them into the examining room, taking vital signs, and generally assisting with any other work that the physician needs to have done. In order to improve the training of the medical assistants, HCHP instituted an in-house certification program, of which the *Vital Signs* project is one component.

HCHP decided to teach these skills through interactive media for many of the same reasons that many companies choose multimedia for training:

- Students are dispersed. It was difficult to gather students together for a traditional group class, because they worked in many different departments all over the area, and they were usually hired only a few at a time. With a multimedia program, individual students could view the program as they needed it and did not have to wait for a group and a teacher.

- Students have varied backgrounds. The backgrounds of trainee medical assistants range from high school graduates to individuals with master's degrees. For some of the trainees, English was their second language. This wide mix of educational levels would make a traditional class nearly impossible to pace without either confusing the slow learners or boring the more advanced students. With multimedia, each student can learn at his or her own pace. Some can skip material; others may want to replay certain sections several times.

- Importance of keeping information consistent. Taking vital signs is an essential skill in all medical departments. It was important that all medical assistants perform this service in the same way and with the latest techniques. If all assistants watch the same multimedia program, this is ensured.

- Cutting training time. It was difficult to take a large group of medical assistants out of their jobs at any one time. It was much easier if they could come individually at slow times in their departments. In addition, for skills such as these, independent studies have documented that students complete multimedia courses more than 30 percent faster than covering the same material in a traditional course. (*Bank Technology News 25*)

- Cutting expenses. Once the program is completed, major training costs are over until the program has to be updated. This is far cheaper than hiring teachers for every new group of students. Studies have documented that "multimedia cost an average of 64 percent less to develop, maintain, and deliver than traditional training" ("Multimedia Sights and Sounds" 25).

PROGRAM DEVELOPMENT

This piece was developed by MediaViz productions, a production company specializing in the design and production of multimedia training programs for corporate clients. This project was designed by instructional designer John Cosner of MediaViz and written by Fred Bauer. Cosner also functioned as the project manager, along with HCHP's Comma Williams, who served as client contact and in-house project manager.

The development of this project followed a standard training model. The information in the program was based on several print training documents that HCHP had already produced. Using this material and additional research, the designer developed a design document. This document included a content outline, which laid out the structure of the course in standard hierarchical outline form. There was no flowchart for this project, although more complicated training programs commonly use flowcharts.

The design document was refined in several design meetings with the writer, the client, the instructional designer-project manager, and eventually the graphic artist. The writer developed several drafts of the treatment based on these meetings and, when the final treatment was approved, wrote several drafts of the script.

THE INSTRUCTIONAL DESIGNER

The instructional designer is an important figure in multimedia training. According to John Cosner, the instructional designer on this project, there are different conceptions of what an instructional designer is. Many instructional designers have an advanced degree in instructional design and/or a teaching background. Other instructional designers have not been formally trained in the field.

On some projects, instructional designers do not write the script but instead deal with high-level instructional design, such as audience analysis, needs, and goals. In these cases, once the treatment and outline are taken care of, the project is handed over to the writer, with the instructional designer editing the material after it is completed. The role of the instructional designer depends on the attitude of the developer, the type of content, and the complexity of the project. Sometimes, there is no formal instructional designer, and the writer assumes the duties normally assigned to that position.

GOALS AND CHALLENGES WRITING AND DEVELOPING *VITAL SIGNS*

CHALLENGES

The key challenges developing this project arose from the type of content, the time limitation on the program, and the nature of the students.

Content

The content involved teaching a specific process: taking vital signs. This process is an essential part of health care and the first thing the physician wants to know about the patient. This information had to be delivered precisely. A general or partial understanding of the topic would not be sufficient.

Time Limit

The client wanted the students to be able to complete this program in less than an hour. This was the amount of time that the stand-up class in the same subject took, so if the interactive program took longer, it would defeat the purpose of limiting the amount of time training takes from work. This time limit restricted the amount of material that could be placed into a program and meant that students wouldn't have time to learn the rules of an elaborate game or simulation. The program would have to be simple and clear.

Audience Issues

A number of issues affected the design of this project:

- Some students had English as a second language.
- For many of them, this was their first introduction to this kind of material.
- Most were not college graduates.
- There were three different types of students: internal medicine, pediatrics, and OB/GYN. After the introductory material, each student needed specialized information for his or her department. This meant a greater variety of information in the program, and a need to identify and track each individual student clearly.

WRITER AND INSTRUCTIONAL DESIGNER'S GOALS

Instructional Designer

Although the writer and the instructional designer shared many concerns, the instructional designer's primary focus was the overall content and design of the program. The instructional designer, John Cosner, had the following concerns on this project:

- Content driven. The serious nature of the content set the tone of this piece, and the process of taking vital signs set the sequencing of information. The importance of a precise understanding of the information dictated that the same material be presented in a number of ways.
- Clear navigation. A primary goal for any training piece is to make the navigation clear and easy to use for the student. If the program feels complicated to a user,

then it has failed. In a good training program, the students should be learning the material, not the program.

- Humanize. In a piece dealing with human interaction, such as this, it's a good idea to put a human face to most of the procedures. For example, the pediatrics section uses the same young girl through several scenes.

The Writer

The writer, Fred Bauer, had input into the overall design of the program. For example, he agreed with the instructional designer that clear navigation was a primary concern; students cannot learn if they are lost. His major concern, however, was with successfully realizing the overall design by achieving the following goals:

- Pace. A key to interactive multimedia is to pace the program in a way that keeps people involved. Users should not passively watch the screen for longer than 25 to 30 seconds before they are asked to interact with the program in some way. It's also important to vary the length and tempo of scenes and the length of time between actions required of the user.

- Humor. In education, humor can be effective in a number of ways: as a reward for a successful performance, as a memory aid, and as a way to help people relax. The opening of this piece is a good example. (See the humorous Introduction script sample later in this chapter.)

- Emotion. It is essential not only to present information but also to present feelings and to elicit an emotional response. In *Vital Signs*, it was important for the students to feel that, as medical assistants, they are a crucial part of the medical service provider team. Another goal was to make the students aware of the feelings that the patient has and to help the students look at the patient as a human being and not just part of the job. The pediatric section of this piece was particularly effective in achieving this.

- Aligning program's voice with viewer. The writer thought that users would feel more comfortable if he could match the program's voice with the users' emotions and expectations. The voice of a program is basically who seems to be talking to you through the program. A voice can be neutral, simply presenting the information without attempting direct contact with the viewer. A neutral voice is fine for an informational program, but in a training piece, it helps the user if the voice can be separated from the content and align itself with the user. For example, in this project, text on the screen frequently questions what was said in the dialogue or the narration. Sometimes the screen text will even attempt to sympathize with a student's confusion if the student gets a question wrong. Actual tone of voice also helps here; the narrator should never talk down to or lecture the student.

- Style of presentation. A multimedia program is usually experienced as up close and personal. A student sits inches away from a screen and is connected via keyboard or other input device. It is also usually a one-on-one experience. Because of this, the writer said that multimedia programs should be more intimate. They should not be developed in the same style as a film or a TV program that will be viewed in a group from a much greater distance. Ways to increase this intimacy include more close-ups and using the screen as a window on the world rather than an artificial stage. With a window, characters' entrances and exits are framed in such a way that the users get a sense that there is a larger world beyond the borders of the screen. This is the same experience as looking out a of window of a house. Some critics call this "open form framing." Intimacy is also increased through the quality of the program's voice.

MEETING THE CHALLENGES AND ACHIEVING THE GOALS

OVERALL DESIGN

As you read the descriptions and script samples that follow, be aware of the overall design. One of the strongest aspects of this piece is how the same information is introduced numerous times, but each time the information is presented, it is demonstrated in a more challenging manner. The program builds from simple linear demonstrations and definitions to highly interactive simulations and testing, as described in the following outline of the program (there are also additional script samples included in the Chapter 16 area of the "Chapters" section of the *Writing for Multimedia and the Web* CD-ROM):

1. Registration
2. Pretest
3. Humorous Introduction
4. Overview
5. Basic Terms
6. Detailed Instruction
7. Practice
8. Case Study Experience
9. Posttest

REGISTRATION, PRETEST, AND HUMOROUS INTRODUCTION

Students register for the program with their employee number and department. This information helps to focus the material to their needs. For the purposes of demonstration, you, the reader, will register in the pediatric department. This means that after the general instruction, the program will link you to pediatric information.

After registration, students take a multiple-choice pretest on vital signs. The purpose of this test is to get them thinking about the subject. This test is not numerically graded. Instead the subjects are listed with a bright bulb or dim bulb next to the topic, depending on how well the students know that specific material. This feedback makes them aware of their strengths and weaknesses.

The pretest is followed by a humorous introduction in which users monitor the vital signs of Norman. (Light lines divide sections; heavy lines divide pages.)

Humorous Introduction Script Sample

```
Unit: Vital Signs Introduction (Video)
Lesson:
  Topic:
  Title:
```

Screen: I1.1
Type:
Graphic File:

(**GRAPHIC/VIDEO:** Photograph of a young man, mid-
twenties, asleep. A panel opens in the upper right of
the frame. It contains four running graph lines
labeled:
"Temperature," "Pulse," "Respiration," "Blood Pressure."
All are moving, but quiescent. Temperature and pulse
are steady, respirations peak with each inhalation,
blood pressure shows almost no variation.) (NOTE: In
general, 4 heart beats per 1 respiration. Pulse is
usually constant during sleep.)

Text:

NORMAL VITAL SIGNS: SLEEPING

If we wake Norman, will his vital signs . . .
  Remain the same
  All show an increase
  Some remain the same, and some increase

AUDIO: NARRATOR (VO): (SOFTLY, SO AS NOT TO WAKEN
NORMAN) Shhh—Normal Norman is sleeping. His normal
vital signs-temperature . . . blood pressure . . . pulse . . .
and respiration—are flowing along in that panel to the
upper right. These values reflect body changes you can't
always see just by looking at a patient. We take vital
signs to spot early warnings, like high blood pressure—
often, these warnings allow us to give preventative
care. Norman's vital signs are normal for sleeping.
What do you suppose will happen to them when we wake
Norman up? Will his vital signs remain the same, all
show an increase, or some remain the same and some
increase? SELECT your choice, and we'll see.

Feedback: (AUDIO + Text) **NARRATOR (VO):**

Same = Close but not quite. Watch. All = A good guess,
but not quite. Watch. Some = Very good. Watch.
After all answers = (CALLING) Wake up, Norman! (SFX:
snorts and grunts from Norman.)
Branching:

I1.2
Special Instructions:

Unit: Vital Signs Introduction (Video)
Lesson:
Topic:
Title:

Screen: I1.2
Type:
Graphic File:

(**GRAPHIC/VIDEO:** Photograph of young man sitting up in bed and yawning. Vital signs show waking norms.)

Text:

NORMAL VITAL SIGNS AWAKE

Button = "Breakfast, Norman!"

AUDIO: (SFX: Music assumes a more upbeat tempo.)
NARRATOR (VO): (IN REGULAR SPEAKING VOICE) In the morning, our temperature is at the lowest point of the day. Norman's waking pulse, respiration, and blood pressure are higher than when he's asleep. No surprises there. Well, time for breakfast. SELECT the breakfast button and we'll see what happens to Norman next.

Feedback:

Button = **NARRATOR (VO):** Breakfast, Norman! (SFX: clanging triangle, as in Western movies chuck wagon call.)

Branching:

Button = 11.3
Special Instructions:

In the next scenes in the script, which are not shown here, Norman's temperature rises as he drinks hot coffee. When Norman suddenly realizes he's late for work, his blood pressure goes up and his pulse increases. When he gets a flat tire, his vital signs go crazy.

Analysis of Humorous Introduction

The major function of this sequence is to introduce the topic in a light manner to initiate users' interest and get them relaxed and ready to learn. This sequence also gives students a chance to concentrate on learning how the program operates without having to learn complex course information. This makes program navigation clear to the students.

In the audio on the first page, the writer quickly sets up a friendly voice for the program and connects directly to the user. By creating the character Norman, whose vital signs the user monitors, the writer puts a human face on the information.

Under the feedback section on the same page, the user is asked to guess what will happen next, adding interactivity and greater audience involvement to what is essentially a linear sequence. The breakfast button on the next page works the same way and helps to maintain the pace.

OVERVIEW

After the humorous introduction, the piece turns more serious, outlining the importance of the topic and the objectives of the program. This is followed by a video overview showing an experienced medical assistant taking a patient's vital signs.

The overview puts a human face on the experience by creating characters for the patient and medical assistant. It also gives the students a general view of what they will be learning in a nonthreatening environment in which little is being asked of them in terms of answering questions and providing information. It is, however, more serious and fact-filled than the humorous introduction. This is part of the slow and careful buildup of the information presentation.

BASIC TERMS

After the overview, it is time for users to roll up their sleeves and start learning the nuts and bolts of taking vital signs. The lessons are first listed in the following interactive menu, which gives users an option of what to study first:

- Temperature
- Pulse
- Respiration
- Blood pressure

If the user clicks on Blood Pressure, a series of screens that define this topic's basic concepts appear.

Basic Terms Script Sample

> (**GRAPHIC/VIDEO:** Repeat animated diagram of heart showing flow of blood.)

> **Text:** Blood Pressure Lesson (small heart symbol) (CALL OUTS)

Right Atrium   Left Atrium
Right Ventricle   Left Ventricle
  The pressure of blood—
    at height of wave from ventricles
    as heart relaxes between beats

AUDIO: NARRATOR (VO): While pulse and respiration are
taken directly, blood pressure is measured indirectly
using a device called a manometer. It is actually two
values. Blood pressure is the measurement of the
highest force of the blood on the walls of the blood
vessels, at the height of the wave from the ventricles,
and the lowest force of the blood on the walls of the
blood vessels, as the heart relaxes between beats.

Feedback:

Branching:

u1.4.2

Special Instructions:

  Unit: u1
  Lesson: Blood Pressure
  Topic:
  Title:

  Screen: u1.4.2
  Type:
  Graphic File:

GRAPHIC/VIDEO: (Animated diagram of artery with red
dots flowing left to right, and vein, with blue dots
flowing right to left.)

Text:

Blood Pressure Measurements:
Systolic and Diastolic
    Artery
    (Muscle)
    Vein
    (Valves)

AUDIO: NARRATOR (VO): Blood flows from the heart in
arteries, which have muscles to help keep it moving.
Blood returns to the heart through veins, which don't
have muscles, but do contain valves that prevent blood
from flowing backwards. Blood pressure consists of two
measurements—systolic and diastolic. SELECT each to
learn more. (When you've finished, SELECT "GO AHEAD" to
continue.)

Feedback: (AUDIO + Text)
Highlight term when chosen.

Systolic = **NARRATOR (VO):** (ARTERY AND VEIN FREEZE AT
HEIGHT OF FLOW) Systolic values measure the pressure at
the height of the pulse wave.
Diastolic = **NARRATOR (VO):** (ARTERY AND VEIN FREEZE
DURING PAUSE) Diastolic readings measure the pressure
during the relaxation period between beats.

Branching:

u1.4.3

Special Instructions:

Analysis of Definition of Basic Terms
Because of the audience for this program, no scientific knowledge is assumed. Basic
terms are explained clearly and simply. The interactive animation on the second page
of the example is a good use of instructional multimedia.

DETAILED INSTRUCTION

Once basic terms and processes are explained, the program moves to the next level
of complexity, which focuses on the medical assistant's specialty, such as pediatrics or
OB/GYN. For example, a user who registered from the Pediatric Department, would
receive detailed instructions on how to take vital signs from a child.

PRACTICE

Immediately following the detailed instruction is a highly interactive sequence in
which the user takes a little girl's blood pressure. It starts off with the challenge: "Now
it's your turn." Enough sitting around watching, it's time to do it.

Practice Script Sample

Unit: u1
Lesson: Blood Pressure

Topic:
Title:

Screen: u1.4.13p
Type:
Graphic File:

(**GRAPHIC/VIDEO:** Colette looking apprehensive)

Text:
Meet Colette, age 7.
You're going to take her blood pressure. You've
explained the procedure to her. What do you use next?

(CAPTIONS)
    Cuff   Ball Pump   Valve on cuff   Doll

(**AUDIO: NARRATOR VO**): Now it's your turn. Meet Colette,
age 7. You're going to take her blood pressure. You've
explained the procedure. What do you use next—the cuff,
the ball pump, the valve on the cuff, or the doll?
SELECT your choice now.

Feedback: (VO and text)

Cuff, Ball Pump, Valve = (SFX: Little Girl's Voice) **(VO
audio ONLY)**: No. I don't want that. It's going to
hurt! **NARRATOR (VO)**: Apparently, Colette didn't buy
your explanation. Try again.
Doll = **NARRATOR (VO)**: You're good. That's right. From
the look on her face, you can tell Colette didn't buy
your explanation, so you demonstrate on a doll. (SELECT
"GO AHEAD" to continue.)

Branching:

u1.4.14p

Special Instructions:

Unit: u1
Lesson: Blood Pressure

Topic:
Title:

Screen: ul.4.14p
Type:
Graphic File:

(**GRAPHIC/VIDEO:** Animated graphic of manometer column at 110 mm)

Text:

SELECT the valve, listen to the heart sounds, watch the mercury, and read Colette's blood pressure. SELECT O.K. when you have it. O.K.

(**AUDIO:** (SFX: 7-year-old heart sounds.) **NARRATOR (VO):** SELECT the valve, listen to the heart sounds, watch the mercury and read Colette's blood pressure. SELECT O.K. when you've got it.

Feedback:

Branching:

ul.4.15p

Special Instructions:

Unit: ul
Lesson: Blood Pressure
Topic:
Title:

Screen: u1.4.15p
Type:
Graphic File:

(**GRAPHIC/VIDEO:** Animated graphic of manometer column at 110 mm)

Text:
What is Colette's blood pressure?

94/68
92/66
92/68

(AUDIO: NARRATOR VO): What is Colette's blood pressure—
94/68, 92/66, or 92/68? SELECT your answer now.

Feedback: (AUDIO + Text)

NARRATOR (VO):
94/68 = That's not right. Try again.
92/66 = That's not right. Try again.
92/68 = That's right (SELECT "GO AHEAD" to continue.)

Branching:

u1.4.14 (Orthostatic)

Special Instructions:

Analysis of Practice

This piece allows you as the student to practice what you've just learned by choosing the right approach to the child. It makes you aware of the feelings of the patient and helps you to see her as a human being and not just part of the job. It also lets you actually "take" her blood pressure with an ingenious, interactive animation. If you get the pressure wrong, you can try again.

CASE STUDY EXPERIENCE

The case studies present the information in yet another way. This time the student watches videos of a medical assistant taking the vital signs. The challenge is to catch the medical assistant's errors.

Case Studies Script Sample

Unit: u2
Lesson: Case History—Pediatric
Topic:
Title:

Screen: u2.4.1
Type:
Graphic File:

(**GRAPHIC/VIDEO:** CLOSE-UP SHOWS RUTH PROPERLY FEELING
FOR PULSE AND FINDING IT. 1) DISSOLVE TO MEDIUM SHOT
OF RUTH. SHE NOTES HER WATCH, THEN LOOKS AWAY,
CONCENTRATING ON THE HEARTBEAT. 2) DISSOLVE TO MEDIUM
SHOT. SILENTLY, SHE BEGINS TO CONCENTRATE ON THE RISE
AND FALL OF COLETTE'S CHEST. 3) CAMERA CUTS TO
COLETTE'S CHEST. 4) DISSOLVE TO CLOSE-UP OF RUTH'S HAND
AS SHE WRITES PULSE AND RESPIRATION ON ENCOUNTER FORM.
DISSOLVE TO SHOT OF RUTH REACHING FOR MANOMETER CUFF.)

Text:

(AFTER RUTH FASTENS CUFF. ACTION FREEZE.)
Error

(**AUDIO:** (SFX: NORMAL, REGULAR CHILD'S HEARTBEAT OVER
PULSE. NORMAL, REGULAR CHILD'S BREATHING MATCHES RISE
AND FALL OF COLETTE'S CHEST. RUTH SPEAKS AS SHE TRIES
TO WRAP TOO LARGE A CUFF AROUND COLETTE'S ARM, FINALLY
FASTENING IT LOOSE, AND REACHING ALMOST TO THE CHILD'S
ARMPIT. **RUTH (ON CAMERA):** I'm going to take you're
blood pressure now, Colette. What's going to happen is,
I'll put this cuff around your arm, and pump it up.
You'll feel a little squeezing, like when your mommy
gives you a big hug. Just nod if you're ready.
(COLETTE NODS "YES." RUTH PLACES CUFF ON ARM AND
FASTENS.)

Feedback:
[Selection before Ruth fastens cuff] **NARRATOR (VO):**
(Track 2) Sorry, no error yet but stay alert. (SELECT
"GO AHEAD" to continue.)
(Selection when Ruth fastens cuff) **NARRATOR (VO):**
(Track 2) Good work. You've helped Ruth become a better
medical assistant. (SELECT "GO AHEAD" to continue.)
[MISS] **NARRATOR (VO):** (Track 2) You missed an error.
We've stopped the time so that you can step in and
help Ruth. If you think you know what that error is,
you can choose to continue. If you'd like to see it
again, choose replay.
Branching:
HIT, OR CONTINUE = u2.4.1q
REPLAY = u2.41
Special Instructions:

    Unit: u2
    Lesson: Case History—Pediatric
    Topic:

    Title:

    Screen: u2.4.1q
    Type:
    Graphic File:

(**GRAPHIC/VIDEO:** FREEZE FRAME OF ERROR)

Text:

What error did you spot?
Using wrong size blood pressure cuff
Unprofessional attitude
Failure to tell patient she's counting respiration

AUDIO:

Feedback:
Unprofessional, or Failure = Not correct. Try again.
Using = That's right. What would you do to correct
this error?

Note on Encounter form that cuff is wrong size.
Get proper size cuff.
Wait until it's time to remove thermometer, then get
proper cuff.

Note, or wait = Not quite. Try again.
Get = That's right.

Branching: u2.4.2

Special Instructions:

    Unit: u2
    Lesson: Case History—Pediatric
    Topic:
    Title:

    Screen: u2.4.2
    Type:
    Graphic File:

(**GRAPHIC/VIDEO:** HOLD FROZEN ACTION)

Text:

Using wrong size blood pressure cuff. Ruth has applied a cuff that's too wide and too long. This will lower the patient's blood pressure. SELECT "GO AHEAD" to help her get it right.

(AUDIO:)

Feedback:

Branching: u2.5. 1
Special Instructions:

    Unit: u2
    Lesson: Case History—Pediatric
    Topic:
    Title:

    Screen: u2.5.1
    Type:
    Graphic File:

GRAPHIC/VIDEO: REPEAT ACTION AS RUTH TRIES CUFF.

    Text:

(WHEN RUTH PLACES CUFF ON ARM. FREEZE ACTION)
ERROR

(**AUDIO:** Just nod if you're ready. (COLETTE NODS "YES." RUTH TRIES CUFF, REALIZES IT'S TOO BIG.) Colette, somebody must have been taking the blood pressure of a giant—look how big this is. I'm going to get a nice new cuff for you—one that fits. I'll be right back. (DISSOLVE or WIPE TO RUTH RETURNING WITH PROPER CUFF, PLACING IT ON COLETTE'S ARM.) That's better.

Feedback:

[Selection before Ruth places cuff on arm] **NARRATOR (VO):** (Track 2) Sorry, no error yet but stay alert. (SELECT "GO AHEAD" to continue.)
[Selection when Ruth places cuff on arm] **NARRATOR (VO):** (Track 2) Good work. You've helped Ruth become a better medical assistant. (SELECT "GO AHEAD" to continue.)
[MISS] **NARRATOR (VO):** (Track 2) You missed an error. We've stopped the time so that you can step in and help Ruth. If you think you know what that error is, you can choose to continue. If you'd like to see it again, choose replay.

Branching:

HIT, OR CONTINUE = u2.5.1q
REPLAY = u2.5.1

Analysis of Case Study

This section has a number of branching possibilities, which increases student involvement, but perhaps the best feature is that the students have the power to stop the disc and replay it. The chance to replay the material helps the students focus on the material and provides a sense of accomplishment when they finally find the error. Without the possibility to replay the material, the students would simply miss the information and experience failure. This approach is mirrored in the feedback answers that suggest "try again" or "choose replay." This section of the program also continues the emotional quality of the previous segment by using the same little girl as a patient.

POSTTEST

The program ends with a multiple-choice posttest. This is the same test students took as a pretest, but the questions are rearranged. Like the pretest, the posttest is not numerically graded in order to reduce test anxiety and increase learning. Instead of grades, the subjects are again listed with a bright bulb or a dim bulb next to the topic, depending on how well the students knew that specific material. This device makes them aware of their strengths and weaknesses and gives them a chance to return to specific topics for additional study. The supervisors can, however, get a numerical grade for their workers if they want. Final certification of this skill, however, must occur in practice.

CONCLUSION: RESPONSE TO THE PROJECT

Written and verbal responses from the medical assistants who have used it are very positive. They like going though it at their own pace. They like the privacy. Students who speak English as a second language enjoy the opportunity to replay difficult sections. Other students said that the interactive visualization helped them learn the material. Based on this initial response, the program has been made available in all of the HMO's facilities.

REFERENCES

Bauer, Fred. Telephone interview with the author. November 1995.

Cosner, John. Telephone interviews with the author. November 1995.

"Multimedia Sights and Sounds Bombard Banks." *Bank Technology News* 7 (February 1994).

Williams, Comma. Telephone interview with author. November 1995.

CHAPTER 17

KEY POINTS FROM PART II: HOW TO WRITE NONNARRATIVE INFORMATIONAL MULTIMEDIA

GATHERING INFORMATION

As in any other information-based project, the first thing to do when writing an informational multimedia program or Web site is to gather as much information as possible on the subject and the audience. Study that information, and let your approach emerge from the material. If you are writing for a client, you also need to learn as much as you can about their expectations of the project.

CLARIFYING THE GOAL AND UNDERSTANDING THE USERS OF THE PROJECT (CHAPTER 7)

Be clear what the program is trying to achieve. Most programs have a combination of goals, but be sure your primary goal is clearly defined. Possible general goals include to entertain, to teach a specific topic, to inform about a broad topic, or to perform an online transaction, such as selling a product. Within these general goals each type of multimedia can have more specific goals. For example, commercial Web sites tend to be focused as consumer sites, transactional sites, marcom sites, or content sites. (See Chapter 11.) Be sure to understand potential users and what their information and task needs are.

DISCOVERING AN APPROACH

If it suits your goals and your type of information, attempt to find an approach that goes beyond click-and-read to utilize the full power of multimedia to engage the audience. (See Chapter 7.)

SIMULATION (CHAPTER 14)

If your information is focused on a process, consider a simulation, such as *The Nauticus Shipbuilding Company*. In a simulation, you first assign a role and a task to the user, such as a naval architect building ships. You then define all the elements of the task and describe the attributes and behaviors of each element. For example, the elements of the shipbuilding process include choosing hulls, propulsion systems, and superstructures. An attribute of an air cushion hull is that it is has shallow draft; a behavior is that it will sink in rough seas. Once the attributes and behaviors are defined, the user can perform the simulated task and receive realistic feedback.

DATABASE (CHAPTER 15)

If your information is on a broad, loosely related subject, such as flight and space exploration as in *Sky High*, the key concern is organizing information into discreet units or categories and making this information accessible to the user. One way to do this is to organize the information around a concept map, such as the journey through time in *Sky High*. Another way is to use a guide or agent to lead the user through the material. It also helps the user's comprehension to present information with a variety of media (video, text, graphics, audio) and in a variety of ways, such as games, quizzes, and explorable spaces.

TRAINING (CHAPTER 16)

If the information is narrowly focused and is on a subject the audience needs to learn precisely, consider a training model, such as that demonstrated in *Vital Signs*. A classic approach to training is to present the material in a variety of ways, starting at the simple and moving to the complex. This is the structure of *Vital Signs*. Its sequences are: (1) Registration, (2) Pretest, (3) Humorous Introduction, (4) Overview, (5) Basic Terms, (6) Detailed Instruction, (7) Practice, (8) Case Study Experience, and (9) Posttest. You also need to present information in a variety of ways to accommodate each user's learning pattern.

It might serve students well to make the multimedia education process resemble the interpersonal education process by giving your program characteristics, such as immediacy of response, nonsequential access of information, adaptability, feedback, options, and interruptibility (Chapter 7).

CONTENT WEB SITE (CHAPTER 11)

If your product or service is information-intensive and the information needs to be constantly updated, consider going online, such as the T. Rowe Price Web Site, which offers daily updates on stock information and other financial news. Attempt to present your information dynamically, allowing the user to customize the presentation of information. For example, instead of offering a general list of stocks, the T. Rowe Price site allows users to customize the information they receive by choosing the degree of investment risks and the number of years that they want to invest.

WEB SITE FEATURE STORY (CHAPTER 12)

If you want to discuss a specific topic in depth and reach a large audience, consider a multimedia feature story on the Web. This is the approach that *The Harlem Renaissance* Web site took to present material about black history. Instead of a broad overview, such as was used in *Sky High*, this site presented a large topic, black history, by telling a detailed story about a key event in that history, The Harlem Renaissance.

ONLINE ADVERTISING (CHAPTER 13)

If the primary purpose is to present information to customers and get them interested in your product, consider online advertising. In this case be aware of the standard structure of the banner and the Web site. Try to use the many advantages of online advertising to present your information in the best way possible. These advantages include measurability, rotation, direct contact with customers, interactivity, reduced cost, and unlimited space.

ARCHITECTURE (CHAPTER 8)

Once your basic approach is determined, then you need to decide what type of structure and navigation will work best for your material. Several different types of structure and navigation are often combined in one piece. Some possible structures and navigation include linear, linear with scene branching, hierarchical branching, multi-path navigation, single-level linking, worlds structure, and simulation.

WRITING THE PROGRAM (CHAPTERS 10 AND 14)

The writing formats for information programs vary, but a fairly standard approach for multimedia programs is demonstrated in *The Nauticus Shipbuilding Company* (Chapter 14). After an initial proposal is approved, writers produce a design document. This document often includes the design objective, creative treatment, project schedule, and a navigation/program flowchart. The final stage is usually a complete script, which includes all the dialogue, narration, and descriptions of the images and actions. There are a number of script format options (Chapter 5), depending on the type of project and degree of interactivity.

Writing a Web site can require many different types of writing, such as writing proposals, outlines, flowcharts, on-screen text, and site maintenance manuals. The Web writer may also have to write the site in such a way that it will show up well in search engines and directories. This includes writing page titles, page text, meta tags, and alt tags. (See Chapter 10.)

MECHANICS OF WRITING (PART I)

There are many organizational devices that help in the planning of informational presentation, such as flowcharting and databases (Chapter 3). You also have to keep in mind the basic techniques of the print, radio, and script writer, such as keeping sentences short, using the active voice, and writing visually (Chapter 2).

PART III

WRITING INTERACTIVE NARRATIVE

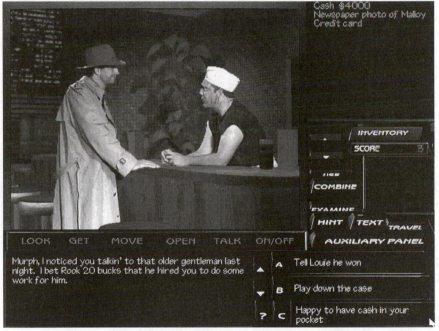

An interactive dialogue scene from *The Pandora Directive*. Courtesy of Access Software, Inc. © 1996 Access Software, Inc.

C H A P T E R   1 8

INTERACTIVE NARRATIVE AND LINEAR NARRATIVE

Portions of this chapter originally appeared in the *Journal of Film and Video.*

CHAPTER OVERVIEW

A narrative is what we commonly refer to as a story. An interactive multimedia narrative allows the user to explore several variations of a story or stories. Interactive narratives are produced for computer games, the Web, and interactive TV. Interactive narratives share many elements with linear film and video narrative. Because of this, it is useful to understand the basic elements of linear narrative before exploring the intricacies of interactive narrative.

NARRATIVE AND INTERACTIVE NARRATIVE DEFINED

"Narrative" and "story" are terms that we intuitively understand but are hard pressed to define. Critics have written many books defining narrative, but for our purposes we will define a narrative as a series of events that are linked together in a number of ways, including cause and effect, time, and place. Something that happens in the first event causes the action in the second event, and so on, usually moving forward in time.

Narrative multimedia involves telling a story using all the multimedia elements we've discussed in previous chapters, including the use of many media and interactivity. In narrative multimedia the player explores a story in the same way the user explored information in the programs discussed in Part II, "Writing Informational Multimedia and Web Sites." Often the player is one of the characters in the story and sees action from that character's point of view. But even if he or she is not a character, the player still has some control over what the characters will do and how the story will turn out. Interactive narratives can be used for pure entertainment or to present information in an experiential way.

INTERACTIVE NARRATIVES VERSUS SIMULATIONS AND WORLDS

A narrative or story is an ancient form of communication, but multimedia can also utilize two newer forms that are sometimes confused with narrative. These new forms are simulations and worlds structures. As David Riordan, the designer of *Voyeur*, points out, an interactive narrative, a simulation, and a worlds structure are three distinct forms.

In a virtual world program, such as *Myst*, the player explores an environment. The designers of a virtual world create a physical space, such as a mysterious island, where the player has the freedom to move about and interact with various elements, such as opening doors, examining objects, and even talking to people if any are present.

In a simulation, such as *The Nauticus Shipbuilding Company* (Chapter 14), a player explores all the different possibilities in an activity, such as building a ship or flying an aircraft. Simulations are not narratives. Even if they have a script attached to them, if the elements in the program come up in a random pattern, they do not comprise a narrative.

In an interactive narrative, a player explores a story. Interactive narratives have beginnings, middles, and ends, even though each user may experience these elements differently. There is nothing unplanned in an interactive narrative. Someone who plays the program long enough will eventually see all the material the writer created. An interactive narrative essentially allows each player to discover the story in a different way.

Simulations, worlds, and narratives can, of course, be combined. *Dust: A Tale of the Wired West*, profiled in Chapter 24, integrates a narrative into a virtual world. And *Wing Commander* gives players just enough narrative to engage them in the fantasy before going into a flight simulation.

INTERACTIVE MULTIMEDIA NARRATIVES AND COMPUTER GAMES

Interactive multimedia narratives are primarily found in computer games. But a distinction needs to be made between games that simply have story elements and those that have fully fleshed out narratives. Marc Laidlaw, the writer of the action-adventure game *Half-Life*, explains it this way:

> If we distinguish stories from storytelling, I'd say that lots of games have stories, but not many games do a good job of storytelling. A story can be very simple, summed up in a screen or even a single line of text. You read it, forget it, and wade into the game. But storytelling is the deliberate crafting of a narrative, with attention to rhythm and pacing, revelation, and detail (Bunn and Herz).

The major types of games that include story elements are action games, role-playing games, and adventure games, with adventure games being the only genre primarily devoted to storytelling. The main focus of action games, such as *Doom* and *Quake*, is speed and action that usually takes the form of shooting other characters or blowing things up. These games are also sometimes called shooters. Role-playing games (RPG), such as *Baldur's Gate*, involve a character taking on a role and exploring a world usually as part of a mini-quest with limited plotting and development of other characters.

As Aaron Conners, the writer of the game *The Black Pearl* explains, "In an adventure game, telling the story is the primary focus. There are strong characters and sophisticated story development. Characters overcome obstacles to achieve a final quest. Puzzles are also an important element."

After a golden age in the mid-1990s, adventure games fell on hard times. A number of adventure games were released to rave review and critical acclaim but did very little business. Because of this, many game publishers started turning their backs on interactive narrative to focus on action games. Fortunately for lovers of interactive narrative, one of these action games, *Half-Life*, became a smash hit by including more story elements than a typical action game. *Half-Life* is more action game than interactive narrative, but it showed that there was still a hunger for stories in the audience. *Half-Life*'s success made popular the hybrid genre: action-adventure—a game that has extensive action elements and a story. Most action-adventure games do not have the sophisticated stories of the classic adventure games of the mid-90s, but they have at least pointed the direction for the creation of commercially successful interactive narratives. Several designers see this erosion of the traditional game genres continuing with a blending of genres becoming the norm. For example, Aaron Conners' new game, *The Black Pearl*, will be an action game with elements of role-playing games and adventure games.

INTERACTIVE MULTIMEDIA NARRATIVES, THE WEB, AND INTERACTIVE TV

Although interactive narratives have been struggling for survival in the computer game industry, in the near future, they may soon blossom on the Web and on interactive TV. There are already some interesting attempts at interactive narrative on the Web. *MysteryNet* and *Nancy Drew Online* both have text- and graphic-based branching stories on the Web. These stories allow you to click images for clues and to choose alternate stories at the end of scenes. Another interesting attempt is *Homicide: Second Shift*, an original online series based on the *Homicide* TV show. Although the interactivity is limited, this online series makes good use of graphics, animations, and page design to tell a story effectively on the Web. Another example is Warner Brothers multi-path movie channel, which shows 3-D animated movies where you control the action.

Low bandwidth is holding back the success of online interactive narrative. Video, audio, animations, and sophisticated interactivity simply take too long to download onto the user's computer screen. With the increased use of broadband access to the Web, however, this problem may soon disappear and make possible sophisticated online narrative.

This greater bandwidth is also going to affect what can happen with interactive television. After years of experiments with dedicated hard-wired systems, interactive television is finally emerging as a convergence of television and Web technologies. Major players such as Microsoft's WebTV, AOL, and @Home Network have launched efforts that allow you to watch the Web and television at the same time on your TV. The ultimate goal of these efforts is to let you interact with shows on television in a sophisticated way. Disney has already made a modest step forward in this direction with its *zoogdisney* Web site, which is built around a block of Disney Channel shows. Viewers can surf the Web site, play games, get information about the programs, but most importantly, they can participate in E-mail and chats about the zoog TV shows. Some of these E-mails are later shown on the television shows, usually in a black strip at the bottom of the TV screen. Matthew Costello, the writer of the *zoogdisney* site, said that the goal is to make the Web experience an extension of the TV world so that it feels to the user as if it is one world (Costello).

Steve Perlman, the founder of WebTV, had a similar vision when he said:

> The line between what we today think of as a video game and what we today think of as a TV show will blur. Some shows will have people from around the country and to some degree around the world, participating in stories and experiences together. (Maloney 109)

When this happens, I think the demands for interactive narratives, and thus the demand for the interactive narrative writers, will radically increase. The television audience is a much larger audience than the video game audience, and this television audience is oriented towards well-developed stories.

CLASSICAL LINEAR NARRATIVE ELEMENTS DEFINED

Although there are many different types of narrative, such as realist and modernist, successful interactive narratives have largely focused on classical narrative, the same type of narrative that dominates linear film and video. Because of this, interactive narrative shares many of the elements of narrative film and video. Since these are forms that most readers already have some familiarity with, I will first review the basics of classical linear narrative in film and TV before diving into the intricacies of interactive narrative.

CHARACTER

Classical linear narrative film and video are character driven. It is the character who grabs our attention and whose situation we are drawn into. Most successful films and videos today clearly define their characters early in the piece: Who are the characters? Where are they from? What do they want or need, and why do they want it? What the character wants usually provides the action story of the film or video; why they want it provides the motivation for the actions and the underlying emotional story.

As an example, the pilot for the *Murphy Brown* television series, one of the hit shows of the 1990s, establishes her character as a hard-driven, hard-headed, Motown-loving, liberal, successful TV reporter and a recovering alcoholic who is just returning from the Betty Ford Clinic. We learn all this information about Murphy through the items in her office, her colleagues' comments, her clothes, and her interactions with others. What Murphy wants (her action need) is to get an interview with the man who may have had an affair with the vice president of the United States. Why Murphy wants this interview is to prove that she is still a top reporter—her emotional need. If we are going to care about the story, it is important that we identify with this character and her needs. Identification can be achieved in a number of ways, including casting an appealing actor, creating sympathy for an underdog, and having the character do positive things. The best way to achieve identification, however, is to develop the character so that the audience clearly understands the character's needs.

STRUCTURE

Once the character's needs are established, then the writer can begin to structure the script. The key elements of classical narrative structure are exposition, conflict, climax, and resolution. Figure 18–1 lays out the basic structure of the vast majority of film and TV shows produced today.

Exposition or Setup

The beginning of the story must set up the lead character, the setting, and what the character wants—the goal to be achieved or the problem to be solved. Current films and videos tend to limit pure expositional sequences at the beginning and jump right into the story, integrating the story with the exposition. Some pieces open with an action scene and then slow down the pace in the next scene for exposition. However it is done, near the beginning of a script, the audience must learn who the character is, where he or she is, and what he or she wants.

Conflict

Once the writer knows the lead character and his or her goal, then he or she can start the character on the way to achieving that goal. Of course, if the character achieves the goal in the first scene, it will be a very short story. To avoid this happening, the writer introduces conflicts or obstacles. There are three basic types of conflict:

1. Person versus person.
2. Person versus the environment.
3. Person versus self.

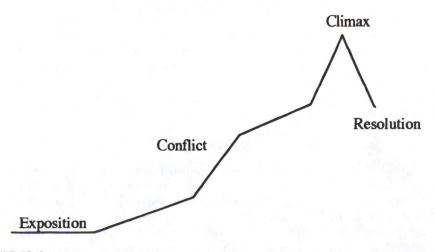

FIGURE 18–1

Classical linear structure.

In the *Murphy Brown* example, the people who oppose her goal of getting an honest interview with the vice president's lover include Murphy's boss, her colleagues, and the interview subject himself. The environmental obstacles include the frantic pace of the newsroom and the high pressure of the TV ratings game. Action stories are built around environmental obstacles where the hero has to climb mountains, ford rivers, and battle the elements. The last type of conflict, person versus self, is a way of adding considerable depth to a piece. In the case of Murphy, she has inner doubts as to whether she is still the hot reporter she was before dealing with her alcoholism.

A number of writing critics, particularly Syd Field in *Screenplay*, point to a key plot point or event in the exposition that shoves the character out of the exposition and into the conflict. In Murphy's case, it is when her boss sets up a meeting with the potential interviewee. Once the conflicts begin, then each conflict or obstacle should be more challenging than the last obstacle so that the story rises in intensity.

Climax

Finally the story nears the peak of intensity, and a final event jacks it up to the climax, which is where the character either achieves the goal or not. In Murphy's case, the climax takes place at the actual interview in the TV studio. Murphy asks the questions she wants and gets the honest interview, achieving her action goal and her emotional goal: to prove to herself that she still has it as a reporter.

Resolution

The resolution wraps up the story after the climax. The resolution of *Murphy Brown* involves a talk with her boss and, more importantly, a talk with her painter back at her house, where we learn that she achieved her emotional goal and is once again confident of her skills as a reporter. In most stories, the character changes or travels a character arc, as did Murphy; she changed from being unsure about her abilities as a reporter at the beginning to having renewed confidence at the end.

SCENES AND SEQUENCES

A narrative is comprised of individual scenes and sequences. A scene is an action that takes place in one location. A sequence is a series of scenes built around one concept or event. In a tightly structured script, each scene has a mini-goal or plot point that sets up and leads us into the next scene, eventually building the sequence. Some scenes and most sequences have a beginning, middle, and end, much like the overall story.

JEOPARDY

The characters' success or failure in achieving their goals has to have serious consequences for them. It is easy for the writer to set up jeopardy if it is a life-and-death situation, such as escaping a murderer or blowing up a death star. It is harder to create this sense of importance with more mundane events. This is accomplished through properly developing the character. As in the Murphy Brown example, we care about her getting the interview because her emotional need for getting the interview is great. In a well-written script, if something is important to the character, it will be important to the audience.

POINT OF VIEW

Point of view defines from whose perspective the story is told. The most common point of view or POV is third person or omniscient (all-knowing). In this case the audience is a fly on the wall and can flit from one location to another, seeing events from many characters' points of view or from the point of view of the writer of the script.

The other major type of point of view is first person or subjective point of view. In this case, the entire story is told from one character's perspective. The audience sees everything through his or her eyes. The audience can experience only what the character experiences. Used exclusively, this type of point of view has numerous practical problems. The primary one is that we never get to see the lead character's expressions except in the mirror. Because of this, stories that are told in subjective point-of-view narrative are sometimes shot in third-person point of view in terms of the camera. This allows us to see the lead character. Voice-over narration is often used with subjective point of view.

PACE

Pace is the audience's experience of how quickly the events of the narrative seem to move. Many short sequences, scenes, and bits of dialogue tend to make the pace move quickly; longer elements slow it down. Numerous fast-moving events in a scene also quicken pace. Writers tend to accelerate pace near a climax and slow it down for expositional and romantic scenes. A built-in time limit accelerates pace and increases jeopardy by requiring the protagonist to accomplish his or her task in a certain time frame. For example, Murphy Brown had to decide what to do before the live broadcast of the interview that night.

CONCLUSION

This chapter has only scratched the surface of a complex topic, but it should be an adequate foundation for the multimedia narrative discussion that follows. A key issue we will be looking at is how the writing of multimedia narrative differs from writing linear narrative.

REFERENCES

Bunn, Austin and J.C. Herz. "The Frontiers of Game Design." CNET Gamecenter. May 12, 1999. http://www.gamecenter.com/Features/Exclusives/Frontiers/ss03.html.

Conners, Aaron. Telephone interviews with the author. December 1995, October 1999.

Costello, Matthew. Phone interview with the author. July 1999.

Field, Syd. *Screenplay*. New York: Dell Publishing, 1982.

Fitch, Stephan. "Cinema Server = s/t (story over time)." Master's thesis, Massachusetts Institute of Technology, 1993.

Garrand, Timothy. "Scripting Narrative for Interactive Multimedia." *Journal of Film and Video 49* (Spring–Summer 1997).

Gilligan, Shannon. Telephone interview with the author. July 1994.

Halliday, Mark. "Digital Cinema an Environment for Multi-threaded Stories." Master's thesis, Massachusetts Institute of Technology, 1993.

Homicide "Second Shift." Original Online Series. http://www.nbc.com/homicide/.

Jensen, Jane. Telephone interview with the author. July 1994.

Maloney, Janice. "Perlmania." *Wired* 7.07. (July 1999):102–109.

Nancy Drew Web Site. http://www.NancyDrew.com Mystery.net. Web site.
    http://www.mysterynet.com/.

O'Meara, Maria. Interviews with the author. Brookline, MA, July 1994, October 1995,
    December 1995.

O'Meara, Maria. Letter to the author. June 1994.

Platt, Charles. "Interactive Entertainment: Who Writes It? Who Reads It? Who Needs It?"
    Wired 3 (September 1995): 145–197.

Pousette, Lena Marie. Telephone interview with the author. December 1995.

Riordan, David. Telephone interviews with the author. June 1994, October 1995,
    December 1995.

Sherman, Tony. Telephone interviews with the author. July 1994, September 1995.

Stalter, Katharine. "*Voyeur.* A Look into the Creative Process Behind the CD-I Game from
    POV Entertainment Group." *Film and Video* (April 1994): 64–120.

Warner Brothers Multi-Path Movie Channel. http://www.warnerbros.com/.

CHAPTER 19

THE ELEMENTS OF INTERACTIVE MULTIMEDIA NARRATIVE

Portions of this chapter originally appeared in the *Journal of Film and Video*.

CHAPTER OVERVIEW

The major elements of interactive narrative that must be understood by the writer are:

- The role of the player
- Character development
- Structure
- Pace
- Time
- Genres

LINEAR VERSUS INTERACTIVE NARRATIVE

The key difference between linear narrative and interactive narrative is interactivity. Amy Bruckman of the MIT Media Lab writes, "In making a story nonlinear, the story teller relinquishes the power to control the flow of information to the viewer . . . A balance must be struck between giving the viewer freedom and maintaining narrative coherence" (Bruckman 12). Finding this balance—giving the player some control over the narrative, while allowing the writer to perform the necessary functions of the classical storyteller, including establishing characters and an engaging story structure—is the key challenge for the writer of interactive narrative.

CHARACTER AND THE ROLE OF THE PLAYER

Character is as important in an interactive piece as in a linear piece, but characterization is vastly more complex because of the role of the player. Lena Maria Pousette, the writer of *Voyeur*, identified the key questions the writer must begin with: "what is the [game's] objective? who is the player? And what does the player get to do?" (Willis 9). In an interactive piece, the player expects to be one of the characters in the story, or at least to have significant control over the characters.

PLAYER CONTROL

The degree of the player's control over the characters is one of the first decisions in writing a program. The basic types of control the player is allowed are choice of scenes, the character's actions, or all the character's behavior.

Scenes

In this approach, the player can decide which path of the story the characters will choose, but once launched on that path, the characters function independently until the next branching point. *Boy Scout Patrol Theater*, an interactive narrative at the National Boy Scout museum, is a good example. The Boy Scouts in the story must decide whether to search the farm, the neighborhood, or the school. Once the player makes the choice to search the school, the characters function on their own until the next interactive point. The characters are usually seen in third person. See the following script sample.

BOY SCOUT PATROL THEATER

SCENE 2—TROOP HQ

2-1. WS GROUP

                        ALEX
    Okay. We all know why we're here.

CU GRAPHIC HIGHLIGHTING THE THREE AREAS BRENDAN IS
TALKING ABOUT: ONE IS THE SCHOOL, TWO IS THE FARM,
THREE IS THE NEIGHBORHOOD.

                        BRENDAN
    Here's a map of the area we're covering. Let's
    divide it up into parts and cover each one. This
    is where she was last seen—the school. Here's
    where she lives. Between the two is the old Wilson
    Farm.

WHICH PART DO YOU WANT TO SEARCH? [IF A. THE SCHOOL]

SCENE 2A
2A-1. CU ALEX

© 1988 National Scouting Museum of the Boy Scouts of America. Note: See the Boy Scout Patrol area of the "Chapters" section of the *Writing for Multimedia and the Web* CD-ROM for the full script.

                             ALEX
   Chas and Don, you guys go see if she's not still
   hanging around the school.

M-1.
TRANSITION MONTAGE TO SCHOOL
1. POV HALLWAY
2. POV SCIENCE ROOM
3. POV POOL
4. POV STAIRS

SCENE 3—THE SCHOOL
3-1. 2 SHOT BOYS enter a classroom.

Actions

In some programs, the player can control the actions of the characters. *Kings Quest VII: The Princeless Bride* functions this way. The player sees the Princess and her mother in third person. If the player clicks on another person in the scene, the Princess will talk to the new character, but the player has no control over what the characters say. If the viewer moves the on-screen arrow to the edge of the screen, the Princess or her mother will walk in that direction. The scene tends to be seen in long or medium shots so that the player can direct the action.

All Behavior

This is the highest degree of interactivity. In this mode, the player chooses what the character does and says. In *Dust: A Tale of the Wired West* (Chapter 24), the interactivity is almost always done in first person, which allows the player to become the character. In the shot from *Dust* shown in Figure 19–1, the player is talking to a gambler and must respond by choosing one of the tough guy lines on the bottom of the screen.

Combinations

Few programs function purely in one of the approaches above. Some programs, such as *Burn: Cycle*, a futuristic adventure game, effectively combine approaches. This program appears to be cinematic. Sometimes the character functions on his own, and at other times the player controls the hero's actions, such as where he will run and whom he will shoot. *King's Quest: Mask of Eternity* presents most of the game from a third-person perspective, but you can switch to a first-person perspective at any time by holding down the right mouse button.

Variable Control

In some programs, players can decide on how much control they want. In *Voyeur* the player watches the events in the mansion across the street, sees the news on television, and receives telephone calls. If the player just sits and watches, the corrupt politician is the protagonist of the story. If the player decides to try to stop the corrupt politician, the player can have a major effect on the plot.

IMPACT OF PLAYER OPTIONS

The degree of player control, player point of view, and the type of character played in a first-person point-of-view story all have significant impact on the story.

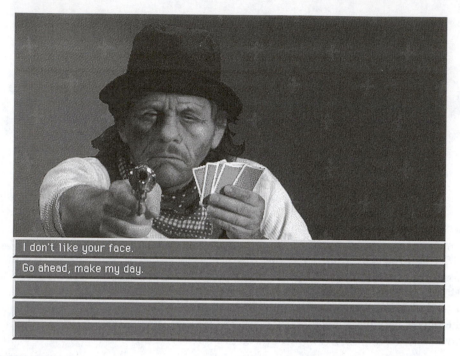

I don't like your face.

Go ahead, make my day.

FIGURE 19–1

Player controlling all behavior.
© 1995 CyberFlix Inc.

Player as Protagonist

To maximize player interactivity and immersion in the story, the best option is to allow the player to become the protagonist of the story by controlling all the character's behavior and seeing the action in first-person point of view. There are, however, drawbacks to this approach. One is that it is difficult to portray certain types of action in first-person point of view. For example, how do you show someone kissing the protagonist? The player also never gets to see the protagonist's expressions and actions, which are the main ways that character is revealed. Because of this, first-person point-of-view interactive stories tend to rely heavily on dialogue. Gender issues are also raised with first-person point-of-view interactive. Is the character male or female? If the character is assigned one gender, as in *Dust*, are there character identification problems for the player? If no gender is assigned, how do the other characters address the player/protagonist?

If the player is the protagonist, it is also difficult for the writer to develop him or her as a complex character. If the writer does develop the protagonist, as in the case of Tex Murphy in *The Pandora Directive*, you/the player are left with "a fictitious version of yourself who isn't like you at all and who does things you have never done in a world you have never visited" (Platt 147). The writer will also have to hope that the goal of the protagonist is something the player can identify with.

The alternative approach for the protagonist, as practiced in *Dust*, is to have a very general character, in this case, the Stranger. The player knows nothing about him, and so can perhaps more comfortably become him. But will the player be able to understand and empathize with the action and emotional needs of this sketchily drawn character?

Player Determining the Character

A way around the quandary of either defining a character that the player cannot fit into or leaving the character vague is to give the player a role in determining the character. Both *Dust* and *The Pandora Directive* do this to some degree. In both cases, depending on what dialogue the player chooses for the protagonist, he becomes nasty or nice. His change in behavior affects how the story progresses.

Some programs give the player even more power to create the characters. In *Caesar's World of Boxing*, the player gets to "interview" potential managers and trainers and choose one. The player also can define the physical appearance and fighting style of the boxers by entering information and adjusting the sliders on a game panel. This approach may not work for every story, but making the player an active part of the characterization process allows for character development while maintaining the interactivity of the narrative.

Player as Minor Character

Instead of being a major character, the player can be a minor character, as in *Voyeur*. The player may not seem so central to the action, but the advantage is that the portrayal of the minor character is not as crucial. If the minor character is only sketchily drawn, it will not have as much of an impact on the story as a poorly developed main character. It is also much easier to show the main action of the story in third person. For certain types of training and education programs, this type of third-person portrayal is essential. *A la rencontre de Philippe* is an interactive language program in which the player takes on the role of helping Parisian friends find an apartment. This allows the player to watch the native speakers interact in French, which was one of the goals of the program and which would have been more difficult if the player was a first-person protagonist.

CHARACTER SETUP AND RELATIONSHIPS

The player is only one of the characters in a program. Many others must be set up, but the demands of the interactive narrative do not make it easy to bring them to life. Space is always at a premium, scenes tend to be short, and character setup tends not to be interactive and thus is kept to a minimum.

An interactive writer needs to be able to introduce the characters quickly and simply. And once the characters are established, the writer also has to keep track of the different relationships of all the characters in all the possible versions of the story. Some writers develop a character matrix, so that they clearly know how all the characters fit together. (See the *Voyeur* character chart near the end of Chapter 22 for an example of a matrix.)

ARCHITECTURE: STRUCTURE AND NAVIGATION

Just as in a linear piece, in an interactive narrative, once the character and his or her goal are established, then the basic structure of the story needs to be developed. In interactive writing, however, this is far more complex than the simple linear structure illustrated in Figure 18–1 in the previous chapter, because in an interactive narrative, the writer must also consider navigation between all the elements of the structure.

Will Wright, the designer of *SimCity*, explains the difference between linear and interactive narrative well:

> When I watch Indiana Jones escaping from the Temple of Doom (in the movie of the same name), it's not what happens to him that I find interesting; it's what might have happened had he slipped in front of the boulder. Dozens of potential failure states are compressed into a few seconds of action and transmitted to my brain with amazing efficiency.
>
> Game players are given the ability to explore a space of possibilities—the phase space—and this is the real strength of the medium. It's sort of like the difference between a roller coaster and a car. The coaster is on a fixed track. It's a very exciting track, but it's always the same. I can add branches to the track, but it can still be viewed as a finite amount of track. If I put someone in a car, however, they can go almost anywhere. Since I can't simulate the whole world in my games, I have to put up barriers and limit where they can go in the car. (Bunn and Herz)

These barriers and the road he describes are essentially the structure of interactive narrative. How the user can move between roads is the navigation. The most common interactive narrative structures are described below:

LINEAR STRUCTURE

Defined: Strictly speaking, this is not an interactive structure but it is often used in interactive projects. Linear structure has no branching choices for the user.

Use: Linear structure is frequently used in narrative multimedia to set up the story. All of the narratives profiled in this book open with linear sequences before user interaction is possible. Linear video is also played during an interactive piece for additional background and to tie interactive scenes together.

LINEAR STRUCTURE WITH SCENE BRANCHING

Defined: This structure allows the user to choose alternative scenes, but after these alternative scenes are played out, the user is always routed back to the same main story line.

Use: This is a common structure in training and educational narratives. In *Boy Scout Patrol Theater* the basic structure is a linear story about trying to find a lost girl. At various decision points, however, the players get to make a choice, such as choosing to search the farm, the school, or the neighborhood. If they choose the farm, then they detour momentarily from the main story and search the farm, but eventually return to the main story. (See Figure 19–2.)

HIERARCHICAL BRANCHING

Defined: This architecture involves taking the story in a completely different direction based on the viewer's choice at a preset decision point.

Use-Complete Story: Using hierarchical branching to take the complete story into different directions has limited options. For example, as illustrated in Figure 19–3, the character comes to a point where she can choose one of three options: marry Alan, marry Bob, or marry Carl. After that choice is played out, then the character can

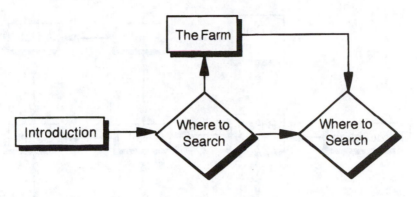

FIGURE 19–2

Linear structure with scene branching in *Patrol Theater*.

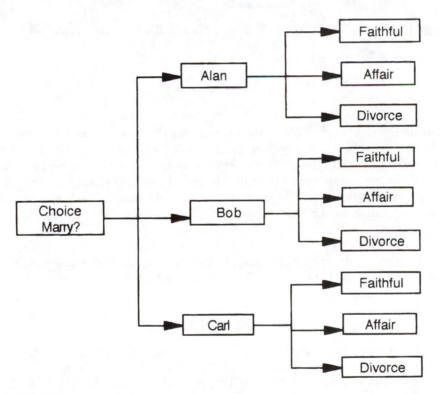

FIGURE 19–3

Hierarchical branching explosion.

choose to be faithful, have an affair, or get divorced. The problem here is obvious: The number of choices increase exponentially. Adding one more set of choices to this chart would mean an additional 27 scenes, the next level would be 81 additional scenes, and the one after that 243 scenes! This is clearly too much material for a writer to present or a viewer to access.

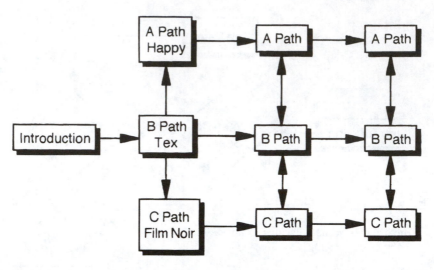

FIGURE 19-4

Parallel path stories in *The Pandora Directive.*

Use-Endings: Although it is rare for an entire story to be completed with hierarchical branching, it is commonly used for the ending of programs. This device gives the viewer a feeling of greater control over the narrative, and branching explosion is obviously limited because the story ends. The end of *The 11th Hour*, where the viewer must choose to save one of three women, is a good example. Each woman equals a different ending to the story. The wrong choice is oblivion; the right choice is bliss.

Use-Dialogue: This type of branching is also used in interactive dialogue. See the flowchart, Figure 23–1, in Chapter 23, "Parallel Stories Narrative Case Study: *The Pandora Directive.*"

PARALLEL PATH STORIES

Defined: With parallel structure, several versions of the same story play parallel to each other. Depending on choices that the player makes in the story, he or she can move from one path to another. This is a way to give the player an option of multiple paths in a story without the branching explosion of hierarchical branching.

Use: *The Pandora Directive* (Figure 19–4) uses parallel path stories. After a linear introduction, the player enters an interactive scene. Depending on the choices that he or she makes, the player can move up to: the A path, which is a Hollywood-type version of the story where the hero wins true love; the C path, a bleak, film noir experience of the story where everything goes wrong; or the B path, which is a middle ground. Each new interactive scene gives the player options to move back and forth between paths depending on the choices they make.

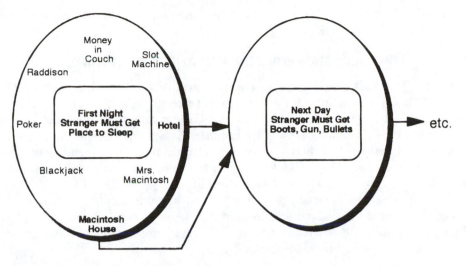

FIGURE 19-5

String of pearls architecture in *Dust: A Tale of the Wired West.*

STRING OF PEARLS ARCHITECTURE

Defined: This approach moves away from simple branching. A string of pearls architecture is a linked series of worlds structures connected by plot points or tasks that the player must accomplish to move forward in the narrative. As defined earlier, the worlds approach lets the user explore a location. By itself, a worlds structure cannot form a coherent narrative, but combined with other forms it can.

Use: *Dust: A Tale of the Wired West* uses the string of pearls approach. When the player/Stranger first comes to town in the middle of the night, he is free to roam the town of Diamondback for as long as he wants. There are poker games to be played, hookers to talk to, and mysterious buildings to explore. This is a clear worlds structure—interesting, but by itself there is no story.

To move to the next day and advance the narrative, the player/Stranger must find a place to sleep. He can either stay at the hotel or get one of the town's citizens to take him in. There are a number of ways to accomplish this goal. To stay at the hotel, he needs money. He can get cash at the saloon if he is lucky at blackjack, poker, or the slot machine. If he is nosy, he might also find the four bucks that somebody lost in the hotel couch. But when he does get the money, the hotel owner says there are no vacancies. To get a room, it helps to meet Raddison, another character who lives there and who will introduce the Stranger (the player) to the owner. An alternative to the hotel is to get a citizen to take the player/Stranger home. To accomplish this, the player needs to sweet-talk the abrasive Mrs. Macintosh.

The player can perform all of these actions in any order desired, but eventually he or she has to find the right combination of actions to get a place to sleep and thus exit from the first night of the story and begin the next day or pearl on the string. In the second pearl, the next day's action, the player must get boots, guns, and bullets before moving on to the third pearl. (See Figure 19–5.) All of the player's accomplishments move the story forward to the final shootout and to solving the mystery in one of six possible endings.

VARIABLE STATE ENVIRONMENT AND TYPES OF LINKS

Defined: The most sophisticated interactive narratives today, which include *Dust* and *The Pandora Directive*, have moved beyond direct links and simple branching to something that Dave Riordan, the designer of *Voyeur*, calls a variable state environment. With the help of software and sophisticated design that responds in a sensitive way to the player's actions, there are multiple outcomes to scenes, depending on where the player has been and to whom he or she has talked. In short, the environment responds to the player, much as it does in real life.

A variable state environment can take into account hundreds of actions as opposed to just the A or B choices in branching. And as each interaction is played differently, it will yield different responses. Different combinations of different interactions will also yield different responses.

Use: In *The Pandora Directive*, if you as the player are tactless with your girlfriend, you will get into a fight. This causes you to get drunk, and because you are drunk, you are unable to save a nightclub singer's life. In *Dust: A Tale of the Wired West*, if you are rude to the mayor, his daughter will like you and later help you solve the mystery. These types of convoluted reactions to the player's actions are far more like real life than the direct reaction to a player's choices in the earlier generation of video games.

EXPOSITION OR SETUP

Exposition is another issue that presents special challenges for the interactive writer. "If you spend time introducing the characters, the viewer is not being asked to do anything. In interactive that is death. Instead you need to discover the back story more as you go" (Riordan).

Tony Sherman said that one reason *Dracula Unleashed* works is that it has a built-in back story. Most people already know the basic story and characters of the original Dracula, and his production could build on that.

If a writer is not dealing with a known story, however, solving exposition problems can be a bit more complex. In the detective story *Under a Killing Moon*, Aaron Conners uses a number of expositional devices that are already established in this genre, but a key difference is that he gives his player the option of choosing them or not. A major device he uses is the voice-over. By clicking the mouse, a player can get the detective's thoughts on other characters, situations, and even objects. Players can also get background through video flashbacks. For example, as a result of clicking on the portrait of the detective's ex-wife, a short scene appears explaining her relationship with the detective.

SETS AND PROPS AS EXPOSITIONAL DEVICES

In interactive narrative, special attention is also paid to sets and props to give exposition. *Voyeur* makes extensive use of these. They can be subtle props, such as a gun in a suitcase, or more overt props, such as a letter the player is allowed to read, or even active props, such as a television set that gives background information on the characters. The use of props in interactive multimedia differs from their use in linear video because in multimedia, the player gets to choose which props to examine, has far more props to choose from, and can do things that would be impossible in linear, such as move closer to a letter to read it.

GUARANTEEING THAT ESSENTIAL EXPOSITION IS SEEN

The danger of players choosing what exposition they'll examine is that it is difficult to guarantee that essential exposition will be seen. One solution is to provide exciting linear exposition scenes for the first viewing that can be skipped on later plays of the game. Another approach is to separate the back story from the multimedia program. In *Gabriel Knight*, exposition is presented in a comic book that comes with the game. *Starship Titanic* includes an in-flight magazine. In other productions, it is the function of the design to lure the player into choosing the essential exposition, often with clever interactive devices.

DEMONSTRATING HOW THE PROGRAM WORKS

Players must be told how to interact with a program. What can they do? How do they move? Can they pick things up? How does the interactive dialogue work? The best programs integrate this information into the exposition and do not make the users read vast amounts of instructions before they can play.

One way to do this is to set up a simple situation at the beginning of the program that shows how the game works. For example, in *Dust*, the player is confronted with a nasty dog as soon as he or she enters the town. To get by this dog, the player must pick up objects, talk to characters, access help, and move about. A less integrated approach is to have a tutorial that plays a scene for the user and shows what to do.

PLOT POINTS

Plot points or beats are story information that moves the plot forward. For example, in *Voyeur*, a key plot point is that Zack is angry at his father because his father fired him from an important research project. In an interactive story, making essential plot points is as difficult as presenting exposition. Because the user can choose which scenes to view, there is no guarantee that the user will choose a specific scene with a certain key plot point.

One solution to this problem is "to put two or three beats in a scene" (Pousette). This way if the user selects a scene, multiple plot points will be established. Another approach is to have the same information appear in a number of different scenes. The difficulty here is that the information can't be presented in exactly the same way or players will get bored if they select several of these scenes. The solution is to feed the essential information into multiple scenes but to do it differently each time.

In a narrative that includes multiple story variations, such as *Voyeur* or *The Pandora Directive*, establishing plot points is even more complex than setting up exposition. Often much of the exposition will be the same for all possible stories. For example, in *Voyeur*, the back story on the corrupt politician and his desire to be president does not change from story to story. Plot points are, however, usually different in each story variation. This means that essential plot points have to be established for each story. It also means that scenes that are common to all variations cannot include plot points that contradict the plot in a specific story variation. Some writers use charts of plot points or beats to keep all of these elements clear. (See the end of Chapter 22, "Cinematic Narrative Case Study: *Voyeur*" for an example.)

SCENES

As the *Voyeur* and *The Pandora Directive* examples above suggest, strong scene writing is important to the interactive writer. Writer Maria O'Meara believes that "crafting a scene well is the most valuable technique of the interactive writer. Every experience in an interactive ought to be a tiny story or scene. Even if it's short, it still needs to have a beginning, middle, and end" (O'Meara letter). Pam Beason of Microsoft agrees: "Every scene must contain a complete thought. An idea cannot be split over two scenes" (Beason). Jane Jensen, writer-designer of the *Gabriel Knight* series, says other characteristics of the interactive scene are that "scenes are smaller and there are vastly greater amounts of them. You have to think nonlinearly. As you approach a given location, think what will occur there" (Jensen).

The interactive writer, in other words, must write vertically as well as horizontally. He or she cannot be concerned only with what scene follows another. The writer also has to be aware of what other scenes in other possible stories might be connected to this one. Some interactive writers script ten or fifteen related scenes at the same time in order to keep tabs on all the connections. And rewriting can be ghastly. Change one element in one of fifteen connected scenes, and all the other scenes need to be rewritten.

Stephan Fitch sums it up: "Interactive writing is more like 3-D writing. The writer has to see the layers and move through the layers of the script, keeping track of parallel actions in a scene" (quoted in Willis 8).

PACE AND TIME

Interactive multimedia has no set running time. It depends on how the player plays the game. The challenge here for the writer is to create a consistent sense of time in the piece when a player might spend twenty minutes in a scene or might skip it altogether. Because time is also an important factor in pace, how does the writer deal with the way this variability of time affects pacing?

PLAYER CREATES THE PACE

Gabriel Knight's Jane Jensen says that there is no way to have the kind of pacing in interactive narrative that there is in linear, in which a writer can carefully create and sequence a number of scenes to create a faster or slower pace. In interactive narrative, the player creates the pace. For example, a player goes into a haunted house and has to find a way out. The writer's job is to make sure that the scenes are dramatic in themselves and that the player is surprised when things happen. The player may think a certain room is safe from the last time he or she played, but this time it might contain a monster (Jensen). How the player interacts with this environment creates the pace of the sequence, but that interaction is affected by the kinds of elements the writer-designer gives the player to interact with.

MULTIMEDIA PACE = MINISERIES PACE

The combined running times of multiple plays of an interactive movie is much longer than the running time of a two-hour feature film. An interactive movie can be thought of more like a miniseries or a serial. For example, the writer can deal with much of the exposition the first time the game is played, which allows the pace to be increased in later plays.

MANIPULATING TIME TO AFFECT PACE

Other writers and designers have actively manipulated time to affect the pace of the story. In Tony Sherman's *Dracula Unleashed*, the player has four days to solve the crime. A clock in the game keeps track of the time. In the real time of playing the game, going to a library and talking to someone may only take thirty seconds, but in game time the player may be deducted an hour. And while he or she is at one location, other scenes happen whether the player sees them or not, just as they would in real life. If the player is knocked out, he or she will miss several scenes and be docked eighty minutes on the clock. Sherman feels that although this time manipulation can add a sense of urgency to the game, the players do set pace. The story material stays the same; it is how it is played that affects the overall pacing.

Dave Riordan designed a similar use of time in *Voyeur*. Players have a weekend to solve or prevent the crime. To do this, they can choose which room to explore in the politician's mansion, but while in one room, events continue to happen in other rooms, unseen by the player.

An even more interesting use of time is in Riordan's *Thunder in Paradise*. In this program, the time spent in one scene affects what happens in later scenes. For example, in one scene the heroes have to battle the villains surrounding an island to save the heroine who is held there. If the heroes take a long time to defeat these villains, the other villains on the island itself have more time to prepare for them, and the heroes' difficulties are increased when they finally land. This use of time is an important step in making games reflect how time is experienced in real life. It can also give the designer more control over pacing. For example, if the player spends a long time on one scene, the next scene could automatically be altered to increase the pace of the sequence.

DIALOGUE AND OTHER SOUND

One of the difficulties of characterization in interactive media is the limited dialogue that is allowed because many scenes are less than a minute, and it usually takes longer to develop a dialogue scene. Shannon Gilligan, the writer of *Who Killed Sam Rupert?* and several other titles in the *Who Killed . . .* series, compares dialogue writing in interactive media to "writing a symphony of snippets." She claims that it is how the writer relates these snippets together through the design that makes a successful sequence (Gilligan).

The potential use of other sounds, particularly nonsynchronous sounds, is much greater than that of dialogue. Sound takes much less storage space than video on a disc, and less time to download from a Web site. To take advantage of this, *Voyeur* has about thirty audio-only scenes that the voyeur can eavesdrop on. *Under a Killing Moon* uses the tradition of the ironic voice-over in the detective story and includes over five hours of voice-over that gives the player information about characters, objects, and situations.

NARRATIVE MULTIMEDIA GENRES

Currently, action adventures and mysteries dominate interactive narrative. *Where in the World Is Carmen Sandiego?*, perhaps the most popular narrative multimedia educational series, is a mystery. The online narratives on the Mystery.net Web site are obviously mysteries. *Half-Life*, one of the biggest action game hits of recent years, owes much of its success to the inclusion of an adventure story line—the hero has to fight his way out of a doomed research facility. The appeal of the mystery and adventure story is clearly that they are strongly goal oriented. The player has something to aim for, obstacles are easy to establish, and jeopardy is built into the genre.

Are other genres also possible? *Caesar's World of Boxing* explores the boxing story. Much of the time in this program is spent preparing the boxer for the final challenge. Other genres, such as the caper film, also follow this character preparation approach and might be worth exploring. Jane Jensen and Maria O'Meara think romance would be a possibility if the writer could find something to drive the story forward (O'Meara; Jensen). Tony Sherman, however, cautions that it will be difficult to expand interactive genres unless the audience changes (Sherman). The primary audience for video games is young males. At present, the video game player makes up the bulk of the audience for the interactive narrative. They are not likely to view a romance program. The larger audience base of broadband Web and interactive TV might make other options possible.

REFERENCES

Beason, Pam. Telephone interview with the author. July 1994.

Bruckman, Amy. "The Combinatorics of Storytelling: Mystery Train Interactive." MIT Media Lab, April 1990.

Bunn, Austin and J.C. Herz. "The Frontiers of Game Design." CNET Gamecenter. http://www.gamecenter.com/Features/Exclusives/Frontiers/?st.gc.fd.bb5.

Conners, Aaron. Telephone interviews with the author. July 1994, August 1995, December 1995.

Fitch, Stephan. "Cinema Server = s/t (story over time)." Master's thesis, Massachusetts Institute of Technology, 1993.

Gilligan, Shannon. Telephone interview with the author. July 1994.

Jensen, Jane. Telephone interview with the author. July 1994.

Mystery.net Web site. http://www.mysterynet.com/.

O'Meara, Maria. Interviews with the author. Brookline, MA, July 1994, October 1995, December 1995.

O'Meara, Maria. Letter to the author. June 1994.

Platt, Charles. "Interactive Entertainment: Who Writes It? Who Reads It? Who Needs It?" *Wired 3* (September 1995): 145–195.

Pousette, Lena Marie. Telephone interview with the author. December 1995.

Riordan, David. Telephone interviews with the author. June 1994, October 1995, December 1995.

Sherman, Tony. Telephone interviews with the author. July 1994, September 1995.

Willis, Holly. "Let the Games Begin." *Hollywood Reporter* (October 1993): S-1-S-32.

C H A P T E R   2 0

INTRODUCTION TO NARRATIVE MULTIMEDIA CASE STUDIES

As discussed in the previous chapter, the golden age of the interactive narrative adventure game was in the mid-1990s. In the video game industry, action games currently dominate with relatively few sophisticated interactive narratives being produced. The Web and interactive television have great promise as media for interactive narrative, but narratives in these media are still in their formative stages. For these reasons, I have primarily used classic interactive narratives for the case studies in this book. These games demonstrate well the variety of different narrative techniques that can be used successfully. The major difference between these games and most current games has more to do with production than writing. Current games tend to be produced as 3-D animations similar to *Dust* in Chapter 24 rather than to the live-action video that is used in several of the case studies in the book.

These programs are examined in the following chapters:

- *The 11th Hour: The Sequel to The 7th Guest*, a puzzle-based, psychological horror game on CD-ROM.
- *Voyeur*, a political thriller on CD-ROM.
- *Dust: A Tale of the Wired West*, a Western on CD-ROM.
- *The Pandora Directive*, the CD-ROM sequel to the sci-fi, detective mystery, *Under a Killing Moon*.

An understanding of how these writers dealt with narrative issues will provide the insight to deal with similar issues when they arise in your work. Each case study answers the following questions:

- Program Description and Background. Is the program a typical example of its genre or is it unusual? Who commissioned, developed, and wrote the program? What was the preproduction process?
- Goals. What were the writers and designers' goals in creating this project? What information or experience were they trying to communicate?
- Challenges. Which goals were particularly difficult to achieve? What approaches were successful in achieving these goals and which were discarded?

- Response to the Project. Did the program achieve its goals? Was it a critical and/or commercial success?

The case studies are documented with script examples, screen shots, and flow-charts. Additional script samples and other material, including color screen shots and working demos, are available for many of the programs in the "Chapters" section of the *Writing for Multimedia and the Web* CD-ROM.

HOW TO GET COPIES OF THE CD-ROMS

Computer games are often released to major stores for a short period of time. To obtain some of the games discussed in this section of the book, you may need to go to online gaming stores and/or buy used games.

Two possibilities are:

- Interact CD-ROM Store

    http://www.interacted.com
- CDROM Softward.com

    http://www.cdromsoftware.com

You can also try searching the Web using the keywords: "computer games," "used," "sale."

C H A P T E R 2 1

PUZZLE-BASED GAME CASE STUDY: *THE 11TH HOUR: THE SEQUEL TO THE 7TH GUEST*

Summary

Name of production: *The 11th Hour: The Sequel to The 7th Guest*
Writer: Story and screenplay by Matthew Costello, revisions by David Wheeler
Developer: Trilobyte, Inc.
Audience: Rated for teenagers (ages 13 and up)
Medium: 4 CD-ROMs, includes *The Making of The 11th Hour*
Presentation location: Home
Subject: Psychological horror story
Goal: Entertain
Architecture: Linear, string of pearls

The script samples and images used in this chapter are courtesy of Trilobyte Inc. © 1994 Trilobyte Inc.

PROGRAM DESCRIPTION AND BACKGROUND

The 11th Hour: The Sequel to The 7th Guest is a psychological horror video game. As stated in the title, it is the sequel to *The 7th Guest*, one of the most popular computer games ever created. *The 11th Hour* uses the same haunted house and many of the same characters as the first game, which was set in the 1920s. But the new game places the action in the present, where a series of mysterious murders and disappearances plagues the towns surrounding the house.

One of the people who disappears is Robin Morales, a successful TV producer. Carl Denning, her ex-lover and the star of her show, goes to the haunted house to find her. The player assumes the role of Denning, directing his search of the house. The point of view alternates between seeing Denning from a third-person point of view, as in a traditional movie, and seeing through Denning's eyes in first-person point of view. The player/Denning is helped in the search by a personal digital assistant

FIGURE 21-1

Foyer of the Stauf mansion.

(PDA), which mysteriously appears at his home. The PDA includes a video screen, VCR-type controls for rewind and playback, a keyboard, an electronic map of the house, and a help button.

This PDA game book plays segments of video about Morales' investigation of the haunted house. To earn these snippets of video, the player/Denning has to solve dozens of puzzles created by Henry Stauf, an evil toy-maker and master of the mansion. A successful player of the game gradually pieces together the video, which shows what happened to Morales. The program ends with a final deadly game between Denning and Stauf.

Examples of many of the game elements can be seen in the video *The Making of The 11th Hour*, which is included in the Chapter 21 area of the "Chapters" section of the *Writing for Multimedia and the Web* CD-ROM.

THE 11TH HOUR: THE SEQUEL TO THE 7TH GUEST AND THE COMPUTER GAME

Unlike some of the narratives described in later chapters, both *The 7th Guest* and *The 11th Hour* are puzzle-based games, which have a strong appeal to a major portion of the gaming audience. The puzzles include word puzzles, board games, and even artificial intelligence games. Most of the puzzles have a limited connection to the story.

Writer Matthew Costello said that what set *The 7th Guest* apart from other video games of this type was that it was one of the first games that actually tried to scare computer game players. *The 11th Hour* continues in this horror tradition, but moves from the Gothic horror of the first game to psychological horror.

PRODUCTION BACKGROUND

Matthew Costello wrote the story and script for *The 11th Hour*. This script was revised by the video director David Wheeler. The project was developed by Trilobyte Inc., whose head designers, Graeme Devine and Rob Landeros, had major input into the script, particularly how it would be used in the overall game. Trilobyte, once a major developer of computer games, has gone out of business. *The 11th Hour* was distributed by Virgin Games, Inc.

GOALS AND CHALLENGES WRITING *THE 11TH HOUR: THE SEQUEL TO THE 7TH GUEST*

The challenge in writing and designing *The 11th Hour* was to tell a compelling, interactive horror story without abandoning the puzzle-based game format that had been so successful in *The 7th Guest*. The developers wanted the story to be interactive, but they did not want to hand over complete control of the story to the user. As designer Graeme Devine said in an interview:

> I've learned, perhaps most of all, that I want to be, need to be, a storyteller, and that means that I want it to be my story—have my start, my middle, my end—rather than allow the stories to be so interactive that there's a zillion endings, a billion middles, and a hundred beginnings. (Demaria 284)

MEETING THE CHALLENGE

THE INTERACTIVE STORY, THE PDA GAME BOOK, AND PUZZLES

The primary way the writers and designers met this challenge was through the use of the PDA game book. The story of Robin Morales' disappearance was originally written as a linear video, but instead of playing it as a linear video, the user can access only bits and pieces of it on the game book. These intriguing bits and pieces lead the user forward in the search for Morales. The player can also play back the video snippets and gradually assemble them into the complete story. The player eventually learns that the game book and its images are an attempt by Samantha Ford, an earlier victim of the house, to help Denning save Morales.

The player needs to understand what happened to Morales in order to make the right choice at the end of the game. This process is not unlike the traditional mystery in which the investigator gradually puts together the story of what happened by piecing together bits of information. (See The *Pandora Directive* case study in Chapter 23.) One difference here is that the game book actually delivers video images as opposed to just getting information about the past through dialogue.

The second major difference in *The 11th Hour* is that the video snippets are not discovered through carefully putting together the evidence and clues related to the event. Instead, the video is earned by solving puzzles in the Stauf Mansion that are unrelated to the Robin Morales story. Many of the puzzles involve a treasure hunt in which investigator Carl Denning must win games and interpret clues to find certain objects, such as a champagne bottle. When he finds that bottle and pops the cork, he is rewarded with a video scene.

Although nothing the player does will alter the Robin Morales story in the game book's video, the player does have the choice of where to explore in the house and which games to play and which games to skip. In order to nudge the narrative forward, however, not all puzzles and not all rooms are open to the player at one time. This is illustrated on the game book map, which indicates which rooms are open at a certain time and place in the game. What video the player can access is also limited by where the player is in the game.

Linear Narrative and Introduction of the PDA Game Book

The game book is introduced in the linear beginning of the story when a package arrives at the home of Carl Denning. Before the package arrives, Denning is watching a TV show that is discussing the disappearance of his producer and lover, Robin Morales.

```
INTRO-1 INT/DENNING'S COUNTRY HOME—AFTERNOON

A UPS truck is pulling away and a package is on the
doorstep. Denning crouches down and picks it up and
goes back inside. He returns to his chair and opens
the package, revealing a small, portable computer of
some kind. He switches it on, and a game flickers to
life on the machine . . . "Funhouse From Hell"—Cartoony
images of mayhem, monsters . . .

Slowly, the computer game changes to an image of Robin
looking frightened in the basement of an old house. She
speaks to him from the small screen.

                         ROBIN
     Carl . . . help me . . . please! . . . I can't get out . . .
     I . . .

The image of Robin fades away and the video screen
goes blank as if the game has shut itself off. Denning
shakes the box and clicks it on and off but it seems
to have died.

                         DENNING
     What is this!?

He sets the game computer on the arm of the chair,
gets to his feet, and begins to pace. The game starts
beeping. He grabs it and switches it on. An image of
the Stauf Mansion appears briefly and fades away and the
game shuts down again.

                         DENNING
     Damn!

Then the screen comes alive for another brief moment:
An image of Robin appears. She mouths the word "Help,"—
but there is no sound and the picture quickly fades.
Denning pulls on a leather windbreaker and stuffs the
game in his pocket as he crosses the room and leaves
in a rush.
```

The remainder of the introduction is also linear until Denning actually enters the Stauf Haunted House.

Interactive Narrative and the Puzzles

Once Denning enters the house, the remaining video has to be earned by solving puzzles and finding objects in a treasure hunt. These puzzles are justified narratively because the evil master of the house, Henry Stauf, is a toy-maker and game designer who likes to torture his guests with difficult and deadly puzzles.

One of the first puzzles occurs when Denning enters the house. The game book beeps, and a creepy male voice (Stauf) says, "Winter coat worn for a mixer?" The words also appear on the game book screen. By touching the help button, the player/Denning gets this clue from a mysterious female voice: "Be warned that 'worn' means *destroyed*." (The player can, of course, make the puzzle more challenging by not pressing the help button.) A second try with the help button elicits, "Mixer might not be a party. What if it's a beverage?" The following hints include: "Something's mixed up here," and "A beverage might be found in the library."

With the help of the map in the game book, the player can find the library but still might need a couple more clues to discover the object of his or her search. The help button offers: "Winter coat is an anagram," and "Winter coat is an anagram of 'Tonic Water.'" Denning (and the player) now knows he is looking for tonic water. But before being allowed to find the tonic water, the player first has to solve a puzzle that involves putting all of the library books of the same color together in a limited number of moves. If he or she succeeds at this, the player is finally allowed to get his or her hands on the bottle of tonic water. The reward is a video clip about Morales played on the game book (in boldface type in the script that follows).

Interactive Video Script Sample

Although the video about Morales is presented interactively to the gamer, it was written and shot as a linear story. In the script sample that follows, the sections in boldface type are examples of video fragments that are triggered by Denning/the player solving puzzles and finding various items. The script sections that are not in boldface type are not initially revealed to Denning, but the player/Denning eventually gets to see all the scenes.

```
MODULE I SCENES: HARLEY-ON-HUDSON

I-1 EXT/COFFEE SHOP ON MAIN STREET—DAY

There is a line of pick-up trucks parked outside a
coffee shop in "downtown" Harley. Like the rest of the
town, the coffee shop seems frozen in time—somewhere in
the late fifties when the freeway went in and traffic
(and life in general) began to pass Harley by. Like a
flash to the present, a convertible driven by a young,
beautiful woman in dark glasses motors down Main Street
and pulls into a parking spot between two beat-up pick-
ups in front of the coffee shop. The coffee shop is
filled with breakfast customers and all eyes are on the
convertible. The woman gets out, and she's dressed in a
fashionable short skirt, heels, and a tailored jacket—
```

all in black—looking as if she'd be more at home in a
Manhattan design studio than the sleepy town of Harley.
It's Robin. She walks up to the front door of the
coffee shop and goes in.

The following boldface segment is revealed to Denning on the PDA when he
touches the tonic water bottle in the haunted house.

1-2 INT/COFFEE SHOP—DAY

**Robin enters the coffee shop and stands just inside the
door next to the cash register, keeping her dark
glasses on. Any motion has come to a complete stop and
everyone is looking at her. Finally a waitress speaks
up. She's a truck-stop woman—kind of voluptuous, a
little rough-edged, and attractive in an earthy sort of
way. She has a prosthetic hand protruding from the
sleeve of her sweater. Her name is Eileen Wiley.**

> **EILEEN**
> **Just sit anywhere, honey. Menus are on the table.**

> ROBIN
> Thanks. Is there a non-smoking section?

There is a slight rumble of laughter. Virtually everyone including the cook is smoking. Eileen grins and
shakes her head.

Robin walks toward a booth by the window. The only
sound is the clicking of her heels and the slight
rustle of her clothing. She sits down, takes off her
dark glasses, and inspects the menu. Slowly, everyone
goes back to their business and the sound level raises
back up to that of a normal coffee shop environment.
Eileen comes over to Robin's table.

> EILEEN
> What can I get for you this morning?

> ROBIN
> Do you have oat-bran muffins?

> EILEEN
> This isn't an oat-bran kind of place, honey. We're
> big on chocolate donuts here.

> ROBIN
> I don't suppose you have any Perrier water.

> EILEEN
> Let me check . . . Hey Slim, we got any Perrier?

Slim is the cook. He sticks his head out from the kitchen.

                    SLIM
    Fresh out of Perrier, Eileen. Had a big run on it
    this morning.
Everyone in the restaurant laughs.

                    EILEEN
    Sorry, honey. How about a San Pellegrino?

                    ROBIN
    Oh? That would be fine.

                    EILEEN
    I'm kidding, hon. The only water we got comes out
    of the tap.

                    ROBIN
    Just bring me a donut and a coffee.

                    EILEEN
    Now you're talkin'. Shall I make that a cappuccino?

                    ROBIN
    Enough with the jokes, okay?

                    EILEEN
    No, I'm serious. As unlikely as it seems, we
    actually have an espresso machine.

Robin smiles and shrugs.

                    ROBIN
    Okay.

                    EILEEN
    Be right back.

She leaves and Robin takes out a small palm-size com-
    puter and begins to type.
Eileen returns with the donut.

                    EILEEN
    Here you go. Be right back with the coffee.

                    ROBIN
    You're Eileen Wiley, aren't you?

                    EILEEN
    Who wants to know?

> ROBIN
>
> I'm Robin Morales. I'm a producer with *Case Unsolved* the TV show.

> EILEEN
>
> Is that the one with Carl Denning?

> ROBIN
>
> Uh-huh.

> EILEEN
>
> Ooh, I like him...Wouldn't mind serving him up a couple of specials.

She laughs and Robin smiles.

> EILEEN (CONT'D)
>
> What's he like?

> ROBIN
>
> He's...uh...he's a man.

> EILEEN
>
> You mean he's a man like you can't live with him or a man like you can't live without him?

Robin thinks about it a moment, then grins.

> ROBIN
>
> He's both.

> EILEEN
>
> Aren't they all?

They both laugh and Eileen sits down.

> EILEEN (CONT'D)
>
> So what are you doing in Harley?

The following segment is revealed to Denning on the PDA when he touches a satyr in a painting.

> **CLERK**
>
> **Hello, Marie.**

An eighteen year old girl moves with a slow sensual saunter toward the desk She has a look of petulant sexuality, dressed in a short denim skirt, white high heels, and a white T-shirt.

MARIE

Where's Chuck?

CLERK

I thought maybe you were here to see me.

MARIE

You wish . . . Is he in his office?

The clerk checks his watch.

CLERK

He's got a meeting in five minutes. He hasn't got time for you today, Marie.

She smirks.

MARIE

Just tell 'im I'm here.

He picks up the telephone and punches a button.

CLERK

Chuck, Marie Wiley's here to see you . . . But you got a meeting at . . . Okay, okay.

He hangs up and reaches behind him for a room key and hands it to Marie.

CLERK

Lucky number 7 . . . Have fun.

She takes the key and turns and leaves without another word. The clerk watches Marie's hips move under her tight-fitting skirt as she goes out the door.

This scene continues, and there are several more scenes in the first module, which is shown during the "Seven O'clock" section of the game.

MULTIPLE ENDINGS

Although the player (and Denning) accesses the video about Morales in bits and pieces, the order in which he or she accesses the video has no affect on the Robin Morales story. Piecing together Morales' story and properly understanding it does, however, help the player make the right choice at the end of the game, where Denning faces three possibilities. Unlike the earlier puzzles, which weren't directly related to the story, this final choice is "a real dramatic choice which goes to the player's values and interests" (Costello). Following are the multiple endings of *The 11th Hour*.

V-8 INT. TEMPLE'S BEDROOM—NIGHT [REAL TIME]

Denning rushes in, hearing the screams of Robin.

                              ROBIN(OS)
        Oh, God—help. Please, no more—no.

                              DENNING
        Robin!

But he enters the room, and there's no one there.
Nothing. The door slams behind him. There is a rumble,
the sound of the house fully alive, a deep bass note
that swells. Denning slowly turns.

And as he turns we see three doors . . . and each door
begins to open . . . slowly . . . End of Module V.

ENDGAME

The opening sequence of the Endgame is triggered after
all scenes of Module Five have been witnessed. Then the
final choices are presented . . .

E-1 INT. THE STAUF MANSION—NIGHT [11:00]

DENNING stands facing the three doors. Stauf material-
izes in front of the doors.

                              STAUF
        Hello, Carl Denning and welcome to "LET'S MAKE A
        REAL DEAL"!

                              DENNING
        Who the hell are you?

                              STAUF
        Why, I'm Monty Stauf, your host on LET'S MAKE A
        REAL DEAL and have I got a real deal for you . . . I
        wonder what this is in my pocket . . . (He reaches
        into his pocket and pulls out a wad of money) . . .
        Six, count 'em, six hundred dollars!

He peels off six bills and hands them to Denning.

                         STAUF (cont'd)
        Now, Carl, here's the deal: You can keep the six
        hundred dollars but you must choose a door, be it
        door number 1, 2, or 3 . . . OR you can pay me two
        hundred dollars and see what's behind the door of
        your choice. What'll it be, Carl?

> DENNING
>
> I'll pay.

He gives Stauf two hundred.

> STAUF
>
> Thank you. Now which door?

> DENNING
>
> The one in the middle.

> STAUF
>
> Okay! Let's see what's behind door number two!

The door opens to reveal a large television set.

> STAUF
>
> A big screen TV! Isn't this fun, Carl? . . . Now, let's make another deal. You can keep the TV AND the four hundred dollars you have left, or you can pay me two hundred dollars to see what's behind another door.

Denning gives Stauf another two hundred.

> DENNING
>
> Let's see what's behind number one.

> STAUF
>
> All right! What a player! . . . Door number one!

The door opens to reveal Marie. She's sitting on a chair dressed in a black bra and panties, garter belt, stockings, and high heels.

> STAUF
>
> It's sweet Marie! She can be absolutely yours anytime, night or day!

> MARIE
>
> Anytime.

> STAUF
>
> Imagine the hours of fun and enjoyment you'll have with Marie! A lot more exciting than watching TV.

> MARIE
>
> You can watch me if you like.

She places her hands on her knees and trails her fingers up the inside of her thighs. She licks her lips and smiles. Suddenly the big screen TV flickers to life, and Samantha [an earlier victim of the house, who has been helping Denning] appears on the screen.

> SAMANTHA
> Be strong, Carl Denning. Don't give in to
> temptation.

> STAUF
> Damn it! I thought that TV was unplugged!

> SAMANTHA
> Choose me.

> STAUF
> What a choice! Marie—sweet, sensuous, sexy Marie—or
> Samantha in a wheelchair! Hah!

> DENNING
> What's behind door number three?

Stauf extends his arm and rubs his fingers together.

> STAUF
> Pay up.

Denning gives him the last two hundred dollars.

> STAUF (CONT'D)
> Door number three!

The third door opens and Robin is there.

> ROBIN
> Carl, I've been so frightened. Please, choose me.
> Save me. I love you.

> MARIE
> I'll give you anything you want . . . Anything and
> everything.

> SAMANTHA
> Don't listen to them. You'll be lost forever.

> STAUF
> Shut up, Samantha!

> SAMANTHA
> He's afraid of you, Carl. Choose me. Destroy the
> power of this hellish house.

> ROBIN
> Carl, you have to choose me. After all we've been
> through . . . I need you, Carl.

> MARIE
> Anytime . . . anyplace . . . any way you want me.

Stauf confronts the player.

> STAUF
> Well, what'll it be, sport? The choice is yours . . .

CUT TO: THE DOORS.

E-2 INT. TEMPLE'S ROOM—NIGHT

(Triggered by choosing Robin)

Note: All choices should be made real choice—all saved positions from Mod Five on will be erased after choosing. The Player is told this. They can eventually see all three endings but not before re-experiencing the last part of the game.

Denning chooses Robin's door. He enters and they embrace. There are tears in her eyes.

> ROBIN
> Thank God.

> DENNING
> Let's go home.

E-3 INT/DENNING'S COUNTRY HOME—DAY

Robin is in Denning's living room watching a newscast on TV. A woman anchorperson is reading the news.

> ANCHOR
> The body of TV reporter Carl Denning was found floating in the Hudson river today. Denning disappeared during his honeymoon in Harley-on-Hudson after his celebrated marriage to Robin Morales, newly appointed president of the Stauf Broadcasting System.

Robin watches without emotion. She clicks a button on a remote control and the picture fades to black.

E-4 INT. TEMPLE'S ROOM—NIGHT

(Triggered by choosing Marie)

Denning moves toward Marie's door. She gets up from her chair and walks away into the darkness beyond, looking over her shoulder with a seductive smile. Denning enters the door and follows her.

E-5 INT/BEDROOM—NIGHT

Denning enters a bedroom. Marie is on the bed, lounging back, inviting. Denning gets on the foot of the bed

and crawls up on top of her. He kisses her and she
responds passionately which unleashes a hunger in him.
She rolls him over so that she is straddling him. She
kisses his neck and chest and unbuttons his shirt as
she works her way down. Denning looks down at the mane
of hair cascading over his stomach. She looks up at
him—but it isn't Marie. It's Stauf in a wig!

                    STAUF
    What a deal!

Denning screams.—THE REST OF THE SCENE IS PLAYED INTO
THE CAMERA AS PLAYER'S POV. Stauf rolls off the bed
and grabs a barbecued rib from a plate on a dresser.
He tosses the wig onto the bed.

                    STAUF
    I'll let you in on a secret—'cause you're so
    special. (smacks his lips) Mmmm . . . these are
    good . . .

He laughs. He offers up a rib.

                STAUF (CONT'D)
    Like a bite? . . . Some choice you made, huh? Oh,
    don't look so sad. I'm not so bad . . . See . . . ?

Stauf metamorphoses back into Marie, still eating the
rib, red sauce dripping off her chin onto her chest.
More lip-smacking.

She holds out the rib, nearly finished.

                MARIE/STAUF
    Sure you wouldn't like a bite . . . ? After all—(she
    laughs) . . . It's you!

Marie laughs uproariously and the laughing voice begins
to sound like Stauf's, then she metamorphoses back into
Stauf, laughing, doubling over. He begins to cough and
it becomes a disgusting, choking sound. As he chokes,
he begins to change into his native form—the alien
creature that's been behind this all along. It looks
up, jaws open, salivating—as it leaps, devouring the
player into blackness.

***E-5-PG INT/BEDROOM—NIGHT [PG VERSION]

Marie leads Denning into a bedroom holding his hand.
When they reach the bed, she pulls him close and they
tumble to the mattress. He kisses her and she responds
passionately. She rolls him over so that she is on
top. She kisses his neck and chest and unbuttons his

shirt as she works her way down. Denning looks down at the mane of hair cascading over his stomach. She looks up at him—but it isn't Marie. . . . etc.

E-6 INT. TEMPLE'S ROOM—NIGHT (Triggered by choosing Sam)

Denning moves toward the middle door containing the TV with Samantha's image. He reaches to touch the screen and there is an explosion of white light.

E-7 INT/SAMANTHA FORD'S STUDIO—DAY

Denning finds himself in Samantha's studio. Samantha looks up at him, sitting in her wheelchair next to one of her monitors. She looks more relaxed than anytime before. She smiles.

> SAMANTHA
> Welcome, Carl Denning. You made the right choice.

> DENNING
> It wasn't easy.

> SAMANTHA
> No.

> DENNING
> I hated leaving Robin behind.

> SAMANTHA
> I know. You risked your life for her . . . But it was too late to save her.

> DENNING
> So what happens now?

She extends her hand.

> SAMANTHA
> Come and see.

He takes her hand and stands behind her as they both look at the monitor. On the screen, the Stauf Mansion is engulfed in flames.

> SAMANTHA
> You won, Carl.

> DENNING
> What about Robin?

Samantha shakes her head.

SAMANTHA
She was lost the moment she said yes to Stauf.

They watch the monitor as the house burns. There are tears in Denning's eyes. Samantha looks content, virtually radiating an inner peace. It's been a long battle for her. On the monitor, there is nothing left but blackness.

THE END

HORROR AND HUMOR

Another element that the writer Matthew Costello thinks makes this game successful is its blending of humor and horror, because "part of horror is to laugh and be scared" (Costello). If a horror viewer has no release from fearful tension, he or she can overload and turn off to the material.

The following example occurs towards the end of the game when the murderer, Chuck, is himself destroyed by the house.

IV-8 EXT. MANSION—DAY

Chuck struggles with his heavy burden in the overgrown field approaching the mansion.

IV-9 EXT/MANSION PORCH—DAY

Chuck drops his bloody bundle on the porch and knocks on the door. This time when he pushes the bundle in, Chuck gets pulled in with it.

IV-10 INT.—INSIDE THE STAUF MANSION—NIGHT

Chuck finds himself in the kitchen.

JULIA HEINE is at the table cutting something with a cleaver. She is dressed as she was in *THE 7TH GUEST*, except the dress is faded, tattered, and stained. She whacks at whatever she's cutting . . . She looks up at Chuck.

JULIA
Are you ready?

CHUCK
For what?

STAUF
Soup's on.

Stauf suddenly appears.

STAUF

  Soup's on!

A head emerges from the soup pot.

HEAD

  Soup's on!

The kitchen starts to change, the walls turning a deep
red, shiny, dripping. And in the cascade of red blood
streaming off the walls, onto the floor, there are
faces, screaming faces in the wall, looking out,
begging. Chuck begins to scream. Julia comes towards
Chuck, her meat cleaver dripping blood.

JULIA

  How 'bout a Chuck roast?

Stauf laughs.

STAUF

  Chuck steak!

HEAD

  Chuck him into the soup!

The cleaver comes down.

THE WRITING PROCESS

The writing processes for *The 7th Guest* and *The 11th Hour* were similar even though
the story structures were different. The scenes in the first game were designed to be
self-contained scenes. In the second game, however, the scenes were meant to be combined to form a complete linear story.

For *The 7th Guest*, the developers had the basic idea about a haunted house
game and an evil toy-maker. They contacted Matthew Costello, a horror novelist, to
develop the story. He created a novella and broke it into scenes, connecting them to
each room.

The 11th Hour followed the same writing process, but the story grew out of the
Stauf files, which were background material for *The 7th Guest*. Costello wrote a
novella based on this material and sent it to the designers, Graeme Devine and Rob
Landeros, who critiqued it. Then Costello wrote a script using film script format, with
the difference in format being that each segment is numbered and tied to a certain
room in the mansion and eventually to the prop in the treasure hunt that triggers
it. This device broke up the linearity of the story and organized the narrative by
the physical environment and by the way that the user interacts with that environment. This script received further comments and revisions by designers Devine and
Landeros and video director David Wheeler.

CONCLUSION: RESPONSE TO THE PROJECT

Critical response to the project was strong. It received raves in most of the major gaming magazines, won a Critic's Choice Award from *CD-ROM Today*, an Invision Award from *New Media*, and it topped many best-seller lists.

REFERENCES

Costello, Matthew. Telephone interview with the author. December 1995.
Demaria, Rusel, and Alex Uttermarm. *The 11th Hour: The Sequel to the 7th Guest—The Official Strategy Guide*. Rocklin, CA: Prima Publishing, 1996.

C H A P T E R   2 2

CINEMATIC NARRATIVE CASE STUDY: *VOYEUR*

Summary

Name of production: *Voyeur*
Writers: Lena Marie Pousette, Jay Richardson, and Michael Halperin
Developer: Philips POV Entertainment Group
Audience: Mature
Medium: CD-ROM
Presentation location: Home
Subject: Political thriller
Goal: Entertain
Architecture: Linear, branching

The script samples and images used in this chapter are courtesy of Philips Media. © 1993 Philips Interactive Media.

PROGRAM DESCRIPTION AND BACKGROUND

PROGRAM DESCRIPTION

Voyeur opens with a special TV bulletin:

```
                    NEWSCASTER
Will he or won't he? This is Tish Van Alden and
that's the hot question on everybody's lips during
this primary season.
Billionaire bachelor and business genius Reed Hawke
has yet to commit himself to the race for the Oval
Office. Well, hang on to your hats, folks, because
he's gathering his flock this weekend to "help him
reach a decision" and when the Hawkes get together,
the feathers are bound to fly.
```

The feathers are bound to fly because Reed Hawke's children, Jessica and Zack; his niece Chloe; and his sister Margaret all have enough dirt to bring him down if they decide to use it. Reed has gathered his family at his mansion to clear the air one way or the other before announcing his candidacy for the presidency.

The player/voyeur lives in an apartment opposite the Hawke estate and, with a powerful video camera, can see and hear what goes on in any room of the mansion. When the user pans the "camera" over one of the mansion's windows and the cursor changes to an eye icon, it indicates that the room holds a video scene; an ear icon indicates an audio scene; and a magnifying glass indicates evidence. The top image in Figure 22–1 shows the view of Reed's mansion through the video camera. The eye icon appears over the foyer. Clicking brings up the foyer video scene in the bottom image.

The goal of *Voyeur* is to figure out which one of Reed's family members is going to expose him, and then to stop Reed before he kills that person for endangering his grab for the presidency. If the player collects enough evidence with the camera, he or she can warn the family member by sending the tape or by contacting the police. If, however, the player contacts the police with inadequate evidence, he or she might be thrown in jail as a peeping Tom. If the player contacts the wrong family member, he or she might tell Reed, and the player could get a visit from Reed's assassin.

Complicating the search for Reed's accuser/victim is that there can be up to six scenes happening at one time in different rooms, so a player watching what is happening in one room will miss what is going on in the others.

Adding to the fun and the replay value of *Voyeur are* the four variations on the main plot, which are loaded randomly each time the game is played. In each variation, a different member of Reed's family attempts to expose him.

VOYEUR AND THE INTERACTIVE NARRATIVE

Voyeur was a major step toward moving multimedia entertainment away from video games for kids and into interactive narratives for adults. It was one of the first programs to use adult themes and subject matter, star actors, and a sophisticated, literate script.

PRODUCTION BACKGROUND

Voyeur was written by Lena Marie Pousette, Jay Richardson, and Michael Halperin. It was designed by David Riordan. Philips POV Entertainment Group developed all elements of the project, except for managing the actual video production and hiring the video production crew, which was handled by Propaganda Films. The program was first released on CD-I, an interactive disc format that is used with a special player connected to a regular TV. *Voyeur* was later released on CD-ROM for both Mac and PC.

GOALS AND CHALLENGES IN WRITING *VOYEUR*

GOALS

The creators of *Voyeur* wanted to develop a narrative, interactive multimedia program that had a sophisticated cinematic quality and to move away from the arcade-type action-adventure game. The goal was to create a story that users can step into and

FIGURE 22-1

Top: The game interface and the voyeur's view of the Hawke Mansion. Bottom: The view of the foyer seen through the voyeur's video camera.

understand who they are in relation to the other characters and what their purpose is in the story, not just an exploratory environment like *Myst*. Through this more sophisticated narrative, *Voyeur* attempted to reach out to the larger audience that watches movies and television.

CHALLENGES

Creating this sense of reality and cinematic quality in an interactive, multimedia narrative presented a number of challenges:

- Overcoming technical limitations.
- Creating a sense of cinematic story complexity and pace, while still allowing repeat play, a key concern for the multimedia audience.
- Giving the program a "real-life" feel.
- Achieving all of the above without losing interactivity.
- Maintaining interactivity while performing necessary story functions, such as setting plot points, characterization, and establishing jeopardy.

MEETING THE CHALLENGES IN WRITING *VOYEUR*

OVERCOMING TECHNICAL LIMITATIONS

Voyeur had a number of technical limitations that were the result of executive decisions and the sophistication of the current technology. Because of limited disc storage space and access speed, the video of the actors could occupy only one-quarter of the screen area. The rest of the image (sets, props, etc.) had to be computer-generated, because computer-generated images take much less disc space than video or photographs do.

This meant that the actors would have to be shot against a blue screen so the computer-generated backgrounds could be later keyed in. Figure 22–2 shows the actors being filmed against a blue screen. The video monitor in Figure 22–2 shows the same image combined with a computer-generated background as it appears in *Voyeur*. This also meant that characters would have to be seen primarily in medium shots and full shots, because close-ups occupy too much screen space.

The writers and designers had to come up with a concept that would turn the technical disadvantages to advantages. Thus the voyeur concept was born. If everything is shot from the point of view of the player, who is a voyeur peering into a building across the street, then it makes sense that the other characters would be seen primarily in medium shot or full shot. (See Figure 22–1.)

The voyeur idea solved the major problem, but another idea to conserve disc space was to put curtains on all the windows. When they are completely closed, the voyeur can still hear what is going on in the room, as in the following audio-only script example. This device saved disc space because sound occupies much less room than video. However, an audio-only scene requires the writer to use the skills of a radio dramatist to spark the user's imagination and create the images in the user's mind.

FIGURE 22-2

Actors shot against blue screen.

```
(No Video—Audio only)
E1/210/200 Chantal and Frank in passion. A symphony of
excited sounds.

                    CHANTAL
     You like it when I use my tongue, don't you?

                    FRANK
                 (moaning)
     Yeah, mmmmm. . . . Ahh.

                    CHANTAL
     Give me your full attention.

                    FRANK
                 (sucking in breath)
     Ooohh.

                    CHANTAL
                 (teasing laugh)
     You call that "full attention"? Let's see if this
     gets your attention.

                    FRANK
     What's that? . . . You're not gonna use that?
                 (freaking out)
     Chantal . . . you're not serious? I don't think—
```

There's a gasp, heavy breathing and lots of moans.

                          FRANK
     Yeahhhhh.

                          CHANTAL
     That's a good boy. Say thank you.

                          FRANK
                        (melting)
     Mm . . . hmmm. Thank you. Oh, thank you.

                          CHANTAL
     Shut up, Frank.

                          FRANK
     Okay . . . Shut up . . . I'll be quiet.

CREATING A COMPLEX CINEMATIC STORY AND PACING

With a workable solution for the major technical limitations in place, the writers and designers still had to come up with a way to give *Voyeur* a complex cinematic story and pacing. One of the problems with many interactive titles is that the story stops while the user makes an interactive choice. This interruption kills the pace of the story and destroys any illusion that these are real people on screen, living out their lives—the kind of illusion that linear movies create so successfully.

Simultaneously Playing Multiple Scenes in Real Time

Voyeur achieves cinematic pace and the illusion of real life by playing multiple scenes simultaneously in real time. This means that up to six different scenes can be playing in the various rooms of the Hawke mansion at any one time. The player/voyeur chooses which room to peer into, but while the voyeur is looking at that room, the other five scenes continue on. Each day of the weekend is broken up into several time zones, such as "Saturday 8:00 A.M." (See Figure 22–1.) The player has a limited amount of time to explore each time zone before that time zone cuts to black and the next time zone, such as "Saturday 2:00 P.M.," begins with a title card. A voyeur/player who spends too much time in one scene will risk missing other scenes altogether. If the voyeur misses key information, he or she will not be able to catch Reed and save the threatened family member.

An added advantage of multiple scenes playing at once was to increase replay value. Because users could not see everything the first time through, they wanted to play the game again to see what was in the other rooms. This is an important consideration if the price of a multimedia program is going to be several times the price of a videotape or a music CD.

Following is an outline of the first five time zones, showing all the scenes that would play simultaneously. The numbers refer to the single time zone in which scenes were played simultaneously. For example, in the first time zone, only one scene was played; in the fourth time zone, there were three scenes. Some of the time zones later in the program (not shown here) have as many as six scenes playing at the same time.

SCENE OUTLINE

ACT ONE:

1a INT. SECURITY ROOM:

FRANK and CHANTAL have a secret relationship. Chantal
is in the shower when someone creeps into her room.
However, it is she who pulls out a gun and directs
Frank to the bed. In the midst of this game, the phone
rings. REED is on his way home. CHANTAL leaves FRANK
tied to the bed.

2a EXT. HAWKE MANOR:

As he makes his way up the front steps, REED is
quizzed by the media about his plans for the
presidency. It is clear that he has been called to run
for the presidency by the people of this country.
Still, he claims reluctance to commit himself as a
candidate until he is sure his family supports this
motion.

3a EXT. ROSE GARDEN/FOUNTAIN:

REED enters the house and makes his way out to the
garden where MARGARET is collecting roses for display
in the house. MARGARET fusses over REED, affectionately
placing a rose in his lapel and expressing displeasure
in his choice of ties. CHANTAL clashes with MARGARET,
explaining that REED's image will be monitored to fit
the presidential image. REED agrees, telling MARGARET
that things have changed.

4a INT. MARGARET'S ROOM:

MARGARET stands in front of her mirror modeling outfits
and judging whether they fit the "First Lady" image to
her satisfaction. All the while she is barking out
orders over the phone directing household matters that
must be taken care of for the weekend.

4b INT. HALLWAY:

ZACK and LARA arrive in the midst of an argument. LARA
does not want to be here, but ZACK says this weekend
is very important to him. While LARA goes off to their
room, ZACK tries to go up in the elevator to see REED.
It is locked. FRANK (over loudspeaker) tells ZACK to
speak with CHANTAL.

```
4c  CHANTAL'S ROOM:

CHANTAL working out.
```

```
5a  INT. SOMEWHERE:

ZACK learns (from LARA) that his room has been taken
over by FRANK and his security division and that he
and LARA have to stay in guest quarters. As ZACK is
obsessed with being CEO, he is convinced that this
rooming situation has something to do with his
position. It is clear that LARA is unhappy with the
marriage.
```

```
5b  EXT. GARDEN PATIO:

JESSICA and MASA arrive together and meet MARGARET on
the patio. MARGARET maintains her air of control by
ignoring MASA. Suddenly, a figure dressed in motorcycle
garb bursts through the door. FRANK wrestles the figure
to the ground, only to find it is CHLOE. Despite this
case of mistaken identity, it appears that FRANK is
uncomfortable about the family gathering. As soon as
CHLOE's identity is revealed, CHANTAL speaks into her
phone: "She's here, Mr. Hawke."
```

Master Story and Four Variations

In addition to playing multiple scenes at one time as in the above example, *Voyeur* *also* has four story variations. Each time the user starts a new game, a different linear story variation loads. The master story of all the characters coming to the house is the same for all variations, but in each variation, a different character decides to take on Reed and gets killed—unless the voyeur intervenes.

The effect of these multiple story lines is to make the game more of a challenge to discover which family member is in danger, because on each playing of the game, it is a different character. It is also intriguing to see the subtle variations in plotting that will push first one character and then another over the edge.

The following script samples illustrate how a variation is developed out of the main story line. Each character has essentially two story lines: one in which they make a deal with Reed and one in which they try to expose him. The game is programmed so that every time a new game is started, a different character will try to expose Reed, while the other three characters will make a deal.

The following example illustrates part of the two variations of Reed's daughter, Jessica's story. The "100" at the end of the number code at the top of the page indicates that this is the main story line in which Jessica sells out to Reed. The "520" at the end of the number code indicates that this is the alternate scene that could be played, Jessica's variation on the main story in which she tries to expose Reed. These are not the only scenes that run during this part of the program. Other characters also have scenes, but they are not shown here for the sake of clarity. In the actual script, each new scene starts on a new page. They are divided here by a line.

(MAIN STORY)

START: 02:00:10:00   END: 02:00:43:20

P1/325/100—Jessica takes Reed up on his proposition for the foundation.

REED'S OFFICE NIGHT—DAY 2

REED and JESSICA enter the room. He gestures for her to sit down as he positions himself in his swivel chair.

> JESSICA
> (terse, business-like)
> I've decided to take your offer on the condition that you use your power to clear Masa of all charges against him. He's innocent.

> REED
> He may not be guilty. But, I can assure you, my dear, that your friend Masa is far from innocent.

JESSICA'S about to protest—

> REED
> However . . . I agree to your terms. So, I'll draw up the papers and put money into escrow.

> JESSICA
> Look . . . Dad. I'm, uh, sorry that—

> REED
> Never apologize, Jessica. Sign of weakness.

JESSICA turns and exists. Reed exits camera right.

(JESSICA'S VARIATION)

START: 02:01:39:01   END: 02:02:01:20

P1/325/520—Reed listens to a recording of Jessica's call to the press. (Taped scene/Jessica)

REED'S OFFICE—NIGHT—DAY 2

REED steps into frame with a SMALL TAPE RECORDER and places it on the desk. He inserts a TAPE and pushes PLAY. We hear:

> JESSICA'S VOICE
> Hello, Mr. Greenblat.

                    GREENBLAT'S VOICE
Greenblat here.

                    JESSICA'S VOICE
Jessica Hawke.

                    GREENBLAT'S VOICE
Do you have it?

                    JESSICA'S VOICE
Yes, I have that material we talked about.

                    GREENBLAT'S VOICE
It's your father, right?

                    JESSICA'S VOICE
Yes, yes, it clearly implicates my father.

                    GREENBLAT' S VOICE
Well, listen. Meet me at seven.

                    JESSICA'S VOICE
7 A.M.?

                    GREENBLAT'S VOICE
Seven.

                    JESSICA'S VOICE
Fine.

REED turns off the player, touches the intercom button
on the speaker phone.

                    CHANTAL (OS)
Yes sir.

                         REED
I need you.

Reed exits.

_____

(MAIN STORY)

START: 02:06:18:23   END: 02:06:44:05

Q1/260/100—Jessica and Masa make love in celebration of
the deal with Reed.

JESSICA'S BEDROOM—NIGHT—DAY 2

JESSICA comes out of the bathroom dressed in Japanese
silk robe. Room is lit in CANDLES, INCENSE is burning.

MASA is kneeling on the BED engaged in deep breathing exercises. His hands at his sides. Jessica without a word straddles his lap, pulling his robe open and then her own. She takes oil from a SMALL JAR and anoints MASA's brain chakra, heart chakra, and then her own. They look deeply into each other's eyes.

> MASA
>
> You are my love. You have freed me from my past life.

> JESSICA
>
> And you mine.

Their lips meet.

(JESSICA'S VARIATION)

START: 02:06:56:12   END: 02:07:06:01

Q1/260/520—Lead in to Jessica & Masa's Murder Scene

JESSICA'S BEDROOM—NIGHT—DAY 2

JESSICA and MASA are lying together on the bed. Masa starts to rise and Jessica makes a complaining noise. Masa kisses her and finishes rising, walks to bathroom dressed in pajama bottoms. Jessica curls up around his PILLOW.

FREEZE SCENE.

(JESSICA'S VARIATION)

START: 02:06:56:12   END: 02:07:06:01

Q1/260/720—Jessica's MURDER SCENE—Continuation of Q1 /260/520

JESSICA'S BEDROOM—NIGHT—DAY 2

JESSICA uncurls herself from MASA'S PILLOW, stretching.

> JESSICA
> (calls off to bathroom)
> So . . . the foundation's going to need a name. We could name it in honor of your village. The Sangatsu Foundation . . .

REED steps in. JESSICA is startled.

> JESSICA
>
> Dad

CHANTAL stands framed in the doorway. She reaches up to whisk the hair out of her eyes and we see the BLOOD-SOAKED HARA-KIRI KNIFE in her hand.

JESSICA starts to scream as REED puts his hands around her neck. Chantal closes the blinds.

(JESSICA'S VARIATION)

START: 02:12:26:29   END: 02:13:25:25

Z1/1 10/520—Reed announces. Jessica's dead.

EXTERIOR HAWKE MANOR—APPEARS ON PLAYER'S TELEVISION SCREEN

Graphic SPECIAL BULLETIN appears on the T.V. screen

CLOSE on Reed

> REED
> Ladies and gentlemen. I only have . . . a brief statement to make. My daughter Jessica and I used to spend many happy hours together talking about the future of this grand and glorious country.

Fights down the emotions.

> REED
> . . . excuse me . . . We are tempered in our lives by hardships. As you all know, last night my daughter's life was cut short by the hand of a suicidal terrorist . . . So many times she said to me, "Daddy . . . you must listen to the voice of the American people."

Composes himself.

Therefore, I have decided to run for the office of President of the United States. Jessica, I know you're listening . . . this one's for you.

[If Jessica followed the main story—her "100" scenes—and sold out to Reed, then one of the other characters, such as Reed's son Zack, would have tried to expose him and ended up dead, and the scene that follows would end the program instead of Jessica's scene above.]

START: 02:13:40:23   END: 02:14:33:12

Z1/1 10/530—Reed announces. Zack's dead.

EXTERIOR HAWKE MANOR—APPEARS ON PLAYER'S TELEVISION
SCREEN

Graphic SPECIAL BULLETIN appears on the T.V. screen

CLOSE on Reed

> REED
>
> As some of you may know, my son Zack was killed
> last night. We had been working around the clock
> to put the finishing touches on Hawke Industries
> Missile Defense Systems. He must have taken his
> computer into the bathroom; apparently it slipped.

He composes himself.

> REED
>
> There is nothing I can do for my son now, but his
> selfless commitment to the security of this country
> has made me realize that I must follow my
> commitment to the welfare of its people. Therefore
> I have decided to formally announce that I am a
> candidate for the Presidency of the United States.
> I only wish my son could be here to see his work
> completed. Thank you. Thank you.

MAINTAINING INTERACTIVITY WITHIN A COMPLEX CINEMATIC STORY: THE *VOYEUR* CHARACTER

The multiple story lines and the simultaneous playing of scenes in real time give *Voyeur* a cinematic story and pacing. Interactivity is maintained through the character of the voyeur. The voyeur sees the activities at the mansion through first-person point of view so the player becomes the voyeur.

First-person point of view is fairly common in interactive narratives (see the case studies for *The Pandora Directive* and *Dust: A Tale of the Wired West* in Chapters 23 and 24, respectively), but what is unusual here is that the player/voyeur is a minor character as opposed to being the protagonist. The advantage of the player being a minor character is that it is possible to see the main action of the game in third person, as a viewer normally would on a cinema screen. What is lost is that the player is not central to the action. Both approaches have validity, depending on the goal of the program.

The voyeur/player can videotape what he or she sees in Reed's mansion. The voyeur can also hear what goes on there and read letters and examine props. The voyeur can do several things with the information gathered. Adding to the tension is the real-time pacing of the game in which the voyeur has only so much time to look for clues before the game moves on to the next part of the day.

The Voyeur Character's Interactive Options

The voyeur has several options, which give this piece a wide range of interactivity and add personal jeopardy for the player/voyeur.

Option #1: Just watch. The voyeur can just watch the action and do nothing; in that case one of the family members is murdered, and Reed announces for the presidency. (See the Jessica and Zack endings in the previous script samples.)

Option #2: Warn a family member. The voyeur can warn the family member that he or she thinks is threatened by mailing the videotape of the evidence collected. If the voyeur warns the threatened family member, he or she is saved, and Reed is exposed, as in the following variation on the Jessica ending:

Z3/115/520—Jessica exposes Reed

EXT. HAWKE MANOR /ALLEY—NIGHT—APPEARS ON PLAYER'S TV

Graphic SPECIAL BULLETIN appears on the T.V. screen.

> REPORTER #1
> Excuse me, Miss Hawke, why are you leaving . . .

> JESSICA
> I have material that proves that Hawke Industries,
> with my father's knowledge, was responsible for
> poisoning an entire village in Japan.

> REPORTER #1
> Is this going to affect your father's decision to
> run for president?

> JESSICA
> Well, I intend to present this evidence at the
> highest level in Japan, where I am sure criminal
> charges will be filed. But that's all I have to say.

> REPORTER #1
> But what about the reports—

They exit.

THE END

If, however, the player/voyeur mistakenly warns one of Reed's allies, the voyeur could get a visit from Reed's assassin, Chantal:

Z2/320/100—REED LOOKS OUT HIS WINDOW INTO VOYEUR'S
APARTMENT

REED'S OFFICE

REED stands looking out his office window—making eye
contact with the VOYEUR (player). The sound of the
VOYEUR'S apartment door opening is heard. The VOYEUR
turns around to look at the door (animation of his/her
POV).

```
Z2/905/300—CHANTAL KILLS VOYEUR/PLAYER INT. VOYEUR'S
APARTMENT
```

CHANTAL steps into the doorway.

                         CHANTAL
      You came close, eh?

She pulls out a nasty-looking gun and begins screwing
on the silencer with a gloved hand.

                         CHANTAL
      Yah, very close.

She smiles enticingly as she raises the gun and aims
it at YOU.

                         CHANTAL
      . . .Compliments of Mr. Hawke.

SHE PULLS THE TRIGGER. THE SCREEN GOES BLOOD RED.

THE END

Option #3: Contact the police. The voyeur can also contact the police before or after the murder and give them the evidence. The police may think the voyeur has adequate or inadequate evidence. In the case of inadequate evidence, the voyeur could go to jail. Following is an example of inadequate evidence:

```
START: 02:20:46:21    END: 02:20:54:18

Z4/915/100—Cop asks to see the tape
```

VOYEUR'S APARTMENT

Cop appears at player's door.

                         COP
      You the one that called with the stuff on Reed
      Hawke? So show me the tape.

```
START: 02:21:09:20    END: 02:21:23:26

Z4/915/200—Cop negatively reacts to player's tape
```

VOYEUR'S APARTMENT'

COP negatively reacting to PLAYER'S tape.

                         COP
      This tape doesn't prove anything. I should haul you
      in, you pervert. I wouldn't be surprised if Mr.
      Hawke presses charges.

Cop exits.

If the voyeur has enough evidence for the police, Reed is exposed:

START: 02:21:38:24   END: 02:21:50:08

Z4/915/300—Cop positively reacts to player's tape.
VOYEUR'S APARTMENT

COP positively reacting to PLAYER'S tape.

                              COP
    I never would have thought Reed Hawke was capable
    of this, but this tape nails him. We'll take it
    from here.

Cop exits.

Following is the ending if the voyeur/player contacts the police after the murder:

START: 02:17:37:06   END: 02:18:16:27

Z3/110/100—Reed responds to the fact that Player has
evidence on tape.

EXTERIOR HAWKE MANOR/ALLEY—NIGHT—DAY 2

Reporters' MICROPHONES are thrust into REED's face as
he is being hauled away in HANDCUFFS.

                         REPORTER #1
    Mr. Hawke, Mr. Hawke, what is your response to
    these allegations of murder?

                              REED
    I categorically deny any and all charges brought
    against me as a result of this so-called
    eyewitness.

                         REPORTER #2
    But is this going to change your plans to run for
    President, Sir?

                              REED
    I guarantee you that I will clear my name of any
    and all charges and be back in the forefront of a
    new movement to bring the power of government back
    to the people.

Reed is dragged away.

                         REPORTER #1
    Well, here you have it. Total denial of all
    charges. However, sources inside the police

department say that they have the murder scene on
tape. Looks like Reed Hawke is finished. But, stay
tuned for further developments.

THE END

ESTABLISHING CHARACTERS, PLOT POINTS, AND CONFLICTS

In addition to developing multiple story paths and interactive options for the player, the writer of interactive narrative must also perform most of the writing tasks common to linear narrative, such as setting up characters, developing rising conflicts, and establishing key plot points. The complex story structure and simultaneous playing of scenes in real time make these tasks much more difficult in *Voyeur*.

CHARACTER CONSISTENCY

The complexity of four different story lines and a large cast made it essential to find a way to keep track of the various characters' attitudes toward each other. Sometimes characters never meet, but even references in conversation have to be consistent, particularly because the purpose of the game is for the voyeur/player to evaluate the evidence that he or she gathers from the scenes.

The following character matrix (just a portion of the entire matrix is shown) helped the writers achieve this consistency. The chart is read from left to right showing what each character feels about the characters listed on top of the chart. For example, Reed thinks of himself as a messiah, of his sister Margaret as entrapment, and of his daughter Jessica as a thorn in his side.

		VOYEUR CHARACTER CHART			
	REED	MARGARET	JESSICA	ZACK	CHLOE
REED	Messiah	Entrapment	Thorn in side	Disdain	Fear of self
MARGARET	Symbiotic	Unheralded	Threatened	Protective	Enabler
JESSICA	Unrequited	Shame	Needful	Rival	Big sister
ZACK	Obsessed	Maternal	Threatened	Deserving	Abscess
CHLOE	Vengeful	Betrayal	Foolish	Clown	Desperate

REPEATING PLOT POINTS

With the character matrix to keep the relationships clear, the writers next had to integrate this character material into the script. In interactive narrative, and particularly in *Voyeur*, the writer can never be sure what material the viewer has or has not seen. This constraint required that the same plot points be placed in several scenes, but written in such a way that if the player did see more than one of these scenes, they would not be redundant.

The information about Zack's stormy relationship with his dad, for example, is introduced in at least four scenes. The writers keep the material fresh by changing the

locations of the scenes and by making the Zack plot point a minor part of two of the
scenes, as the following examples show.

Variation 1

This is the first we hear of Zack's problems with Dad. It is integrated into a newscast
with other family members and accessed by the voyeur/player clicking on his or her
TV set.

```
START: 02:34:41:23    END: 02:36:19:09

A2/050/100—Gossip about Reed and family.

INT. VOYEUR'S APARTMENT—DAY—DAY 1

ANGLE on Voyeur's T.V. The screen has a SPECIAL
BULLETIN graphic on it. Tish Van Alden appears on
background shot of Hawke Manor.

                    TISH
    Will he or won't he? This is Tish Van Alden and
    that's the hot question on everybody's lips during
    this primary season.

                (Snapshot of Reed)
    Billionaire bachelor and business genius Reed Hawke
    has yet to commit himself to the race for the Oval
    Office. Well, hang on to your hats, folks, because
    he's gathering his flock this weekend to "help him
    reach a decision," and when the Hawkes get
    together, the feathers are bound to fly.

                (Snapshot of Zack)
    I mean, imagine how his son Zachary must feel
    after his sudden promotion off the Missile Defense
    System project, just in time for it to propel dear
    old dad into the White House. Getting a little
    chilly in Daddy's shadow, Zack?
```

Variation 2

The first time we see Zack. He is arguing with his wife about his father.

```
START: 01:05:16:24    END: 01:06:12:13

C1/220/100—Zack and Lara arrive in the midst of an
argument

FOYER—DAY—DAY 1

ZACK and LARA, carrying OVERNIGHT BAGS, enter the FOYER
and head toward the elevator. ZACHARY HAWKE is Reed's
only son, and he's a little too tightly wrapped for
his own good. LARA, his wife, is in her late twenties,
```

fresh-faced and normally optimistic. But it's clear
that this couple has arrived in the midst of an
argument.

                    LARA
    Why do you continue to do this to yourself . . .

                    ZACK
    Look, we're not going into this again. I told you
    how important this weekend is to me. We're staying
    here and that's it.

Preoccupied, ZACK goes to the elevator and punches the
button. It doesn't respond.

                    ZACK
              (turns and sighs, trying)
    Look . . . Lara, please just let me deal with my
    father—

                    FRANK'S VOICE
              (over the intercom)
    Mr. Hawke. Can I help you?

ZACK's attention shifts back to the elevator.

                    ZACK
    What the hell is with the elevator, Frank?

                    FRANK'S VOICE
              (cordial in an androgynous way)
    I'm sorry, Mr. Hawke, your father's orders.

                    LARA
    Come on, Honey, you can see your father later.

                    ZACK
              (agitated)
    Look, Lara, will you please just go upstairs and
    unpack.

He turns back to the elevator. LARA walks off.

                    ZACK
    Open up, Frank.

                    FRANK'S VOICE
    I'm afraid Mr. Hawke doesn't want to be disturbed
    at the moment. He asked me to have all
    appointments scheduled through Chantal.

                    ZACK
    Schedule an appointment? That son of a bitch! . . .
    Lara, wait up.

```
He storms off.
```

Variation 3

In case the player missed that scene, then the same information is included as the minor part of a scene between two of Reed's staffers. This time we only hear when Zack's voice comes out of the intercom in the staffers' office.

Variation 4

A little later in the script, the same information is presented again, but this time through Zack's wife, Lara, and in a different context. The problem is that Zack's room has been given to Reed's personal assistant. When Lara tells him about this, he blows up about his Dad.

MULTIPLE PLOT POINTS IN ONE SCENE

Another way to ensure that the player sees key information is to include multiple plot points in one scene, so if the player does access a scene, much key plot information has been established. In order for the scene not to be overly dense with information, however, the writer has to find a number of different ways to present the material.

The following example sets up Jessica's relationship with Margaret, Margaret's relationship with Jessica's fiancé, Chloe's relationship with them both, and Frank and Chantal's relationship with them all. Notice how what is not said is as important as the dialogue. Margaret clearly does not listen to Jessica and completely ignores her fiancé. Chloe's costume and actions set her distinctly apart from the rest. (This scene is illustrated in Figure 22–1 at the beginning of this chapter.)

```
START:01:07:52:00  END: 01:08:53:06

D1/220/100—Chloe arrives, disturbing gathering of
Margaret, Jessica, Masa, & Frank

FOYER—MAGIC—DAY 1

Margaret steps out, followed by Frank who is carrying a
BOTTLE OF RED WINE and a TRAY OF WINE GLASSES. He puts
the tray of glasses down on an off-screen table.

                    MARGARET
    Put it right there. I want this weekend to be
    perfect. It's been so long since the family has
    been together.

A couple steps into the atrium. JESSICA HAWKE is in
her mid-thirties and dresses with a style that reflects
her self-assured manner. Her companion, MASA, is a
tall, attractive Japanese man in his late twenties.

                    JESSICA
    Hello, Margaret.

MARGARET turns, sees Jessica, and swoops over to greet
her, pulling her from Masa who's left in the
background.
```

MARGARET

Jessica You're here. You look more mature every time I see you.

JESSICA

Where's Dad?

MARGARET

Reed's upstairs. He'll be joining us later.

MARGARET leans in, kissing the air to the side of her cheeks. She turns her back on JESSICA'S COMPANION and toward the wine tray. JESSICA gestures to him.

JESSICA

You remember Masa.

MARGARET, ignoring MASA, leads JESSICA toward the wine service.

MARGARET
(to Frank off stage)
Frank, do be a dear and take Jessica's bags.

FRANK moves to follow out the order, but MASA intercedes.

MASA

I will get Jessica's bags. And mine.

He exits.

MARGARET
(to Jessica)
It must be miserable for you over there...

Off-stage we hear the sound of doors bursting open. A LEATHER-CLAD FIGURE in a hooded sweatshirt, carrying a DUFFEL BAG and a MOTORCYCLE HELMET, enters abruptly. With the reflexes of a pit bull, FRANK attacks the intruder and wrestles him around. As the intruder spins around, the sweatshirt hood falls off, revealing long blonde hair. FRANK sees the intruder's face and his mouth drops open, his hands frozen on the intruder's chest. He's a she.

FRANK

Hey!...Chloe?

CHLOE

Frank, I never knew you cared.

Now FRANK sees that his bands are cupped to CHLOE'S breasts. She knees him in the groin. She dusts herself

off and picks up her bag as Frank tries to get his
wind back. She saunters over to MARGARET, who, for the
first time, is speechless. CHLOE grabs the wine bottle
out of her hand.

>   CHLOE
>   Jessica. Mother . . .

Before MARGARET can regain her composure, CHLOE downs a
swig from the bottle and leaves. JESSICA leaves.
MARGARET hurries after her. CHANTAL steps into frame
speaking into her MOBILE PHONE.

>   CHANTAL
>   She's here. Come on, Frank, up we go.

CHANTAL goes to Frank and helps him up off the ground.
They walk off, leaving Margaret alone.

>   MARGARET
>   (frustrated)
>   OOOHHH!!!!

She storms off after Jessica.

ESTABLISHING RISING ACTION IN ALL FOUR STORY VARIATIONS

In any story, it is not enough to ensure key plot points; those beats must be carefully
orchestrated in rising action that builds to a climax. In *Voyeur* with its four variations, this process became particularly complex. To ensure smoothly rising action in
all the story variations, the writers broke the story into five acts and twelve key beats.

```
ACT 1 INTRODUCTION

Introduction of situation
Development of relationships
Foreshadowing of conflict

ACT 2 RISING ACTION

First action points
Angling for positions
Turning point

ACT 3 CRISIS

Main action point confrontations

ACT 4 TRAGIC FORCE

Repercussions from confrontations
Force of last suspense
Revelations
```

```
ACT 5 RESOLUTION

Climax: pay-off, point of highest emotional activity
Conclusion
```

Once the beats were laid out, the writers developed a chart (see the following) to make sure that the key beats were developed for each character's story variation. The chart numbers refer to the scenes where the beats are located.

ACT ONE: INTRODUCTORY BEATS			
	INTRODUCTION OF SITUATION	DEVELOPMENT OF RELATIONSHIP	FORESHADOWING CONFLICT
MARGARET	Demonstrates her control over Household. 4a	Has a softer side. 3	Some of her powers have been usurped. 3
ZACK	Attempts to wield power he doesn't have. 4b	Has abandoned Lara emotionally. 5a	Obsessed with becoming CEO. 5a
JESSICA	Feels like an outsider. Margaret rearranged her room. 6a	Masa is her strength and grounding. 6a	Has evidence that threatens Reed. Feels conflicted using it. 6a
CHLOE	Enjoys being the black sheep. Acts for effect. 5b	Reed is notified of her arrival. 5b	Something about this house causes her tremendous pain. 6b
REED	Will announce presidential candidacy tomorrow morning. 2	Is charismatic and has been called to the presidency. 2	Is concerned about family's reaction to his announcement. 2
FRANK	Is head of security. Has long-standing relationship with Reed. 4b	Has secret relationship with Chantal. 1	Is uncomfortable about this family gathering. 5b
CHANTAL	Controls all access to Reed. Is Reed's personal assistant. 4b	Has secret relationship with Frank. 1	Isn't afraid of confrontations with family members. 3

CHARACTERS, PLACE, AND TIME

The challenge of properly developing rising conflict is shared to a large degree with linear scriptwriting. The problem of having the same character in two different places at the same time is, however, unique to interactive narrative, and a particular problem with a piece as interactive as *Voyeur,* which has multiple scenes playing simultane-

CHARACTERS & SCENES CHART

MARGARET	JESSICA	ZACK	CHLOE	REED	MASA	LARA	CHANTAL	FRANK
				2a / w/Marg			w/Frank	1a
3a								
4a		4b					w/Marg	
w/Chloe		5a	5b			w/Zack	4c	
w/Jessica	w/Chloe		6b		w/Chloe	w/Zack	w/Chloe	w/Chloe
7a	6a	7b	7c	w/Marg	w/Jessica	w/Chloe		
8b	w/Zack	w/Chantal	w/Marg	w/Frank	8c		8a	w/Chantal / 9a
10a		10b		w/Marg		w/Zack		
11a	w/Chloe		11b	w/Marg				
w/Zack	12b	12a		w/Jessica	w/Jessica		w/Reed	
	13a		15a	13b		14a		
		16a		w/Lara				
				w/Chloe				
				w/Zack				

ously. To avoid having the same character in two different places at the same time, the writers developed a characters and scenes chart.

The numbers refer to the time line, explained earlier in this chapter in the "Simultaneously Playing Multiple Scenes in Real Time" section. In the first time line, there is only the one scene (Chantal and Frank). In the fourth time line, there are three scenes happening at the same time: 4a with Margaret, whose name is at the top of the sheet; 4b with Zack, which also includes Lara; and 4c with Chantal. This was only the first draft of this structure. The final draft was much denser, with as many as six scenes playing in a single time zone. The final script had about 100 scenes. Thirty to forty of these scenes were common to all the scenarios and were always available to be seen. There were ten to fifteen unique scenes for each of the four variations that were played only when that scenario was loaded.

CONCLUSION: RESPONSE TO THE PROJECT

All of the careful planning and skilled writing helped *Voyeur* become a much-honored interactive narrative, winning seven Academy Awards from the Academy of Interactive Arts and Sciences, including awards for best interactive program, best drama, best direction, and best story. It also won a gold medal Invision award and a gold Cindy award from the International Association of Audio Visual Communicators. This success spawned a sequel called *Voyeur II*.

REFERENCES

Pousette, Lena Marie. Telephone interview with the author. December 1995.
Riordan, David. Telephone interviews with the author. June 1994, October 1995, December 1995.

C H A P T E R   2 3

PARALLEL STORIES NARRATIVE CASE STUDY: *THE PANDORA DIRECTIVE*

Summary

Name of production: *The Pandora Directive*
Writer: Aaron Conners
Developer: Access Software Inc.
Audience: General audience
Medium: CD-ROM
Presentation location: Home
Subject: Tex Murphy detective mystery
Goal: Entertain
Architecture: Parallel story paths, linear, hierarchical dialogue branching

The script samples and images used in this chapter are courtesy of Access Software Inc. © 1994, 1996 Access Software Inc.

PROGRAM DESCRIPTION AND BACKGROUND

PROGRAM DESCRIPTION

The Pandora Directive is the fourth interactive movie in the Tex Murphy science-fiction mystery series. The program is released on CD-ROM and intended for home use. It is played by one person and is highly interactive. Much of the game is played in first person. Users can choose where Tex goes, what he does, and even what he says.

At the beginning of *The Pandora Directive,* Tex is hired to find Dr. Thomas Malloy. Tex soon learns that Malloy has secret information that the National Security Agency (NSA) and others are willing to kill for. To safeguard his secrets, Malloy sent out five puzzle boxes, each carrying a component of the Pandora Directive, which will explain his project. Tex's search for Malloy quickly turns into a quest for those boxes, which seem to have a bad habit of getting their owners killed. Romantic complication ensues between Tex and Malloy's daughter, Regan, which doesn't exactly thrill Tex's girlfriend, Chelsee. The climactic ending takes place in a Mayan labyrinth where Malloy's project is hidden. The plot has three basic story paths with seven possible endings, so Tex's success in love and war depends on how you play the game.

PRODUCTION BACKGROUND

The Pandora Directive was developed and produced by Access Software Inc. of Salt Lake City. Since the production of *The Pandora Directive*, Access has been purchased by Microsoft, but it continues to develop multimedia programs under the Access name. In addition to the Tex Murphy series, Access produces the best-selling *Links* golf series and a number of other successful adventure games, including *The Black Pearl*.

Chris Jones, the cofounder of the company, produces and stars in the Tex Murphy series, which includes *Mean Streets, Martian Memorandum, Under a Killing Moon* (the first collaboration with Aaron Conners), *The Pandora Directive,* and *Tex Murphy Overseer*. Conners wrote and codesigned the *Pandora Directive* based on his novel of the same name, which was published by Prima Publishing. Chris Jones codesigned the game. The video sequences were directed by Adrian Carr.

GOALS AND CHALLENGES WRITING *THE PANDORA DIRECTIVE*

GOALS

One of writer Aaron Conners' goals was to present a complex story that combined the best elements of the detective genre with off-beat science-fiction material reminiscent of *The Twilight Zone* and *The Outer Limits*. Some critics have compared the Tex Murphy series with *The X Files*. Conners also wanted to present well-developed characters, particularly in Tex, but also in his love interests, Chelsee and Regan.

So far this sounds like any good movie. But we are talking interactive movie here, and Conners also wanted to allow for maximum interactivity on the part of the user. His goal was interactive choices integrated in a way that disturbs the flow of the narrative as little as possible. He hoped to achieve this by having the choices affect the story in the same way that such choices affect us in real life.

Although not strictly a writing goal, Conners, as writer-codesigner, and his codesigner, Chris Jones, also wanted this video game to capture the feeling of a theatrical movie. They achieved this through heavy use of close-ups, video, and action sequences. These space-hungry elements required the game to be released on six CDs.

CHALLENGES

The key elements of these goals and the major challenges are:

- Developing a complex interactive story and characters.
- Creating smooth and realistic interactivity at the shot and dialogue level and the scene and sequence level.

- Making the complex story and interactivity work together in an engaging and coherent fashion.

WRITING *THE PANDORA DIRECTIVE*: MEETING THE CHALLENGES

Although this case study will be focused primarily on *The Pandora Directive*, comparisons will occasionally be drawn with the previous Tex Murphy mystery, *Under a Killing Moon*.

DEVELOPING A COMPLEX INTERACTIVE STORY AND CHARACTERS

The Novel

Writing *The Pandora Directive* novel first, said Conners, gave him a chance to develop the story and characters thoroughly. He started the novel writing freehand in a smoky Salt Lake City bar with red vinyl seats and sparkly counter tops, the kind of place Tex Murphy might hang out in. Conners first roughly outlined the story, listening to snatches of conversation and sometimes jotting down lines of dialogue.

He also developed the basic characters at this stage. He decided what he wanted them to be like and what their signature character quirks would be, such as using faulty grammar. Finally, he laid out how he wanted the characters to progress and develop in the story. He generated a lot of pages in this preparatory stage.

Once this preliminary work was done, he sat at the computer and developed an extended hierarchical outline broken down by acts and scenes. He determined what would happen in each scene and gradually laid out the story. He wrote the novel based on this outline.

The Script

This is one of the more complex interactive narrative programs produced, and the writing process reflects this complexity. After Conners completed the novel, his codesigner, Chris Jones, cut key story elements out of the novel to make a rough script, which was just one path of the story and conversation (the B path, the same as the novel). Screenwriter Scott Yeagamn polished this script, and Conners completed it.

The script serves primarily as a reference for people outside of Access Software, such as actors, so they can understand what the program is about. The script includes few interactive elements and comprises only 20 percent of all the material written for the project. A script sample follows.

```
INT. BREW AND STEW—DAY (Interactive Scene #22)

...Tex sidles up to the bar.

                        LOUIE
          Hey, Murph. How goes the battle?

                        TEX
                  (a forced grin)
          Louie, you wouldn't believe it if I told you.
                  (Louie doesn't ask)
          Say, did Chelsee leave some things of mine...
```

LOUIE
(retrieves a couple items from under the bar)
You bet . . .
(lays them on bar top)

LOUIE (Cont'd)
Amongst the items . . . Looks like someone's business
card . . . and your lucky Pez dispenser.

TEX
(Picks things up. Inspects Pez dispenser)
Wondered where that went to. Thanks.

TEX
(on a more serious note)
So how's she doing?

LOUIE
Yuh mean Chelsee?
(weighs it)
She just turned 30. She thinks it's the end of the
world.

TEX
I don't understand it.

LOUIE
You're not supposed to. Just accept that she's
having a hard go of it and leave it at that. She's
looking for something more in her life, that's all.
(beat)
Tell me somethin', Murph? You ever been in love?
I'm talking about "True Love."

Tex twists his neck nervously, plays with his Pez
dispenser.

TEX
I dunno, Louie. What the hell's that mean anyway,
true love?

LOUIE
Nothin'. It's all just chemicals. Endorphins or
whatever. Fallin' in love's simple as one, two,
three. Any idiot can do it. What's hard is gettin'
ta know someone, and after all that, still likin'
'em.

TEX
No kidding.

LOUIE
But that's not even the hardest thing. Hardest
thing is what makes all the difference.

```
                              TEX
What's that?


                             LOUIE
...Finding someone you can trust.

Tex thinks about it.


                          LOUIE (Cont'd)
Chelsee's givin' you a shot,...but she's not
gonna wait forever. There's a whole load of guys
who'd give their right arm for one minute of
Chelsee's attention. You know it.

CLOSER ON TEX...

...as he continues to reflect on what LOUIE has said.
```

The Walkthrough

After the script, Conners developed the walkthrough (part of which is included at the end of this chapter). This is a description of the story line and the key interactive elements. A walkthrough of a computer game is similar to a linear film/TV treatment, which gives the basic story line without extensive dialogue or calling shots. The *Pandora* walkthrough primarily explains how to get through the B path, but it also refers to key interactions with the other paths.

Conners divided the walkthrough story into days. This device not only makes the transitions between the program's multiple discs easier, but the writer also feels that this structure makes good sense for an interactive movie. Because an interactive movie can include as much as sixty hours of game play, it should be thought of not as a feature film but rather as a miniseries with a number of small conflicts and cliffhangers at the end of each day that gradually lead to the major climax at the end.

Puzzles

After developing the basic walkthrough storyline, Conners came up with puzzles that the player must solve to advance in the game. Integrating puzzles into interactive narrative is one of the challenges that faces writers of interactive movies. Many of the users of a program, such as *The Pandora Directive*, are primarily interested in following the interactive story. For dedicated gamers, however, the challenge of solving difficult puzzles and racking up high point scores is a prime appeal.

Conners and his codesigner solved this problem by coming up with two levels of play: a game player level and an entertainment level. On the game player level, there is no access to hints, there are additional puzzles, and the solutions to the puzzles are more difficult. For their extra effort, the game players can earn twice as many points as the entertainment-level players, who in addition to having hints and easier puzzles can skip the puzzles altogether by simply typing, "I am a cheater," on their keyboard. Both categories of user earn points by solving puzzles and making the right choices to advance the story. A running tally of points scored is constantly on the screen.

Interactive Conversations

For Conners, the last phase of writing an interactive movie is coming up with the characters' interactive conversation. To do this, Conners makes a list of the characters and develops the interactive dialogue, flowcharts, and Ask Abouts (key information that the player/Tex can ask other characters about). Each of these elements is explained in detail later in this chapter under "Making a Complex Story and Interactivity Work Together" and "Creating Smooth and Realistic Interactivity."

Game Play Addendum

Another document that the writer created during development of this project is the addendum, which consists of 500 pages explaining all the rules of interaction and game play. These clarifying inserts are sometimes referred to in the walkthrough or other production material to make it clear to the people putting the program together how the game is supposed to work.

There is no unified document that unites all of these written elements on which the game is based. That is the job of Conners and his codesigner, Chris Jones.

CREATING SMOOTH AND REALISTIC INTERACTIVITY

Interactive Dialogue

One of the more innovative elements of *Under a Killing Moon* and *The Pandora Directive* is the degree of interactivity that is allowed at the dialogue level. In an interactive dialogue scene, the viewer is given a list of three Response Attitudes for Tex's dialogue. Clicking one of these attitudes causes Tex to respond in a certain way. If the player does nothing, there is a default path, a middle ground between the bad Tex and the good Tex.

Under a Killing Moon **Interactive Dialogue Examples** In the following examples from *Under a Killing Moon,* the dialogue in parentheses is Tex's girl, Chelsee, speaking. The empty brackets indicate that Chelsee's dialogue at the top of the list can initiate each of Tex's responses. The Response Attitudes are in all capitals. Clicking on one of those Response Attitudes causes Tex to respond with that line of dialogue to Chelsee. This is the list of all the Response Attitudes for a scene. Of course, the player would see only one list of three Response Attitudes in the menu at a time, and would not see all the dialogue written out. Tex would speak it in response to the attitude choice (see Figure 23–3) later in this chapter.

Conners decided to use this approach as opposed to having all the dialogue options written out because it would slow the story too much if players had to read three lines of dialogue before making a choice, and the Response Attitudes maintain the element of surprise. Players don't know what line they will get when they click an attitude. Surprise is essential for humor and shock.

(See the flowchart in Figure 23–1, for a sense of how the scene below would play out interactively.)

```
(Tex/Chelsee)

Chelsee: ("Well, hello, stranger.")
Tex:    [ ] SUBTLE INNUENDO Hey sweetheart, know
            anyone who could use my services today?
```

[ ]   LOVESICK PUPPY Chelsee, you're breaking
      my heart.
[ ]   CHARMINGLY CURIOUS Tell me, gorgeous,
      has the new *True Detective* come in yet?

Chelsee: ("I guess that depends on which services
               we're talking about, big guy.")
Tex: [ ] BLATANT INNUEND0 Join me for a drink
               and I'll go over all the great services
               I have to offer.
          [ ] SLEAZEBAG OFFER You know, I'm a certified
               love mechanic . . .
          [ ] PLAY STUPID Well, duh. I guess you
               forgot—I'm a P.I.

Chelsee: ("Why? Because I've got a steady job?")
Tex: [ ] MAKE A PASS No. You're just so beauti-
               ful it makes me ache.
          [ ] SARCASTIC RETORT Ha ha. You're a riot,
               Chelsee. You ought to be doing standup.
          [ ] DEEPLY INSULTED Sure, kick me when I'm
               down. You think it's fun being broke?

Chelsee: ("Yeah, but you've gotta pay for it
               this time. When you finish a magazine,
               it's in no condition to sell.")
Tex: [ ] SARCASTIC RETORT Ha ha. You're a riot,
               Chelsee. You ought to be doing standup.
          [ ] DEEPLY INSULTED Sure, kick me when I'm
               down. You think it's fun being broke?
          [ ] MACHO P.I. TALK Think of it this way,
               Chelsee. Reading *True Detective* . . .

Chelsee: ("Gee, Tex, that kind of talk could get
               you into trouble, but I don't drink
               with customers.")
Tex: [ ] STUD RESPONSE Not even the hottest P.I.
               in town?
          [ ] BLUE COLLAR OFFER I'd be happy to throw
               in a chili dog with that drink.
          [ ] PRICKED BY CUPID'S ARROW It's quite
               painful, the way you toy with my emo-
               tions, Chelsee.

Chelsee: ("Did you hear that Rook's place got
               robbed?")
Tex: [ ] ON THE CASE I . . .
          [ ] NO, BUT EAGER FOR INFORMATION No, I
               didn't. What do you know about it?
          [ ] YES, BUT UNCONCERNED Yup. Darn shame. I
               hope the cops find out who did it.

Chelsee: ("I hear you took care of Rook. Pretty
               impressive.")

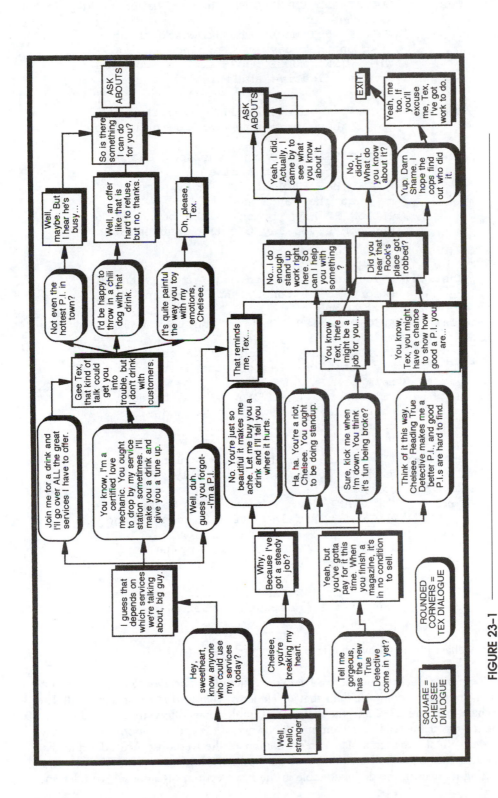

FIGURE 23–1

Dialogue Flowchart for *Under a Killing Moon.*

Tex: [ ] MODEST AND UNEMPLOYED Thanks. Maybe word
            will get around...
      [ ] MODEST, BUT MANLY Oh, it was nothing.
            Just another day at the office.
      [ ] WINK WINK, NUDGE NUDGE Let me show you
            my investigative abilities . . .

Chelsee: ("Oh, I'm sure it will. Maybe then
            you'll have some money and quit mooching
            off me.")
Tex: [ ] TENDER HEARTED C'mon, Chelsee. Let me
            savor success for awhile.
      [ ] RUGGED BANTER Admit it, doll, you love
            me just the way I am.
      [ ] INDIGNANT Hey, I don't like being broke.
            Why don't you lay off the insults and
            help me.

Chelsee: ("You know, Tex, it must take quite an
            effort to be lonely and broke and still
            be so smug.")
Tex: [ ] RUGGED BANTER Admit it, doll, you love
            me just the way I am.
      [ ] INDIGNANT Hey, I don't like being broke.
            Why don't you lay off the insults and
            help me . . .
      [ ] REEKING OF CONFIDENCE I have talents
            that money just can't buy. And some I
            charge for.

Chelsee: ("I'm sure I would, but I just don't
            date my customers. Especially ones with
            no money.")
Tex: [ ] INDIGNANT Hey, I don't like being broke.
            Why don't you lay off the insults and
            help me . . .
      [ ] REEKING OF CONFIDENCE I have talents
            that money just can't buy. And some I
            charge for.
      [ ] GOING FOR THE HARD SELL Did I ever tell
            you that I'm a gourmet chef . . .

The flowchart for the above dialogue is in Figure 23–1.

The Pandora Directive **Interactive Dialogue Example**   *The Pandora Directive* dialogue is even more complex than that of *Under a Killing Moon* just discussed. The flowchart in Figure 23–2 and the dialogue examples that follow are from a *Pandora* scene for the character Louie Lamintz, the owner of the greasy spoon Brew & Stew. In order to make the example clearer, I combined the Response Attitudes and dialogue lists into one. Find a number on the flowchart and then look for the corresponding number in the dialogue table in the next section, "Response Attitudes and

Interactive Dialogue for *The Pandora Directive*," to understand the flow of the conversation. On the flowchart, grey blocks are Louie's dialogue, and white blocks are Tex's dialogue.

Interactive dialogue in *The Pandora Directive* follows the same general structure as that in *Under a Killing Moon*. The screen shot from *The Pandora Directive* in Figure 23–3 shows the dialogue on the bottom left and the response attitudes on the right.

The interactive dialogue in *The Pandora Directive* is, however, even more complex than that in *Under a Killing Moon*. It is broken down by character and written in three separate documents:

- A flowchart with the boxes numbered and shaded
- A numbered list of the other characters' and Tex's dialogue
- A numbered list of Tex's Response Attitudes

There are several possible responses to certain lines of dialogue, depending on which story path (A, B, or C) the player/Tex is on. In the dialogue table in the following section, the Response Attitudes are in italics. The dialogue they elicit follows immediately after. (The complete list of dialogue and response attitudes is available in the Chapter 23 area of the "Chapters" section of the *Writing for Multimedia and the Web* CD-ROM.)

Interactive Dialogue and Story Paths

The A1 before the first line of Tex's dialogue in the table above refers to which story path Tex is on. Lines 1, 2, and 3 are the three possible lines of dialogue for a player on the A path. Lines 2, 3, and 4 are the three possible lines for a player on the B path, and lines 4, 5, and 6 are for the C path. There is some reuse of lines in different paths. (The different paths will be explained later in this chapter.) This is only the interactive dialogue for one scene for one character. This has to be done for every scene for every character.

Effect of Interactive Dialogue

The Response Attitude chosen and the resulting dialogue spoken mold Tex into the kind of character the player wants him to be. He can be a jerk or a hero, depending on which attitudes are clicked. The dialogue choices also have far-reaching effects on the story. These choices at the micro-level ultimately affect Tex's life (and the flow of the plot) at the macro-level. This is a more natural type of branching than that seen in many other interactive games, where the user simply chooses major actions, such as shooting the sheriff or the outlaw.

In *Pandora*, such larger action choices often become inevitable because of smaller choices made earlier in dialogue. This is one way that this game embraces the fatalistic viewpoint of its hard-boiled detective genre. In this genre, characters rarely make clear choices for their future. Instead they make a series of small choices that set off major consequences that shove them in one direction or another.

Emily's murder sequence is a good example of the effect of interactive dialogue. The steps that lead up to the death actually occur well before the actual event, and when the death does happen, it affects the rest of the story.

Tex stumbles onto the dark path that leads to Emily's death long before he ever sets foot in her nightclub, the Fuchsia Flamingo. The trouble starts in the linear

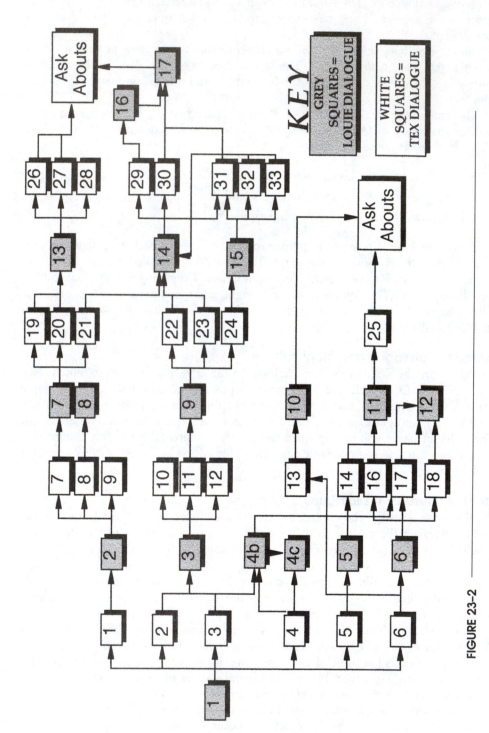

FIGURE 23–2

The Pandora Directive: Louie Scene 7, interactive dialogue flowchart.

Response Attitudes and Interactive Dialogue for *The Pandora Directive*

LOUIE
1. You just missed Chelsee.She stopped in to say goodbye. Apparently, she's off to Arizona. Everything OK with you two?

TEX
1. Definitely maybe
1. (A1) Let's see . . . Chelsee came by my office and redefined the word "frustration" and now she's headed off to Phoenix. I'd say things are going pretty darn well

2. Dumb male response
2. (A2-B1) It's kind of hard to tell . . . Chelsee being a woman and all.

3. Look to Louie for illumination
3. (A3-B2) I have absolutely no idea. What did Chelsee have to say?

4. Nuptial worries
4. (C1-B3) We had a bit of a tiff at the Fuchsia Flamingo. Felt just like we were married.

5. Condensed explanation
5. (C2) No. We decided to go with the *Readers' Digest* relationship and break up on our first date

6. Hard-boiled attitude
6. (C3) I don't want to talk about it. I'm so sick of dames I could puke.

LOUIE (Response to Tex #1)
2. That's kinda what I figured. She looked happier than I've seen her in quite awhile.

TEX
7. Pessimistic viewpoint
7. Well, she should. she's got a leash on most of my vital organs. That always makes women happy.

8. Play it down
8. Well then, my work is done. It's always been my mission in life to make anyone I can just a little happier.

9. Express total confusion
9. So, of course, she leaves town, just when things are picking up steam. I don't get it.

LOUIE (Response to Tex: #2 or 3)
3. Well, she and I talked for a bit. She's havin' a rough go of it.

TEX
10. Be moderately offended
10. Should I take that personally? I think I'm

11. Trivialize Chelsee's plight
11. Oh, you mean the unbearable trauma of turning thirty?

12. Manly incomprehension
12. Maybe I'm just not in touch with my feminine side. What exactly is so rough?

introduction to the program. Tex and Chelsee are sitting in Louie's diner. Chelsee, about to turn thirty years old, is feeling stuck and confused. She tries to get a response from Tex that would let her know that he really cares about her. But being an unsubtle male, Tex misses the point; she gets angry and leaves. Louie and Rook, who are also in the diner, however, understand her completely and lay into Tex after she has left: "Tex, you idiot, what she meant was . . ."

FIGURE 23-3

Interactive dialogue and response attitudes in The *Pandora Directive*.

Once the game goes into the interactive mode, the player Tex can go back and talk to her at her newsstand. Tex knows that she is upset, and really wants to go out with her. He has wanted to go out with her for years. What the player/Tex chooses to say to Chelsee at this point can send Tex down the dark path to Emily's death or to the light path and Emily's rescue.

The response attitude choices are: ATTEMPT AN APOLOGY, PRETEND NOTHING IS WRONG, or LIGHTEN THE MOOD. If Tex pretends nothing is wrong and just asks, "Any new detective magazines?" he has stumbled onto the dark path because this waffle makes Chelsee angry, and she'll respond with, "Sure, I've got Butthead Detective, you ought to like that one." Continuing this pattern of dialogue choices sets off an argument, which plants a seed of mistrust in Chelsee. Tex does, however, eventually calm her down enough to set a dinner date.

The player/Tex can take another step on the dark path when talking to Leach, Emily's boss. If Tex is rude to him, Leach gets mad and later will block Tex's entrance when he tries to rescue Emily.

After talking to Leach, Tex searches a room and gets knocked out, causing him to miss his dinner date with Chelsee. She, of course, is angry: "I can't believe you stood me up." At this point, Tex can try to explain and move up to the light path, or he can stay on the dark path by saying, "Look, that's the way it is. I'm a PI," causing another argument between them.

When they finally do get to the nightclub, he tells Chelsee he wants to see if he can get backstage to see the singer, Emily. Chelsee snaps, "You're here with me, and you're watching another woman." She says this because she is still angry about the argument they had before they went to the club. They have a huge fight. She leaves. Tex stays and gets drunk.

When he finally does see Emily at the club, he is in a totally different frame of mind than he would have been if not for the fight with Chelsee and being drunk. Because of this, and because Leach (mad from their earlier interaction) blocks him from Emily's room, he is unable to save her life.

After failing to save her, his whole perspective changes. He says, "I've got to get out of this business; it's killing me." He's now in for the kill, trying to get money so he can quit the PI business. He also loses Chelsee and later hooks up with the dark woman, Regan. If he continues on this path, he is killed at the end of the story.

Dialogue Explosion and Reusability

Although interactive dialogue is an excellent way to give the viewer a high degree of control and create realistic interactivity, it is not without its drawbacks. This degree of interactivity demands that a vast amount of dialogue be scripted. *Pandora* has six to twelve totally unique paths of conversation, depending on the scene. This doesn't mean there are twelve different choices per line of dialogue, but it does mean that there are twelve possible dialogue sequences or paths that could be charted through a scene. (Take some colored highlighters and chart a few paths through the *Pandora* flowchart in Figure 23–2 to see what I mean.)

A writer who isn't careful can be buried in a dialogue explosion of hundreds of lines for just one scene. The conversation grows vertically and requires massive amounts of dialogue writing. On the *Pandora* flowchart (Figure 23–2), notice the towering vertical stack of boxes 7 to 18, a total of eleven different lines of dialogue. *Pandora's* writer, Aaron Conners, said that the extra work of writing all these dialogue options doesn't actually pay off with viewer satisfaction. It is rare for the viewer to access all lines of dialogue, and because of the number of lines of dialogue in a scene, the lines had to be quite short.

Because of this limitation, Conners tried to make the *Pandora* dialogue branching more horizontal by reusing the same lines in different situations. Notice on *The Pandora Directive* flowchart (Figure 23–2) the number of places where multiple arrows go into one box. This means that the same line is being reused several times, such as Louie's shaded box #14, which is a possible response to three of Tex's dialogue lines.

The Mechanics of Flowcharting

Conners uses the software *ABC Flowcharter* to draw his charts. In *Under a Killing Moon,* he used flowcharts with dialogue typed in and indicated different characters by different-shaped boxes. Because the *Pandora* charts are more complex, he used numbers in the chart that refer to numbered lines of dialogue in a list. He indicated different characters by shading boxes. This technique makes it easier than the different-shaped boxes to distinguish the characters.

First-Person Point of View and Control of Character Movements

The *Pandora Directive* also gives the viewer a high degree of control over Tex's actions. Most of the interactive scenes are shot in first person. The player becomes Tex. He or she sees what Tex sees, and as Tex, the player can move all around the room and examine objects. The player can also click on items, such as a painting, to get Tex's sarcastic voice-over about art. Or the player can click on a picture of Tex's ex-wife, which might trigger a flashback video sequence. See the list of player options just above the dialogue in Figure 23–3.

Interactivity at the Scene and Sequence Level: Multiple Story Paths

These interactive choices at the dialogue and movement level launch the Tex character on one of three main story paths with seven possible endings. There are three main paths:

A—Light Path: This is the basic Hollywood ending in which Tex saves the world and wins the good woman, Chelsee.

B—Middle Path: This is middle ground. He doesn't lose Chelsee, but he doesn't win her either.

C—Dark Path: This is film noir—a chance to explore the negative possibilities. Tex fails to save Emily. He loses the good woman, Chelsee, takes up with the bad woman, Regan, and dies at the end.

As Tex (the player) continues to make choices in dialogue and movement, he will hit key dialogue lines or flags that will shift him back and forth between paths. And redemption is hard won. Once entrenched in the dark C path, the best he can hope for is to move up to B. The saintly A path is out of reach.

The player molds Tex into what he wants him to be: good, middle, or bad. Sometimes one choice can mean the difference between life and death. For example, which of the seven endings the player gets depends to a large degree on whether Tex sleeps with the bad woman, Regan. If the player has been on the A or B path and says no to Regan, then Tex solves the final puzzle on the spaceship before escaping safely. If the player follows the C path throughout the game, but says no to Regan, the player gets the B ending: Tex is wounded and sent limping off the ship by Fitzpatrick. If the player follows the C path throughout the game and Tex says yes to Regan, depending on the player's choices in the last scene, Tex could end up dead.

MAKING A COMPLEX STORY AND INTERACTIVITY WORK TOGETHER IN AN ENGAGING AND COHERENT FASHION

A detective story is very information-based. It requires readers or viewers to keep track of many characters, clues, and locations. This problem is exaggerated when the story has a high degree of interactivity, as in *The Pandora Directive*. Aaron Conners does a number of things to keep the audience well-oriented, such as voice-over for exposition and character background, a hints file, a travel list and map, and Ask Abouts.

Ask Abouts

As a detective, Tex is constantly asking people questions. If Tex/the player, chooses the right questions and goes to the right places, he gets key information. Where a real detective might scribble something in a notebook, Tex's key information automatically appears in his Ask Abouts list, which the player can access from the main interface at any time. See the top right in Figure 23–4.

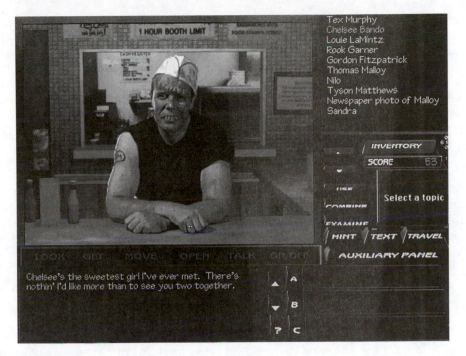

FIGURE 23–4

Ask Abouts in the *Pandora Directive*.

The following example from the *Pandora Directive* walkthrough explains how the Ask Abouts work. All the Ask Abouts are in bold. They appear on the on-screen Ask Abouts list (Figure 23–4), when someone tells Tex about them. He can then ask others about these Ask Abouts.

When Tex finds a scarf, he takes it to the Brew & Stew and shows It to LOUIE, who tells him about a **young blonde woman. Young blonde woman** is automatically placed in your Ask About list. When Tex asks him more about the young blonde woman, he responds with, "She was real pretty, though a little heavy on the makeup. I think she said her name was Emily." This puts **Emily** in your Ask About list. You can now ask anyone about Emily including Louie, but all he has to say is, "I don't know anythin' else about her."

However, when you ask another character, Clint, about Emily, he'll tell you she works for Gus Leach. **Gus Leach** is now placed in your Ask About list. Ask Clint about Gus Leach and he'll give you the **Leach's Key** Ask About. Ask Clint about Leach's key to get the key. You now know that the scarf belongs to the girl who sings at the Fuchsia Flamingo and that her name

```
is Emily. You also know that the Flamingo is run by
Gus Leach.
```

The Ask Abouts not only help the player keep track of key clues, they also limit the player to questions that the characters might have answers for. Otherwise, the viewer would be faced with the irritation of characters' constantly saying, "I don't know," or the writers would have to write Ask Abouts for everything mentioned in the game. The Ask Abouts also give a convenient way to ask questions. Simply click on the item on the list.

Louie's Ask Abouts Example   Following are some of the responses that the Louie Lamintz character can make if questioned on various Ask Abouts. Note that in some cases, as in the Chelsee Ask About, his responses depend on what path Tex is on (A, B, or C). Refer back to the *Pandora* flowchart (Figure 23–2) and you'll see that all the interactive conversations eventually end up in Ask Abouts.

```
If Tex Murphy asks about:

1. Tex: (Louie answers) You're OK in my book, Murph...
   no matter what anyone else says.
2. Chelsee: (1) Chelsee's the sweetest girl I've ever
   met. There's nothin' I'd like more than to see you
   two together.

      (2a)  Just between you and me, I get the feelin'
            she's sweet on ya.
      (2b)  I don't know what to tell ya, Murph. The
            mind of a woman can be a great mystery.
      (2c)  She called awhile ago. I guess she's gonna
            make her visit to Phoenix permanent. Sorry.
   (3a/b)  Yeah, I've heard from her. She wanted me to
            say hi.

3. Louie: What are ya askin' 'bout me for? I ain't
   nothin' special.
4. Rook: Rook's just an ornery son-of-a-gun, but,
   believe it or not, he's pretty soft underneath.
```

(The complete Ask Abouts list is in the Chapter 23 area of the "Chapters" section of the *Writing for Multimedia and the Web* CD-ROM.)

Sometimes Ask Abouts involve more than just asking about a name. They can involve showing things. What is shown and in what sequence affects Louie's response:

```
Offer photo of Malloy: Yeah. I've seen this guy. Lemme
think...He came in here a week or two ago. Had a
young blonde girl with him. Ordered liver and onions if
I remember correctly.
Offer untranslated letter: Well Murph, if I had to
guess, I'd say this is written in Yucatec. It's a
```

Mayan language, spoken in southern Mexico. I can't help ya with the translation, though. You know who might be able to help ya is Clint. I heard he's quite a world traveler. Might give it a try.

Offer scarf:
   If Tex offers Photo of Malloy first: Yeah, I remember this guy. Came in here to eat a couple times. Probably a month ago.
     Then Scarf: Oh, yeah. I remember this scarf . . . and the perfume on it. Young, blonde girl . . . In fact, she came in here with the guy in the photograph.
     If offer Scarf first: Oh, yeah. I remember this scarf . . . and the perfume on it. Young, blonde girl. Came in here awhile ago.
     Then Photo of Malloy: This guy was with that young blonde girl who wore the nice-smelling scarf.

Ask About Lead-Ins   You as the player can't just walk up to and start quizzing a character about Ask Abouts. Like a real detective, it usually requires a bit of chatter to warm up the source and get to an Ask About. In the example that follows, the numbers refer to the *Pandora* flowchart (Figure 23–2).

Louie:
17. My point is, fallin' in love don't mean a lot. What's hard is knowin' someone real well and still likin' 'em. But that ain't even the hardest thing. The hardest thing is findin' someone you can trust. Remember that. [beat] Now I'll get off my soapbox. . . What can I do for you?

Tex:
25. Yeah, I'll keep that in mind. Not to be rude, but can I ask you a few questions before I go?

Sometimes, getting to the Ask Abouts requires quite a bit of smooth talking. Refer to *The Pandora Directive* flowchart (Figure 23–2) to see the twisted path it takes to get to the Ask Abouts in that scene. Other times, Ask About lead-ins are fairly short, such as when Tex dials a telephone number and the person appears on the videophone ready for questions. But even these brief lead-ins can have relevance to the plot or character development.

THE PANDORA DIRECTIVE NARRATIVE WALKTHROUGH

To get a sense of how all of the elements discussed (complex story, interactivity, and Ask Abouts) work together, read the walkthrough sample that follows. The walkthrough is a rough description of the story and key interactive elements. It is an attempt to provide an overview of how the program is going to work. This is essential, because much of the other written material for an interactive program can be simply lists of dialogue, flowcharts, and phrases.

The walkthrough is broken down by days, as is *The Pandora Directive*. This makes it easier to use multiple CDs and to get the miniseries type of pacing that the writers and designers were looking for. Following is Day One of the walkthrough. (The complete walkthrough has ten days and is available on the *Writing for Multimedia and the Web* CD-ROM.)

Options are frequently listed for the character in the walkthrough, such as, "Your options at the outset (in likely order of importance) are (1) find out about Malloy staying at the Ritz, (2) pay the rent to Nilo, (3) pay Rook and/or Louie, (4) go to the newsstand and talk to Chelsee, or (5) go to the Electronics Shop." In the actual game, these options are clear because of the situation or are explained through Tex's voice-overs (VO). There are different versions of voice-overs for the different paths. Voice-overs are enclosed by brackets.

THE PANDORA DIRECTIVE WALKTHROUGH

Day One

After the Introduction is finished, we have met Louie, Rook, Glenda, Chelsee, and Fitzpatrick. You have also seen Sandra Collins (dead) and the Black Arrow Killer (Dag Horton).

In the introductory conversation with Chelsee, you learn that she is about to turn thirty years old and is in an emotional quandary about it. After she leaves, Louie and Rook lead us to believe that Chelsee is romantically susceptible.

In the introductory conversation with Gordon Fitzpatrick, you learn that he is looking for a Dr. Thomas Malloy, who recently stayed at the Ritz Hotel. Fitzpatrick and Malloy used to work together (where, unspecified). Fitzpatrick then says he saw a photograph of Malloy in the Bay City Mirror and found out that the photograph had been taken at a local university (San Francisco Tech). Fitzpatrick gives Tex a copy of the photo. The only person at SFT able or willing to recognize Malloy was a grad student named Sandra (Collins). She said she had worked with the man Fitzpatrick knew as Malloy, but that she knew him as Tyson Matthews. Fitzpatrick arranged to meet Sandra later to discuss what she knew, but she didn't keep the appointment and Fitzpatrick was unable to locate her again. Fitzpatrick then saw another reference to Malloy in the *Cosmic Connection*, an underground paranormal journal, which mentioned an upcoming interview with Dr. Thomas Malloy. The interview never appeared in the magazine and no explanation has been given. Finally, Fitzpatrick says he was able to pay 500 dollars to get Malloy's address at the Ritz, but Malloy had already moved on.

Tex accepts the case and Fitzpatrick leaves. This initiates the first interactive portion of the game. [Play TEX VO—Tex owes $ to Rook, Louie, Nilo.] Your inventory consists of the newspaper photo of Malloy,

$4000 cash, and Tex's Electronics Shop credit card
(from UKM). Your options at the outset, in likely order
of importance, are: (1) find out about Malloy staying at
the Ritz, (2) pay the rent to Nilo, (3) pay Rook
and/or Louie, (4) go to the newsstand and talk to
Chelsee, or (5) go to the Electronics Shop.

Going to Rook, Louie, Chelsee, or the Electronics
Shop can be done in any order at any time. In order to
talk to Nilo, however, you must make a date with
Chelsee (Path: A/A/A/A/C). Until this is done, Nilo
isn't at the front desk of the Ritz.

Note: In order to initiate the A path, you must use
Path C/B/B/ . . . In order to initiate the C path, you
must use Path A/C/C/ . . . When returning to Chelsee
(after initiating one of the alternate paths), you must
use Path C/A/C to make the date.

Once the date with Chelsee has been set, she is still
available at the newsstand for Ask Abouts until Tex
gets jumped at the Ritz. After that, she's no longer
at the newsstand at any point in the game. Also, once
you've set the date, Nilo becomes available at the
front desk in the Ritz lobby.

If you go to the Brew & Stew and talk to LOUIE, you
can choose A, in which case, you lose $20 from inven-
tory; otherwise, you don't lose any money. Once the Ask
Abouts start, you can also offer $200 to pay your tab
to Louie. This is totally optional, though it will earn
you points. At the pawnshop, you must pay Rook $300 in
order to get him to answer Ask Abouts. At the Electronics Shop, you must pay Zack $1230 in order to make
a purchase.

Once you've made a date with Chelsee, you're free to
talk to Nilo. You must pay Nilo $2100 for rent before
doing anything else. After paying the rent, Nilo will
ask for more money in order to get to the Ask Abouts.
You must pay either $300 (choice A or B after "no com-
prende") or $100 (choice C after "no comprende").
Offering the photo of Malloy will get Nilo to tell you
that Malloy stayed in Apartment A, but is no longer
there. [TEX VO—Probably no one else has been there
since Malloy left.]

When you go to Apartment A, you'll find the door
locked. There is a security panel on the wall by the
door, which requires a number code in order to enter.
[TEX VO—Nilo keeps notebook on desk.] You now have two
ways to get into the apartment: (1) Go back to Nilo
and ask for the code, or (2) set off the fire alarm,
getting Nilo to leave the front desk and allowing you
to get his notebook. If you ask Nilo for the code,
he'll ask for another $500. Using Path C/C will get
you the code for free. Any other path will cost you
$500. In order to find the fire alarm, locate the paint-
ing on the wall in the second floor hallway of the Ritz

and move it. Get the screwdriver from Tex's office, and
use it on the face of the fire alarm. This will initiate the fire alarm puzzle. Click the top left nodule,
then the top right nodule. Next, click the second
nodule from the top on the left; then click the bottom
nodule on the right. Next, click the second nodule from
the bottom on the left; then click the second nodule
from the top on the right. Finally, click the bottom
nodule on the left; then the second nodule from the
bottom on the right. This will start the fire alarm. Go
to the front desk in the lobby and get Nil's notebook.
Examine the notebook and find the code to Apartment A
(4827). Go to the apartment and enter the code on the
security panel...then enter the apartment.
   A movie sequence is initiated. Tex is jumped and
knocked unconscious.

CONCLUSION: RESPONSE TO THE PROJECT

The Pandora Directive has been a major success. *Computer Gaming World* and *PC
Games Magazine* named it adventure game of the year, and *PC Gamer Magazine*
named it an Editor's Choice.

REFERENCE

Conners, Aaron. Telephone interviews with the author. July 1994, August 1995, December
    1995, October 1999.

C H A P T E R   2 4

WORLDS NARRATIVE CASE STUDY: *DUST: A TALE OF THE WIRED WEST*

Summary

Name of production: *Dust: A Tale of the Wired West*
Writer: Andrew Nelson
Developers: CyberFlix Inc.
Audience: Rated for teenagers (13 and up)
Medium: CD-ROM
Presentation location: Home
Subject: Western
Goal: Entertain
Architecture: String of pearls, linear, hierarchical

The script samples and images used in this chapter are courtesy of CyberFlix Inc. ©1995 CyberFlix Inc.

PROGRAM DESCRIPTION AND BACKGROUND

PROGRAM DESCRIPTION

Dust: A Tale of the Wired West is an interactive Western set in 1882 in Diamond-back, New Mexico. In the precredit linear video scene, the Stranger catches a gun-slinger, the Kid, playing foul at cards and nails his cheating hand to the table with a knife. Before the Kid can recover, the Stranger flees.

In the next scene, the player becomes the Stranger as the rest of the game is played through first-person point of view. What the Stranger sees, the player sees. When people talk to the Stranger, they are talking to the player.

Running from the Kid, the Stranger stumbles into the town of Diamondback (see Figure 24–1) in the middle of the night with no gun, little money, and a hole in his size-twelve boots. The goal is first to get cash, gun, and boots, and then to defend

---

Parts of this chapter originally appeared in *Creative Screenwriting*.

FIGURE 24-1

The main interface showing the town in *Dust: A Tale of the Wired West.*

himself from the Kid, who is gunning for revenge. If the Stranger survives the high noon shootout, he may get appointed sheriff and lured into helping a Native American schoolteacher recover her tribe's lost treasure.

The town of Diamondback is a three-dimensional world populated with forty animated characters. *Dust's* writer, Andrew Nelson, calls it "*Myst* with people in it." The Stranger can move through the town, exploring most of its buildings and talking to its citizens. They will sometimes help and sometimes mislead; a big part of the game is judging the character of the people the Stranger meets and deciding whose advice to follow.

In addition to the story, this program also has games to play, such as blackjack, poker, slot machines, checkers, and a shooting range. These games are well integrated into the story, and success at them helps the player advance the narrative. For example, on the Stranger's first night in town, he must win enough money gambling to stay at the hotel.

DUST: A TALE OF THE WIRED WEST AND THE ADVENTURE GAME

Dust's writer Nelson says that sophisticated navigability and interactivity sets this game apart from other adventure games. The user in *Dust* enters a world populated by cyberpuppets who have lives and personalities of their own. They do their shopping, gambling, or drinking in real time, whether the player interacts with them or not. If the player does interact, they will address him or her directly, and they will remember how the player treats them. This can cause a chain of events that radically changes the progress of the narrative.

All the buildings in town can be entered whenever they are "open," and objects can be looked at and picked up. Sounds that are heard in the distance will get louder as the player approaches their source. This complex navigability and interactivity is made possible by CyberFlix's DreamFactory authoring program, described in detail later in this chapter under "Creating an Inhabitable, Believable World." *Dust* is the first program to be completely developed in this process.

PRODUCTION BACKGROUND

Andrew Nelson wrote and produced *Dust: A Tale of the Wired West*. Michael Gilmore and Jamie Wicks were the art directors in charge of the design. The program was developed by CyberFlix Inc. of Knoxville, Tennessee. After producing several more successful games, including *Titanic: Adventure Out of Time*, the CyberFlix management decided to concentrate on licensing its DreamFactory software and ceased producing computer games.

GOALS AND CHALLENGES WRITING *DUST: A TALE OF THE WIRED WEST*

GOALS

A primary goal for the developers of *Dust* was to create an inhabitable, believable world with its own constants and laws. They also wanted to give the user the maximum possible freedom to explore this world and interact with its citizens as part of a complex, interactive story. They hoped this program would have broad appeal and reach a wider audience than the typical video game.

CHALLENGES

The key elements of these goals and the major challenges are the following:

- Creating an inhabitable, believable world.
- Giving the user the opportunity to explore this world and interact with its citizens.
- Developing a story within this highly interactive world through establishing plot points, characterization, and other story functions.

WRITING *DUST: A TALE OF THE WIRED WEST*: MEETING THE CHALLENGES

CREATING AN INHABITABLE, BELIEVABLE WORLD

The key to *Dust's* success in creating an inhabitable, believable world is CyberFlix's proprietary, multimedia, authoring tool, DreamFactory. This technology allowed writer Andrew Nelson to "write" *Dust* in a radically different way than most other multimedia programs are written today.

Preliminary Writing

The writing of *Dust* started off with words on paper, as do most other multimedia titles. First Nelson developed the back story on the town of Diamondback, giving the history of the town and the characters. When creating a world such as this town, the designers need to know background on every individual and building, so that they can create a consistent, realistic environment that has a life of its own.

The writer next wrote the walkthrough, outlining the basic story line and key interactions. Then came the game design, which is basically a blown-up storyboard showing the interactive puzzles. Finally came the table of events, which became the basis for the hint book. This book has suggestions that help the player solve key problems and move forward in the game. Up to this point, the writing process on *Dust* is similar to that of other worlds games. But from this point forward, the writer used DreamFactory, and the similarities quickly fade.

DreamFactory® Defined

DreamFactory is a set of multimedia authoring tools designed by CyberFlix's president, Bill Appleton, and used to create *Dust*. DreamFactory is designed so that nontechnical people, such as writers and designers, can develop an interactive multimedia piece without programming.

DreamFactory develops 3-D interactive environments that are peopled by "cyberactors" who interact with the user. The cyberactors are not videos of real people, nor are they traditional, drawn animations. Instead they are created from photographs of real people that are developed into computer-generated animations. The final results are cyberactors who walk around town and talk to the user. (See Figure 24–2 later in this chapter.)

These synthetic actors allow for greater realism than cartoon-style animation, and they allow much higher levels of interactivity than video, because these computer-generated characters, like the letters on a word processor, are simply bits of code that can be instantly assembled and reassembled. This advantage has made 3-D animation similar to that used in *Dust* the most popular approach for video games.

In *Dust* the characters respond smoothly to the user, remember interactions, and change future behavior based on these interactions. Most of the characters develop significantly during the four days of the story. The characters also move about on their own in real time, whether the user interacts with them or not.

DreamFactory has these specialized tools:

- SetConstruction: Builds 3-D digital sets that the player can move through in real time.

- PropDepartment: Creates accurately scaled props that increase or decrease in size as they get closer to or farther from the user.

- CentralCasting: Creates and animates the cyberactors who move through the 3-D sets, speak, and react to the user.

- HeadShot: Animates the close-ups of the talking characters based on photographs of actual actors.

- MovieEditor: Edits animation sequences and can add special effects, camera movement, and transitions.

- SoundTrack: Builds and controls the audio.
- FlatPainter: Creates backgrounds, interfaces, and interactive buttons.

DreamFactory and the Writer

After the writer develops the basic characters, story line, and some of the dialogue on paper, he or she stops writing a plan for a world and instead uses DreamFactory to build the world itself. Once the characters are defined, artists use the HeadShot and CentralCasting tools to create the characters. Other designers use the SetConstruction and PropDepartment tools to create the environment or world of the story (in the case of *Dust*, the town of Diamondback). The newly created cyberactors are placed in this world, and from this point forward, the writer doesn't put words on paper again.

The writer thus functions more like a writer-director. When the writer types lines for a certain character, the appropriate cyberactor on the computer screen will speak the lines. When the writer types in screen directions, the cyberactor will do what he or she is told to do. The writer thus gets to see the world being created come immediately to life.

Editing is just as easy. The writer can click on a cyberactor to get his or her dialogue and reaction to changes in the script. *Dust's* writer, Andrew Nelson, said that there was no other effective way to test all the variables in a program as complex as *Dust*. DreamFactory allows the writer constantly to test game play and interaction all the way up to the alpha stage and beyond. (Alpha stage is the earliest full working version of a multimedia program.)

Nelson estimates that half of the original dialogue and most of the dialogue and story editing occurred in DreamFactory. Once he started working with DreamFactory, he did not work with paper again until the end of the project, when a hard copy of the script was printed out. The final script does not look like a screenplay. It is more like a treatment of the characters and character interactions, off of which hangs huge amounts of dialogue. Nelson estimates that there are about 5,000 individual lines of dialogue in *Dust*.

Writing in DreamFactory requires using a special scripting language, but Nelson says that it was not much more difficult than learning to write in linear screenplay style, which has its own specific formatting and technical vocabulary. Like writing in linear screenplay format, writing in DreamFactory is cumbersome at first, but eventually it becomes second nature. What is difficult (and this is shared by any other highly interactive script) is the need to write mosaically. When a writer is using DreamFactory to develop a worlds program such as *Dust*, there is no linear structure outside of the central story line. The linear progression is built by the user out of the snippets of dialogue and bits of interaction the writer creates.

GIVING THE USER THE OPPORTUNITY TO EXPLORE THIS WORLD

Perhaps the best way to explain the extensive navigability the user has in *Dust* is to describe some of the options available the first night of the story. After the introductory material, *Dust* starts with the Stranger coming into town in the middle of the night. After a few preliminary interactions to orient the viewer to the game, the user/Stranger is free to explore the town. He can wander the streets and talk to people he meets, or he can enter the buildings that are open. Because it is the middle of the night, the open buildings are limited to the saloon, the hotel, and the curiosities shop.

The curiosities shop is owned by a character named Help, who is always there if the player gets stuck. The hotel has no rooms available when the Stranger arrives, but the saloon is hopping with gambling, music, and women upstairs.

Players can visit each of these sites as often as they want and talk to anyone they meet. Because the characters all move in real time and have lives of their own, different characters appear as the evening progresses. However, in order to advance in the story and move on to the next day, the Stranger needs to find a place to sleep.

This can be done in a couple of ways. The Stranger needs money to stay at the hotel. He can get this by gambling or by searching the couch in the hotel, which has four dollars under the cushions. If he loses all his money gambling, he can ask Help for a loan. The other way to get a bed for the night is to be nice to the mayor's wife, who will then ask him home. But this works only if the Stranger sees her on the street and says just the right things. In *Dust*, there is usually an easy way and a hard way to achieve goals.

There are myriad story paths that the user/Stranger could travel the first night, depending on where he decides to go and whom he decides to talk to, but all the story paths will eventually lead to the Stranger's going to bed that night. Nelson describes this structure as a circular experience with several doors that will shoot the player out to the next level of the story. Depending on what the player does on one level of the story, he or she will be better or less prepared to meet the challenges in the next level. Eventually, all of these story paths on all of the levels lead to a common destination, which is a branching of six different endings.

The overall structure can be compared to a string of pearls (see Figure 19–5 on page 227), with each pearl being a set time period and location that the character is free to explore. To leave the pearl and advance the story, the player must achieve certain things, such as get a place to sleep, get a gun, get bullets, and so on.

This type of structure means that the writer and other developers must prepare vast amounts of dialogue, interactions, and places for the user to explore. It also means that it is difficult to create many emotions common to linear video that require a tight sequencing of action, such as suspense. However, Nelson explains that *Dust* offers something different from the linear experience. He compares *Dust* to Disneyland. Whatever players would like to do, they can find it in *Dust*. They can play cards, shoot in an arcade, and if they are lonely, there are lots of folks willing to talk. The experience of *Dust* essentially revolves around getting things, doing things, and having fun. (See the *Dust* demo in the Chapter 24 area of the "Chapters" section of the *Writing for Multimedia and the Web* CD-ROM.)

INTERACTIVE DIALOGUE

Dust's Approach to Interactive Dialogue

A major way to get information and have fun in *Dust* is through talking to the characters. Like the creators of *The Pandora Directive*, the developers of *Dust* decided that interactive dialogue provided the best opportunity for detailed and fluid interaction. The two games, however, take different approaches to dialogue interactivity. In *The Pandora Directive*, the primary dialogue interaction is through the main character, Tex, who has a series of response attitudes that the user can click to elicit different lines of dialogue. The user cannot choose Tex's actual dialogue. The other characters do not have attitudes to click on; their responses are dictated by Tex's lines. They also have considerably less variation in their dialogue than Tex does.

Dust takes the opposite approach. The Stranger's lines are presented in a menu of written choices. We never hear him speak. The other characters speak in response to the Stranger's questions, which the user picks from the menu. For example, when the player first encounters the character Marie Macintosh, she will be in the form of what CyberFlix calls an "actor," which is an animation of Marie going about her daily business in the streets of Diamondback (see Figure 24–2). When the player clicks on her, she will walk toward the player, then dissolve to a more lifelike close-up. At this point she will speak her opening lines: "Why, if it isn't the stranger in our midst! I was out for a stroll."

Once she completes her opening lines, the player will have the option of responding by clicking text questions and comments from a menu at the bottom of the screen. If the player chooses "I could use help" from the menu, in Figure 24–2, Marie will say: "However can I be of assistance?" Now the menu will change to these options:

```
Got any boots?
Got a gun?
Got bullets?
Thanks.
```

The user can choose one of the above menu items, and Marie verbally responds. The conversation continues until the user cuts it off with a menu item such as "Thanks" or "Bye." But the user/Stranger never speaks.

Andrew Nelson chose this approach to interactive dialogue because he thought that the written lines were more neutral than choosing attitudes and hearing the main character speak. He said that with the written text, it is easier to infer that the dialogue would be delivered in the way the player imagines. He also said that he wanted to give the user more choices by: (1) giving the user the option of choosing the specific lines to speak, and (2) giving a number of possible user responses for each line of the other character, as opposed to a limited number of Response Attitudes. Nelson does not, however, rule out all use of Response Attitudes in projects where they are effective. (See Chapter 23, "Parallel Stories Narrative Case Study: *The Pandora Directive*," for a discussion of the Response Attitudes approach.)

Effect of the Interactive Dialogue in *Dust*

The characters in *Dust* remember and react to what the player/Stranger says to them. If the Stranger is rude, they may not give him the information he needs or help when he needs them. For example, when he first meets the mayor's wife, if he flatters her, she'll invite him home to spend the night. If he insults her, she'll run off in a huff.

How the Stranger treats one character may also affect how a character who is connected to that character will treat him. Marie Macintosh hates her father. If the Stranger is rude to her father, she'll like the Stranger. This type of complex reaction to the user's dialogue choices can change the progress of the story.

Possible Dialogue Scene: Marie Macintosh—Day One—Morning

Following is an example of a more complex dialogue scene, but it is only one possibility. (The sequence is from the morning of Day One.) The actual dialogue sequence depends on which questions the user chooses to ask. This conversation is not written out in order like this in the actual script. It was reconstructed here to explain how

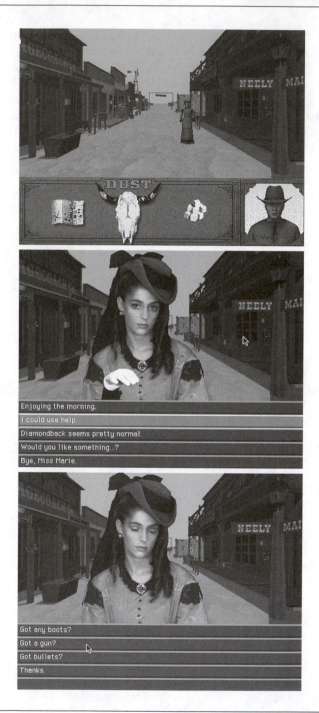

FIGURE 24-2

Top: Marie as "actor" before user clicks on her. Middle: Marie in interactive conversation after the user clicks on her (menu items are the user's questions/comments. In this example, the user clicks, "I could use help"). Bottom: Marie continues interactive conversation (the menu is narrowed to the things the user needs help with).

the interactive conversation works. The complete list of dialogue options as they appear in the actual script follows this example (the Stranger\user's questions and comments in boldface type are answered by Marie Macintosh's comments that have the same number as his questions):

```
MARIE MACINTOSH

MORNING—DAY ONE

                    MARIE: A1. Cheerful greeting
        Why, If it isn't the stranger in our midst!

                    MARIE: B. Question to user
        (She's suspicious) However do you do?

            STRANGER: C1. I'm doing fine.

                    MARIE: C1. Teasing you
        I'm delighted to hear that Diamondback provides all
        that you need, but aren't you curious about us?

            STRANGER: C1a. Should I be?

                    MARIE: C1a. Being mysterious
        (tinkling laugh) Diamondback is a town of secrets.
        Some are useful. Others aren't. But I don't mean
        to imply mystery. You have, no doubt, more pressing
        questions ...
```

[This is an example of the writer nudging the user to ask more questions to advance the story.]

```
            STRANGER: C1b. why is the school deserted?

                    MARIE: C1b. Explaining simple facts of life
        The mission school? Well, once the Yunni left,
        there really was no need for it. Diamondback's
        youngsters go to the Hildago school five miles from
        here. And there are no more Indians ...

            STRANGER: C1b-1. Why was that?
```

[Her answers to some of the questions depend on whether she likes the Stranger, which is based on the types of questions asked earlier. For example, for C1b-1, if she doesn't like the Stranger, she will answer:]

```
        MARIE: C1b-1. Impatient. Not answering him, but
                        speaking from the heart
        Really. That's all in the past.
```

[If she does like the Stranger, however, she will say:]

```
C1b-1a. Confiding in you.
"You know, since you came here I have felt a
(looks for word) kinship with you. I feel you have
known great tragedy, and because of that you, you
understand me.
```

Dialogue Transcript Marie Macintosh—Day One—Morning

This is a list of the Morning Day One dialogue for Marie Macintosh and the Stranger as it appears in the actual script. This is a first draft; the final draft as seen on screen deals with the mission, not the school. Using DreamFactory, most of the editing and revisions are done on screen, and there is no second draft on paper.

In the dialogue that follows, the Stranger's questions are in boldface type, Marie's attitudes are in italics, and her response matches his question of the same number. "Home base" refers to the location where the cyberactor is usually stationed. For Marie, it is outside Bolivar's store, but like the other characters, she can wander about on her day's activities.

```
Marie Macintosh


(Marie is a petulant, spoiled girl who, at 17, is
thoroughly bored with this backwater she finds herself
in. She's very intelligent and wants to appear older
than she is, which makes her very young indeed. With
her alliance with Raddison, Marie can become suspicious
of your motives, guessing you may know about their
pyrite mine scheme. She can also shift her allegiance,
if you choose the right questions to ask her. We meet
her usually in the street where she whiles away the
day fingering the fabrics at Bolivar's or teasing the
cowboys who wander into the Hard Drive Saloon.)


Morning—Day One


A1. Cheerful greeting
"Why, if it isn't the stranger in our midst!"
A2. If unknown from previous night
(offering hand) "I'm the mayor's daughter, Marie."
A1a. if outside home base
"I was out for a stroll ..."
A1b. if outside first destination
"I was out for a stroll ..."
A1c. if inside first destination
"I often come here. To think"
A1d. if outside second destination
"Picking up a few items at Watsons."
A1e. if inside second destination
"I was fetching something."
A1f. if outside third destination
"I'm returning home from shopping "


B. Question to user
(She's suspicious) "However do you do?"
```

C1. I'm doing fine.
C2. I could use help.
C3. Play, if possible
C4. Thanks. Bye.

C1. Teasing you
"I'm delighted to hear that Diamondback provides all
  that you need, but aren't you curious about us?"
C2. Amused
"However can I be of assistance?"
C3. Giving you her hankie, speaking softly "There's
  sweat on your brow. Here ... Take my hankie. A token of
  a friendship?" (She ends this on a provocative note.)
C4. End conversation comment
"Goodbye. I am so very glad you've come to stay in
  Diamondback. If we are lucky, perhaps you'll stay for
  a long, long time."

C1a. Should I be?
C1b. Why is the school deserted?
C1b-1. Why is that?
If Marie likes Stranger
C1b-1a.
C1c. Who is the school teacher?

C2a. You got boots, size 12?
C2b. You got a gun?

C1a. Being mysterious
(tinkling laugh) "Diamondback is a town of secrets.
  Some are useful. Others aren't. But I don't mean to
  imply mystery. You have, no doubt, more pressing
  questions ..."
C1b. Explaining simple facts of life
"The mission school? Well, once the Yunni left, there
  really was no need for it. Diamondback's youngsters
  go to the Hildago school five miles from here. And
  there are no more ..."
*C1b-1. Impatient. Not answering him, but speaking from
  the heart*
"Really. That's all in the past."
If Marie likes Stranger
C1b-1a. Confiding in you
"You know, since you came here I have felt a (looks for
  word) *kinship* with you. I feel you have known great
  tragedy, and because of that you, you understand me."
*C1c. A little irritated to be back on the subject of
  Indians*
"A Yunni called Sonoma, who lived with the Grangers
  until they died. Now I wouldn't know where she was.
  She is, after all, an *Indian*."
C2a. She is amused
(tinkling laugh) "Oh, I do not mean to make light of
  your situation, but your feet [giggles], they are

> *simply* enormous. The only ones bigger belong to the
> Nevans boy, Jay, who has a terrible crush on me"
> [giggles]
> C2b. *Lying sweetly through her teeth*
> "Oh, no! I don't even know how to shoot a gun! Guns
> scare me"
> If Marie is suspicious
> C2c. *She responds*
> "Now, if I don't know a Colt from a Remington what
> would I know about bullets? [laughs] Maybe you could
> borrow a few from some cowpoke!"

Additional dialogue transcripts are available in the Chapter 24 area of the "Chapters" section of the *Writing for Multimedia and the Web* CD-ROM.

DEVELOPING A STORY WITHIN THIS HIGHLY INTERACTIVE WORLD

This level of dialogue interactivity, coupled with the nearly unlimited opportunity to explore Diamondback, creates a highly interactive world in the control of the user. In order to create a story within such a world, the writer must develop a series of devices that nudge the user in the right direction, while still leaving the impression that the user is making the ultimate choice. These nudges establish key plot points, introduce characters, engineer confrontations, guide the user where the writer wants him or her to go, and generally keep the story moving forward.

Help

One of the ways the writer guides the reader in this program is through the Help option. Unlike many other programs where help is a text-hints window that clearly disrupts the story, help in *Dust* is a Chinese gentleman named Help who runs a curiosities shop. He always knows where the player is in the game and gives just the assistance needed. For example, if the Stranger runs out of cash, he'll give him a five dollar loan but also chase him out of the store, calling him a "hopeless case."

Other Characters' Dialogue

It is not only Help who knows where the player is in the story. The other characters are also aware of the Stranger's situation and can prompt him in the right direction. For example, when the Stranger gets a note at the hotel to meet a character outside, the hotel Clerk says, "So you going out again?" The Stranger can ignore the note and the prompt and go to bed, but if he does, he will miss the fun of a fist-fight with a local bully and some key information. Even if dialogue in this piece is not prompting the user in a certain direction, it is usually giving key plot points or setting up character. There is not much room for idle chatter in an interactive program. The same information must be included in a variety of ways in different pieces of dialogue, because there is no guarantee that any one piece of dialogue will be accessed by the user.

Written Material

The note mentioned above is only one example of written material used to prod the character. *Dust* also includes a book on Diamondback in the curiosities shop that gives key information about the town. The town's newspaper also provides updates.

At one point, the user can read in the paper that Congress has passed anti-Asian legislation. A smart user realizes that the Chinese gentleman Help might be endangered and rushes to his store, saving it from being burned. This was also a way to bring in historical events as a context for the story.

The Narrator

The narrator allows the writer to compress and deliver instructions. In *Dust*, the narrator is triggered automatically at key times, particularly at the beginning of each day, telling the user what he or she has to accomplish. This is one way to ensure that the user will get key plot points without intruding significantly on the interactive experience.

Short Linear Movies

Short linear movies also occasionally appear to give important information, such as the opening card game that shows the Stranger's fight with the Kid.

Film Language and Genre

Film has spent a hundred years teaching the audience its visual language. Smart interactive writers can take advantage of this language to communicate meaning. *Dust* makes particularly good use of the icons associated with the Western genre. For example, when the town of Diamondback rises up from the desert, it creates a whole range of associations that users bring from their experience of other Westerns.

CONCLUSION: RESPONSE TO THE PROGRAM

Dust: A Tale of the Wired West was named Best Multimedia Game of the year by *MacWorld*. It has also received critical acclaim in such publications as *Newsweek*, *People*, *Next Generation*, and *CD-ROM Today*, and was a best seller for CyberFlix.

REFERENCES

Garrand, Timothy. "Writing Interactive Narrative." *Creative Screenwriting* (Spring 1997).
Nelson, Andrew. Telephone interview with the author. December 1995, September 1999.
Production Notes. *Dust: A Tale of the Wired West*. Knoxville, TN: CyberFlix Inc., 1995, p. 5.

C H A P T E R   2 5

KEY POINTS FROM PART III: HOW TO WRITE INTERACTIVE NARRATIVE

A STORY WITH INTERACTIVE POTENTIAL

There are no hard and fast rules about what makes a good interactive narrative, but some things that have worked in the past include the following:

- A clearly defined goal to lead the player through the story. Examples: Exposing a corrupt billionaire (*Voyeur*, Chapter 22), rescuing a lover from a haunted house (*The 11th Hour*, Chapter 21).

- An interesting role for the player that allows some control over the narrative flow. Example: In *Dust* (Chapter 24), the player becomes an Old West drifter named the Stranger. The player controls what this character says and does.

- Various plot possibilities and choice points. Scenes can be played out in a number of ways, and the player's choices in these scenes can lead to a number of possible endings. Example: In *The Pandora Directive* (Chapter 23), the player/Tex Murphy can choose to have a fight with his girlfriend and can decide to sleep with the evil woman, but these choices lead to his death at the end.

- A story line into which puzzles and games can be easily integrated. Examples: *The 11th Hour* (Chapter 21) justifies its games narratively by making the antagonist an evil toy-maker who likes to torture his victims with deadly games. Other programs, such as *The Pandora Directive* (Chapter 23), integrate the puzzles into the obstacles facing the player, such as deciphering a secret code to disarm an alarm.

- An intriguing, unusual world to explore. Examples: Part of the fun of immersing ourselves in the multimedia experience is a chance to explore unusual locations, such as a desert town in the Old West (*Dust*, Chapter 24), the mansion of a billionaire (*Voyeur*, Chapter 22), and the urban future (*The Pandora Directive*, Chapter 23).

STRONG LINEAR NARRATIVE (CHAPTER 18)

Most of the writers in the programs featured in the case studies first wrote a linear story, which they later developed into an interactive narrative. The main reason for this approach is to make sure that the idea can be developed into a strong story. All the interactivity in the world won't make a bad idea interesting. It is also sometimes hard to determine the full interactive potential of a story idea until it has been fully developed.

CLASSICAL STRUCTURE (CHAPTER 18)

Many successful interactive narrative programs are based on classical narrative structure. Classical narratives usually have a lead character who has a need or goal that he or she wants to accomplish. When the lead character tries to achieve that need, he or she meets obstacles that create conflict. Obstacles can be another person, the environment, or inner conflicts. The conflicts build until the climax, where the character achieves the goal or not.

CHARACTERS

THE PLAYER (CHAPTER 19)

At the same time as the writer lays out the basic story, he or she needs to define the role of the player(s) clearly. Who are they in the story? The lead character? A minor character? What will they get to do? How much control will they have over the characters' behavior? What is the player's goal? What are the key obstacles to achieving that goal? Will these obstacles be personalized in the form of an opponent?

CHARACTER INTERACTIVITY (CHAPTERS 24, 25)

It's necessary for the writer to devise a way for the lead character/player to interact with his or her environment. If it is limited interactivity, the writer might merely need a menu or map of options. However, if there is to be complex interactivity, the writer has to come up with a more sophisticated approach, such as interactive dialogue. One approach to interactive dialogue, as used in *The Pandora Directive*, is to allow the other characters to speak and give the player/main character a series of Response Attitudes to choose from. What Response Attitude the player chooses determines what line the character will speak.

Another approach, as used in *Dust: A Tale of the Wired West*, is to have dialogue menus for the main character that show the complete dialogue that the user can choose. In addition to dialogue, most programs also give the user other options, such as moving, picking up objects, and clicking on objects and characters to get information or initiate interactions.

ARCHITECTURE: STRUCTURE AND NAVIGATION (CHAPTER 19)

Once the writer has a clear idea of the plot, characters, goals, and conflicts, he or she can decide which interactive structure might work best. The types of structure available depend to a large degree on the authoring system—the story engine that will be used to produce the program.

LINEAR WITH SCENE BRANCHING (CHAPTER 19)

If the story will be primarily linear with occasional branching choices for the users that eventually loop back to the main plot, consider a scene-branching structure. This approach is used in *Boy Scout Patrol Theater*, which is described in the "Chapters" section of the *Writing for Multimedia and the Web* CD-ROM. In this piece, a Boy Scout patrol searches for a little girl. The player assumes the role of one of the scouts and can decide which locations to search, such as the school or a farm. Once launched on the search of a location, the scene is primarily linear until the next branching point. Although interactivity is limited in this approach, it does allow the writer more control over story elements. In this case, the writer thought that limited interactivity was the best way to maintain the suspense of the search for the girl.

PUZZLE-BASED NARRATIVE (CHAPTER 21)

A writer whose major interest is presenting puzzles and games might want to use a puzzle-based narrative. This is the basic approach used in *The 11th Hour: The Sequel to the 7th Guest*. The lead character (player) searches a haunted house for his girlfriend. To win clues to her whereabouts, he has to solve numerous puzzles in this house. The main interactivity is in the puzzles, not in the narrative itself. In this case, the reward for solving a puzzle is a video fragment of the girlfriend's story.

HIERARCHICAL BRANCHING (CHAPTER 19)

If a story has a number of major choices that take it in a completely different direction, then the writer is involved in hierarchical structure. The problem with this structure is branching explosion. Five options with five choices each equals 25 scenes; five choices for each of those scenes equals 125 scenes. This quickly becomes too much to write or produce. This is why hierarchical branching is primarily limited to the endings of stories, as in *The 11th Hour: The Sequel to the 7th Guest*, *The Pandora Directive*, and *Dust: A Tale of the Wired West*.

PARALLEL STRUCTURE (CHAPTERS 19, 23)

A way to have multiple story paths and avoid the branching explosion of hierarchical structure is to have parallel story paths. In this case, there are multiple story paths that the user can explore, but the paths are limited, usually to three or four. Choices the user makes send him or her back and forth between these paths instead of onto completely new story paths as in hierarchical structure.

Parallel structure is useful for showing multiple perspectives on a story or various ways a story could unfold based on user choices. *The Pandora Directive* uses this structure. Its "A" path is a basic Hollywood story where everything turns out all right and the hero gets the woman. The "C" path is bleak film noir, ending in death for the hero. The "B" path is a more realistic, middle-ground compromise story. This approach allows a high degree of interactivity for the user but still allows the writer some control over the story.

STRING OF PEARLS (CHAPTERS 19, 24)

The string of pearls structure combines a worlds approach with a narrative. In this structure, the character is allowed to explore a certain world or portion of a world, but to move on in the story, he or she has to achieve certain plot points. In *Dust: A*

Tale of the Wired West, the first pearl of the story allows the player/lead character to explore a desert town at night. But to advance in the story to the next pearl, the player must find a place to sleep. The next morning is the next pearl of the story. The player/Stranger can continue to explore the town, but now he (or she) must find guns, bullets, and boots. This approach allows maximum interactivity for the player and the least writer control over the narrative.

STORYTELLING DEVICES (CHAPTERS 19, 24)

Structure gives the overall approach to the story, but to develop narrative within that structure, the writer needs to use a number of storytelling devices. It helps the players to have some sort of map of the story and/or location so that they know where they are at any give time. Often this is an actual map, such as the map of the town in *Dust*, or the map of the house in *The 11th Hour*.

Interactive devices help make the user aware of interactive possibilities. These devices can be as simple as text menus or icons that indicate what action is allowed in a certain situation. The Help feature, on-screen text, the narrator, and linear movies are other useful tools for telling an interactive tale.

MECHANICS OF SCRIPTWRITING (PART 1)

There are a number of organizational devices that help in the plotting of narrative, such as flowcharting (Chapter 3) and character charts (Chapter 22). The writer has to keep in mind the basic techniques of the scriptwriter (Chapter 2), such as showing the audience the story with dramatic action instead of simply telling, as in a novel. Finally, the writer must come up with a proposal and script format suitable to the project (Chapter 5).

P A R T   I V

INTERACTIVE WRITING CAREERS

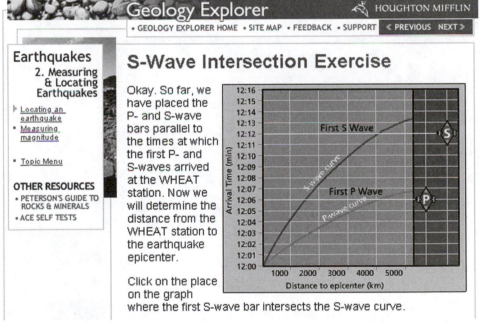

A an interactive Flash animation exercise from the Houghton Mifflin *GeologyExplorer* Web site and CD-ROM. Users can move the slider bar and get feedback. © 1999 by Houghton Mifflin Company. Screen shot courtesy of Houghton Mifflin Company, www.geologylink.com

C H A P T E R   2 6

CONCLUSION: BECOMING A SUCCESSFUL INTERACTIVE WRITER

THE CHALLENGES

This book has explained some of the key challenges that must be faced to become a successful interactive writer. The challenges include:

- Creative challenges
- Technical challenges
- Productivity and organizational challenges
- The challenge of keeping up with the rapid changes in multimedia and the Web

NOTE: See the careers area in the "Chapters" section of the *Writing for Multimedia and the Web* CD-ROM for links to Web sites for the resources discussed in this chapter.

CREATIVE CHALLENGES

The interactive writer has to be able to write for many media, such as video, print, and audio. He or she also has to understand how the elements of interactive media affect communicating information or telling a story. These elements include interactivity, the role of the player, interactive structure, and interactive approaches to material, such as simulations and worlds.

TECHNICAL CHALLENGES

In addition to meeting creative challenges, the interactive writer needs a certain amount of technical knowledge. The writer does not have to be a programmer or have any formal technical training, but he or she does need to have a general understanding of interactive technology to effectively use these tools to communicate. For example, an understanding of the expressive power of Flash animation software made possible the effective exercise pictured on the opening page of Part IV of this book. Some writers become so technically proficient that they become writer-designers or writer-producers. A hyphenate writer (writer-producer, writer-designer, writer-information architect) is also far more employable.

PRODUCTIVITY AND ORGANIZATIONAL CHALLENGES

Whether it is a huge Web site or a video game with an 800-page script, the sheer volume of work that must be produced for an interactive media project can be overwhelming. In addition, an interactive writer has to write quickly to meet production deadlines. Strong word processing skills are assumed. A knowledge of information management software, such as flowcharters and databases, can also help organize a large project.

FUTURE CHALLENGES

As difficult as it is to master the required skills needed for success in this field today, it is perhaps even more challenging to predict changes in the interactive media industry in the future. Nevertheless, a few developments seem likely. The Web and other online networks will continue to grow explosively. Broadband access will allow a true multimedia experience on the Web, including video and sophisticated interactivity. All of these developments will increase the demand for interactive content and thus for the interactive writer. Future changes will also probably require the writer to acquire new, yet-to-be-defined skills.

MEETING THE CHALLENGES

Meeting the challenges described above to become a successful interactive writer will require you to:

- Get new skills
- Network with industry professionals
- Present your portfolio as effectively as possible to clients and potential employers

GETTING THE SKILLS

Whether you are a beginner or an experienced professional, the first thing you have to do is get the needed skills in this field. Studying Web sites and reading books, such as this, are a good first step. This may be adequate for some of you who are good at learning on your own. But for many people who are learning a new skill, formal study can significantly accelerate the learning process.

College Degree

If you have the resources and the time, there are certainly excellent degree programs at universities and colleges around the country. Check out the computer department or communication department of an institution near you and chances are they will have offerings in multimedia or the Web. Two of the top schools in this field include:

- MIT Media Lab (http://www.media.mit.edu/)
- San Francisco State University (http://www.cel.sfsu.edu/msp/MSP2.html)

Certificate Programs

If you already have a college degree, a good alternative to a degree program is a certificate program. Certificate programs are packages of courses in a certain subject areas. These certificates are usually offered by the continuing education departments of colleges and universities. A certificate program may only be a half dozen courses and could be completed by taking classes part-time in a year or two. An added plus of continuing education courses is that many of the people teaching these courses are working professionals who can provide you with contacts in the industry. These schools are examples of good certificate programs:

- The University of Massachusetts at Lowell (http://continuinged.uml.edu/)
- San Francisco State University (http://www.cel.sfsu.edu/msp/MSP2.html)

CyberEd

If you are busy with family and work, or you simply do not live near a college or university, consider online education. A number of colleges and private companies offer courses on multimedia and the Internet via the Web. As long as you have a Web connection, you can take these course sitting in front of your computer at home. There are many sites that offer online education. A few examples are:

- The University of Massachusetts at Lowell (http://continuinged.uml.edu/)
- San Francisco State University (http://www.cel.sfsu.edu/msp/curriculum/msponline.html)
- Smart Planet, founded by Ziff-Davis. (http://www.smartplanet.com/)
- The HTML Writers Guild (http://www.hwg.org/)

Conferences and Professional Seminars

Conferences and professional seminars offered by professional and educational organizations are another resource. Find out more about professional organizations under "Networking" later in this chapter.

Internships

Internships are a great way to get professional experience and build up your portfolio. In many cases, internships are not paid, but often they are. You can learn while you earn, and if you are good, get hired by the company that you are interning for. If at all possible, do your internship full-time for as long a time as you can afford to. If you are a full-time intern, you get full-time responsibilities. If you are a part-time intern, you may end up answering phones and getting coffee. It is usually more difficult to get an internship if you are not at least a part-time student, but if there is a specific company you are excited about, it doesn't hurt to offer your services. Many of the job resources at the end of this chapter also include leads for internships.

CREATING YOUR PORTFOLIO

Even though you might be selling yourself as a writer, most potential employers are going to be reluctant to read scripts. You need to get your interactive writing produced as an effective Web site or multimedia program. Classroom projects are great ways to build your skills, but employers want to see professional portfolios. They want to know that someone, somewhere paid you for your services. Do whatever you can to get your work produced. Be creative. If you have friends with a business, volunteer to write and produce their Web site for little or no payment. If you don't have production skills, team up with a classmate or colleague who does. Once completed, your first Web site is now a professional piece of work, and your friends with the business are clients. If you are currently employed, use your multimedia skills on the job. You can also donate your multimedia or Web services to a nonprofit organization. Obviously, you can't keep working for peanuts forever, but when you are starting out, it helps to get a few professional pieces in your portfolio.

If you have no way of producing your writing, at least try to develop some impressive flowcharts or storyboards to accompany your text. Although professional interactive media pieces are the best to have, professional pieces of any kind—articles, videos, books—can help demonstrate your skills.

Presenting Your Portfolio

Once you have a few pieces to put in a portfolio, the most effective way to actually present your material is to create a portfolio Web site. This site should have a page describing your clients with links to work samples. A portfolio Web site is a good way to go because almost every potential employer or client that you are dealing with will have a browser and access to the Web. If your work is high bandwidth multimedia that will not work well on the Web, try to include some trimmed samples on your portfolio Web site, but also have your material on a CD-ROM or ZIP disk to show clients if your Web site material catches their interest.

NETWORKING

In addition to getting strong skills and a good portfolio, you need to meet people in the industry, because so many jobs are made through personal contact. One way to do this is to join professional organizations and attend their meetings, conferences, and seminars. Most of these organizations have inexpensive student memberships. They also often have print journals and newsletters that list jobs.

- Association for Applied Interactive Multimedia (AAIM) http://www.aaim.org/
  AAIM was created to support professionals who use and develop interactive multimedia.

- The Association for Computing Machinery (ACM) http://www.acm.org/
  The first and still the largest international scientific and educational computer society in the world. They have a special interest group (SIG) for multimedia.

- Association for Educational Communications Technology (AECT) http://www.aect.org
  An organization of professionals interested in the use of educational technology and its application to the learning process.

- Computer Game Developers' Association (CGDA) http://www.cgda.org/
  The Computer Game Developers' Association is the professional society for interactive entertainment, educational software, and multimedia.

- The International Interactive Communications Society (IICS) http://www.iics.org/

The nation's oldest professional organization devoted exclusively to interactive arts and technology professionals.

- Media Communications Association (formerly ITVA) http://www.itva.org/index_new.html
  The organization of nonbroadcast (corporate, educational etc.) television producers is increasingly active in interactive media.
- Society for Technical Communication (STC) http://www.stc-va.org
  STC's members include technical writers, editors, graphic designers, multimedia artists, Web and Intranet page information designers, translators, and others whose work involves making technical information understandable and available to those who need it.

GETTING THE JOB

When you have the skills, a slick portfolio, and a few contacts in the industry, it's time to go after that job. Many useful tools for finding a job exist on the Web. I've outlined some key ones below. Many of these links are also good for internships.

MEDIA JOB WEB SITES

These sites are devoted to media job leads. All have new media sections or are devoted to new media. It is also useful to check on the Web pages of companies you are interested in. Most have a jobs or careers section.

- *The Advertising Age*/Monster Board Job Bank
  - http://adage.com/job_bank/index.html
  - Jobs for advertising, marketing and media professionals.
- Communications Roundtable Career and Employment Page
  - http://www.roundtable.org/jobs.html
  - Jobs page features PR, journalism, academic, new media, and other media jobs.
- Creative Freelancers
  - http://www.roundtable.org/jobs.html
  - Specializes in illustrators, designers, artists, writers, editors, art directors, photographers, proofreaders, and production staff.
- The International Interactive Communications Society—National Job Line
  - http://www.iics.org/docs/job_bank.html
  - Chapter sites also have job listings.
- JobStar San Francisco
  - http://jobsmart.org/silicon/
  - Silicon Valley jobs and career information
- Journalism Jobs and Internships
  - http://www.journalism.berkeley.edu/jobs/
  - Wide range of journalism jobs spanning editorial, design, production, systems, and management; includes print and new media positions.
- New York New Media Association
  - http://www.nynma.org/

- New York job listings are free to search and free for members to post.
- New York Silicon Alley Jobs & Internships
  - http://www.news-ny.com/jobs.ht
    New media jobs in New York, Los Angeles, Washington, D.C., and Europe

General Job Sites with Media Categories

These extensive listings cover all jobs, but they also have new media categories.

- America's Job Bank
  - http://www.ajb.dni.us/
  - America's Job Bank is a partnership between the U.S. Department of Labor and the state-operated, public Employment Service.
- CareerPath.com
  - http://new.careerpath.com/
  - Allows searching of help wanted pages of major newspapers including the *Boston Globe* and the *San Jose Mercury News*, the newspaper for Silicon Valley.

New Media Job Recruiters

These companies find jobs and charge the employer (not you) a fee. They are not useful if you are a beginner, but if you have some skills and professional experience, they can be a good resource for finding employment.

- CDI
  - http://www.cdicorp.com/
  - This is one of the largest placement firms in the U.S., with offices across the country. CDI offers a wide range of career opportunities through its three distinct job banks.
- Clear Point Consultants, Inc.
  - http://www.clearpnt.com/
  - A Massachusetts professional staffing firm that specializes in placing contract and permanent Information Design and Delivery professionals. Job categories include: Online Information Designers, Web Designers, Technical Writers, and Instructional Designers.
- Information Technology Partners
  - http://www.itp-inc.com/
  - A staffing firm serving the IT organization market in the Silicon Valley area.
- InfoTech Contract Services
  - http://www.winterwyman-contract.com
  - Specializes in contract job opportunities on the leading edge of Software Development, Information Technology, Software QA, and Globalization. With offices in the Boston area, Atlanta, Georgia, and Japan.
- Pubsnet
  - http://www.pubsnet.com/hotjobs.htm
  - Pubsnet is a training and recruiting agency that specializes in media writers, primarily technical writers. They are based in Massachusetts and New Hampshire.

- Silicon Alley Connections
  - http://www.salley.com/
  - New media recruiters for the New York Market.

GOOD LUCK

Good luck with your interactive writing career. Feel free to E-mail me (tpg@interwrite.com), and I will look forward to meeting you some day on a project or at a conference. Happy cyber trails.

WRITER AND DESIGNER BIOGRAPHIES AND COMPANY DESCRIPTIONS

The following individuals or companies either contributed script material or gave interviews for this book. They are listed alphabetically by company or individual name. The name of their program or Web site discussed in the book is next to their name. For detailed descriptions of the companies and biographies of the individuals, see the References Section of the *Writing for Multimedia and the Web* CD-ROM.

Peter Adams (T. Rowe Price Web Site)

At the time the first version of the T. Rowe Price site was created, Peter Adams was Director of Interactive and Creative Services at poppe.com/New York, advertising agency Poppe Tyson's interactive division. Adams is also one of the pioneers in the Internet arena, setting up one of the first Web sites on the Internet in 1993.

Access Software (*Under a Killing Moon, The Pandora Directive*)

Access Software Inc. of Salt Lake City, Utah, is a major developer of multimedia entertainment, including the Tex Murphy detective series and *Links* golf series. Microsoft bought Access, and it is now called Microsoft Access Software. It is still a developer of multimedia entertainment.

Encyclopaedia Britannica (Britannica.Com and *The Harlem Renaissance*)

Encyclopaedia Britannica produces Web sites and disc-based media versions of its print encyclopedias and other publications. Its Web site Britannica.com also serves as a research portal.

Fred Bauer (*Vital Signs*)

Fred Bauer has written over 200 scripts for linear video, interactive video disk, and interactive multimedia since opening his Marblehead, Massachusetts-based business, "Fred Bauer, the writer."

Butler, Raila & Company (*Boy Scout Patrol Theater*)

Butler, Raila & Company has specialized exclusively in the development of high-quality custom interactive media presentations since 1985. Markets and application areas served include publishing, sales and marketing, public information, museum exhibition, and learning (medical, technical, consumer).

Aaron Conners (*Under a Killing Moon, The Pandora Directive*)

Aaron Conners joined Access Software in 1991 as its first full-time writer. In addition to writing the Tex Murphy CD-ROMs *Under a Killing Moon*, *The Pandora Directive*, and *Tex Murphy: Overseer*, he is the developer of *The Black Pearl* and the author of Tex Murphy science-fiction novels.

Chedd-Angier Production Company (*The Nauticus Shipbuilding Company*)

Chedd-Angier is a Boston-based media production company.

John Cosner (*Vital Signs*)

John Cosner is an instructional designer and multimedia producer for Consultec, a training and consulting company in Massachusetts.

Mathew J. Costello (*The 7th Guest, The 11th Hour*)

Mathew J. Costello is the author of fourteen novels and numerous nonfiction books. He wrote the script for *The 7th Guest*, an interactive drama that has become a best-selling CD-ROM (nearly 2,000,000 copies). The sequel, *The 11th Hour*, was released in 1995 and also became an immediate best-seller. He is also the writer of the *zoogdisney* Web site and many other interactive media programs.

CyberFlix Incorporated (*Dust: A Tale of the Wired West*)

An interactive storytelling company and CD-ROM publisher, CyberFlix was founded in 1993 and is based in Knoxville, Tennessee. Titles include *Titanic*, *SkullCracker*, and *Red Jack's Revenge*. CyberFlix has ceased game development to concentrate on licensing its story engine software, *DreamFactory*.

Shannon Gilligan (*Who Killed Sam Rupert?*)

Shannon Gilligan is an author of children's and mystery books, founder of the Santa Fe, N.M.-based Spark Interactive, and writer of numerous successful multimedia titles, including *Who Killed Sam Rupert? Who Killed Elspeth Haskard?* and *The Magic Death*.

John Hargrave (ZDU (SmartPlanet) Online Ad Campaign)

ZDNet Editorial Projects Director and principal of the interactive media development company, Media Shower, Inc.

D.C. Heath and Company (*Sky High*)

D.C. Heath and Company has as its basic mission the development, publication, and marketing of materials of instruction to schools and colleges. These include textbooks, computer software, videos, and CD-ROMs. D.C. Heath is an imprint of Houghton Mifflin Company.

Houghton Mifflin Company (*Sky High, Geology Explorer*)

Houghton Mifflin Company is one of the largest producers of textbooks and educational materials, including CD-ROMs and Web sites.

InterWrite (*Prudential Verani Realty Web Site, Geology Explorer Web Site*)

InterWrite of Londonderry, New Hampshire, specialized in the writing, developing, and information architecture of high-content Web sites. InterWrite's owner Timothy Garrand has joined the international Web consulting firm Immersant as a senior Interactive Architect. He has ceased development through InterWrite.

Jane Jensen (*Gabriel Knight*)

Jensen is a writer-designer who has worked on *Police Quest 3, Ecoquest, King's Quest VI,* and *Pepper's Adventures* for Sierra On-Line. She is also the designer of the award-winning *Gabriel Knight I: Sins of the Fathers* and *Gabriel Knight II: The Beast Within.*

Ken Jones (*Prudential Veranni Realty* Web site)

Since working on the Prudential site, Ken Jones has joined Immersant as a Technical Architect.

Ron McAdow (*Sky High*)

Ron McAdow has written books, CD-ROMs, and the award-winning films *Hank the Cave Peanut* and *Captain Silas*. He is currently a multimedia developer for CAST Inc. of Peabody, Massachusetts.

National Scouting Museum (*Patrol Theater*)

The National Scouting Museum, Murray, Kentucky, is a place where history, theater, and technology combine to give visitors an engaging interactive experience of the history of the Boy Scouts of America.

Andrew Nelson (*Dust: A Tale of the Wired West, Britannica.com, Harlem Renaissance*)

Andrew Nelson is producer and writer for *Dust* and writer for *Jump Raven* and *Titanic Adventure Out of Time*. He is currently a producer at Britannica.com.

Maria O'Meara (*Sky High, Patrol Theater*)

Maria O'Meara has been a scriptwriter for twenty years. Her interactive clients include Harvard Community Health Plan, Videologic, Federal Express, Merck, IBM, GTE, Allstate, and Southwestern Bell. She also wrote Kidvidz's *Paws, Claws, Feathers, and Fins,* TV Guide's "Best Children's Videos for 1993."

poppe.com (T. Rowe Price Web Site)

Poppe.com was Poppe Tyson's online development unit dedicated to strategic Web planning, content design, and data capture systems. Some of the Web sites poppe.com has created include The White House, AT&T, Chrysler, IBM, Jeep, LensCrafters, Merrill Lynch, Netscape, T. Rowe Price, and Valvoline. Poppe Tyson has merged with Modem Media to form Modem Media.Poppe Tyson.

Lena Marie Pousette (*Voyeur*)

Lena Marie Pousette is a writer, producer, and designer. Some of the multimedia titles she has been involved with include *Caesar's World of Boxing, Droid Wackers*, and *Endorfun.*

David Riordan (*Voyeur*)

David Riordan has been a creative executive for Disney Interactive, Time Warner Interactive, and Phillip POV. He is the designer of *Voyeur, Thunder in Paradise*, and many other titles. He is currently part of the team working on the Web site/online community *Jenna's Garden.*

Anthony Sherman (*Dracula Unleashed, Club Dead*)

Anthony Sherman was the game designer for Viacom New Media's *Dracula Unleashed* and *Club Dead.*

Steve Street (Prudential Verani Realty Web Site)

Since working on the Prudential site as lead designer, Steve has founded his own company in Londonderry, New Hampshire.

T. Rowe Price Associates (T. Rowe Price Web Site)

T. Rowe Price Associates is a Baltimore-based investment management firm that serves as investment adviser to the T. Rowe Price family of no-load mutual funds, and to individual and institutional clients, including pension, profit-sharing, and other employee benefit plans, endowments, and foundations. T. Rowe Price Internet Services is the in-house group that developed the second-generation site profiled in this book.

ZD Net (ZDU Online Ad Campaign)

ZD Net is the online branch of Ziff Davis Publishing, a major publisher of computer magazines and books.

See the References Section of the *Writing for Multimedia and the Web* CD-ROM for additional appendixes and other information. The CD-ROM table of contents is at the beginning of the book.

INDEX

Wri...

To Start the ...
1) Launch a W...
2) Double clic...
3) Windows: r...
4) Macintosh: ... ...SO 9660 File
Access" extens...

Genre and Title	Scripts & Charts	Imag...	...emos & Videos	WWW Links *
Web Site *Prudential Verani Realty*	●	●		●
Web Site *T. Rowe Price Web Site*		●		●
Web Feature Story *The Harlem Renaissance*	●	●		●
Online Advertising *ZDU Campaign*		●	●	●
Museum Kiosk Simulation *The Nauticus Shipbuilding Co.*		●		●
Multimedia Training *Vital Signs*	●	●		●
Multiplayer Narrative *Boy Scout Patrol Theater*	●	●		●
Puzzle-Based Game *The 11th Hour*	●	●	●	●
Cinematic Narrative *Voyeur*	●	●		●
Parallel Stories Narrative *The Pandora Directive*	●	●		●
Worlds Narrative *Dust*	●	●	●	●
Worlds Narrative *Titanic: Adventure Out of Time*		●		●

Background	Reference
Playback/Delivery Systems	Glossaries of Media Terms
Production Systems and Software	Writers & Production Companies
Accessible Multimedia & Web Pages	Info. for the Teacher & Student
Multimedia & Web Legal Primer	Links To Writing Related Software

* Links to sites on the World Wide Web can be accessed if the reader has an Internet connection.
